English Conversation
for Global Healthcare

의료관광 실무영어회화

한광종 저

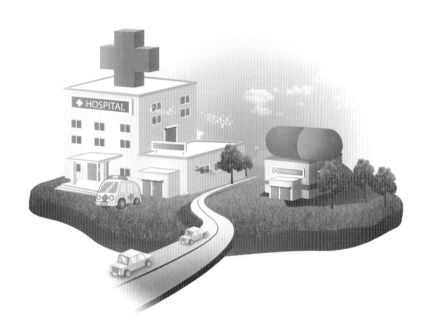

백산출판사

머리말

　의료산업의 국제화와 외화획득을 목표로 외국인 의료관광객을 유치하기 위한 「의료법」이 2009년에 개정된 후 외국인환자 유치업체와 외국인환자 유치의료기관에 종사하는 의료관광코디네이터 인력에 대한 수요가 꾸준히 증가하고 있다.

　의료관광객수의 증가와 의료관광사업의 규모가 확대됨에 따라 많은 의료관광 전문인력이 필요하게 되었고, 현재 대학원, 4년제 대학, 3년제 대학, 2년제 대학뿐만 아니라 대학 부설 평생교육원 및 사회교육원 그리고 의료관광관련 정부산하기관과 지방자치단체 등에서 의료관광 전문인력을 양성하고 있다. 이와 같은 의료관광 전문인력의 능력을 객관적으로 검증하기 위해서 2013년부터 한국산업인력공단 주관으로 국제의료관광코디네이터 국가자격증도 시행되고 있다.

　높은 수준의 의료서비스를 기대하고 한국을 찾는 의료관광객의 Needs에 부응하기 위해서 의료서비스의 수준 향상이 요구되며, 그중에서도 특히 의사소통은 가장 중요한 서비스 중 하나이다.

　본서는 의료관광객과의 의사소통에 중점을 두었다. 즉 영어권 의료관광객을 유치하고 직접 응대·관리하는 데 필요한 여러 가지 영어 표현을 외국인 환자의 유치, 예약, 영접, 예진, 진료, 수술, 회복, 관광, 영송 등 의료관광 진행 프로세스별로 정리했다.

　또한 본서는 외국인환자 유치의료기관의 국제진료센터 직원·간호사·원무과 직원과 외국인환자 유치업체의 의료관광마케팅담당자 그리고 국제의료관광코디네이터가 의료인과 외국인환자와의 의사소통을 하는 데 도움이 되는 표현과 의료관광 통역코디네이터가 직접 의료관광객을 응대하는 경우의 표현을 동시에 고려했다.

본서에서 표기한 MTC는 Medical Tour Coordinator의 약자이며, 의료인(의사, 간호사 등)이 직접 의료관광객과 의사소통하거나 국제의료관광코디네이터가 통역을 한다는 가정 하에 일반적으로 Doctor가 말하는 표현은 MTC(Doctor), 간호사가 말하는 표현은 MTC(Nurse), 의사 또는 간호사가 하는 말을 의료관광통역코디네이터가 통역할 경우는 MTC(Doctor) 또는 MTC(Nurse)로 표기했다. 약사의 표현은 MTC(Pharmacist), 병원의 리셉셔니스트는 MTC(Receptionist), 병원의 방사선사는 MTC(Radiologist) 그리고 외국인환자유치업체 직원 또는 병원 직원이 공히 사용 가능한 표현일 경우는 MTC(Staff)로 표기했다.

본서가 외국인환자 유치의료기관의 의료인뿐만 아니라 외국인환자 유치업체의 임직원 및 국제의료관광코디네이터로 취업하는 데 관심있는 분들과 의료관광분야로의 취업·진출을 준비하는 분들에게 도움이 되었으면 한다.

본서에서의 부족한 부분은 앞으로 개선해 나가도록 노력할 것이며, 어려운 출판 여건에도 불구하고 의료관광 전문 출판사로서의 자부심과 의료관광에 대한 남다른 애정으로 본서의 출판을 기꺼이 맡아주신 백산출판사 진성원 상무님과 편집, 교정 및 디자인 작업에 수고해 주신 편집부 직원 여러분들께 감사드립니다. 1974년 진욱상 사장님이 설립한 이후 꾸준히 성장을 거듭하고 있는 백산출판사가 앞으로도 더욱 발전하기를 진심으로 바랍니다.

본서의 내용에 대해서 궁금한 점이 있거나 문의사항이 있다면 저자에게 fatherofsusie@hanmail.net으로 직접 문의하거나 blog.daum.net/fatherofsusie의 방명록에 궁금한 점과 의견을 남겨주기 바랍니다.

2013년 12월
한광종

차 례

Chapter 1

의료관광 영접

1.1 사증발급

2012년 1월 2일부터는 외국인환자 유치기관으로 등록한 병원 및 유치업자는 외국인 환자를 초청하려면 반드시 휴넷 코리아(www.visa.go.kr)를 통한 온라인 사증발급인정서 신청만 가능하며, 출입국관리사무소 방문신청을 할 수 없다.

구 분	예 약	비 자	비 고
스스로 의료관광 비자를 발급받은 의료관광객	입원 예약	의료관광비자 (C-3-3, G-1-10)	해외 현지 한국 대사관이나 영사관에 비자 신청
외국인환자 유치업체 또는 의료기관을 통해서 의료관광 비자를 발급받은 의료관광객	입원 예약	사증발급 인정서 의료관광비자 (C-3-3, G-1-10)	휴넷 코리아를 통해서 사증발급인정서 비자 신청
한국 거주 의료관광객	외래 예약 입원 예약		주한 외국대사관 직원, 주한 미군
한국 거주 교포 및 외국인	외래 예약 입원 예약		거소 신고한 해외교포 및 외국인 신고를 하고 90일 이상 체류하는 외국인은 국민건강보험 가입 가능
일반 관광객	외래 예약 입원 예약	관광·통과 비자(B2)	

■ 비자 변경

의료관광객에 대해서 좀 더 치료가 필요한 경우, 체류를 연장하기 위해서 C-3-3에서 G-1-10으로 변경하는 경우도 있다.

구 분	비 고
외국인환자 유치 의료기관 및 유치업체	신청서, 여권 원본, 수수료(3만원), 체류기간 연장의 필요성을 소명하는 서류(의사 진단서) 7일 이전에 제출
본인	신청서, 여권 원본, 수수료(3만원), 체류기간 연장의 필요성을 소명하는 서류(의사 진단서) 당일 제출

■ 온라인사증발급인정서 신청방법

① 휴넷코리아(www.visa.go.kr)에 접속
② 로그인
③ 홈페이지 상단 '사증발급인정서 신청' 선택 후 하단의 신청 버튼 클릭
④ 신청가능 체류자격의 의료관광 신청을 클릭
⑤ 사증발급인정서 신청화면 하단 피초청자 추가 버튼을 클릭하고 피초청자 기본정보를 등록 후 관련 첨부서류 등재 후 신청
⑥ 신청 후 처리 결과는 회원의 마이페이지에서 확인 가능
⑦ Reference Number 확인(외국인환자 유치업체 또는 의료기관 비자담당 직원의 핸드폰 문자 또는 E-mail로 통보)

■ 의료관광 진행순서

의료관광 비자는 어느 단계에서 도움을 제공할까?

Steps	Procedure
Initial Contact	• Contact • Collecting data
Confirmation	• Diagnosis and Treatment options • Setting up Visit Plan • Assisting with VISA(비자발급 지원) • Reservation and Scheduling • Airport pick up

Pre-surgery	• Outpatient's Center Or Inpatient Procedures
	• Medical Exam and Consulting
	• Hospitalization and Paperwork
	• Treatment(Surgery)
Post-surgery	• Recovering
	• Discharge

■ 〈Case〉 의료관광 비자 필요 문의

Patient: Hello.

MTC(Staff): Good morning. This is ABC global healthcare center.

This is Nurse Lee speaking.

How may I help you?

Patient: I am a Chinese citizen. I want to have a surgery done(performed) in Korea.

Do I need a VISA?

MTC: China is not under VISA exemption[1] agreements so you need a VISA to stay in Korea.

If you get the medical VISA, you can stay for 90 days.

Patient: How can I get the medical VISA?

What kind of documents do I need to get the medical VISA?

MTC: Medical VISA applications require a completed application form, a recent passport-sized photo, official proof of medical treatment issued by hospitals in Korea, financial[2] documents to prove affordability[3] to pay the medical expenses.

Patient: How can I prove my financial affordability?

MTC: The documents showing approving how much money you deposit in the bank are necessary.

---

1) exemption: 면제

2008년 2월부터 중국인관광객 제주도 무비자 입국 가능

인천, 김해국제공항을 통해 제주도로 가는 환승객(중국인 포함)은 72시간 동안 국내 입국 가능

2) financial: 재정적인

financial capability: 재정능력 = financial affordability

3) affordability: 여력

Such documents will be issued[4] by any banks in China.

Patient: So, I must prove how much amount of deposit I have in the bank.

MTC: Yes.

■ 〈Case〉 의료관광 비자 필요 문의

Patient: Hello.

MTC(Staff): Good morning. This is ABC Clinic.

Nurse Kim speaking.

How may I help you?

Patient: I am interested in a plastic surgery procedure in Korea.

I live in California. I am calling from California

MTC(Staff): America is under VISA exemption[5] agreements so you don't need a

visa if you stay in Korea less than 30 days.

Did you check the expire[6] date of your passport?

Patient: I will.

■ 〈Case〉 사증발급 인정서 설명

Patient: Hello.

MTC(Staff): Good morning. This is ABC Hospital.

Nurse Kim speaking.

How may I help you?

Patient: I am interested in the spinal[7] treatment at ABC Clinic.

Where and how can I get the medical VISA?

MTC(Staff): The medical VISA will be issued by Korean Embassy[8] or Consulate[9]

in China.

---

4) issue: 발급하다.
5) exemption: 면제
6) expire: 만기
   expire date: 만기일
7) spinal: 척추의
8) embassy: 대사관
9) consulate: 영사관
   consulate general: 총영사관

Patient: What kind of documents do I need?

MTC: Your passport, application form for VISA, a 2 by 2 inch size photo[10], official proof of medical treatment requirement issued by Korean hospitals, and financial documents to prove your financial capability[11] to bear[12] the medical expenses during your stay in Korea.

Patient: Thank you for your kind information.

Would you help me get through all the procedures?

MTC: With great pleasure.

First of all, please tell me your e-mail address.

I will let you know what I can do for you.

We can keep in touch by e-mail.

Patient: OK. My e-mail address is fatherofsuise@hotmail.com.

■ 〈Case〉 사증발급 인정서 설명

Patient: Hello.

MTC(Staff): Good morning. DEF Medical Travel Agency.

This is Park speaking.

What can I do for you?

Patient: I am interested in a plastic surgery (procedure) in Korea.

How can I get the medical VISA?

---

10) 2×2 사이즈 사진 : a 2 by 2 inch size photo = 51 by 51 mm size photo

Photos must be 2 by 2 inches in size.

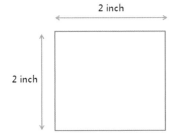

11) financial capability: 재정능력

12) bear the medical expenses
= pay the medical expenses

MTC: DEF Medical Travel Agency is able to submit necessary documents for you to get the medical VISA.

After the Immigration office check if you are qualified, an authorized code will be sent to me.

As soon as I receive the authorized code, I will inform you of the code by cellular phone or e-mail.

Patient: I understand.

MTC: Korean Embassy or Consulate in China will issue you the medical VISA based on the authorized code.

■ 〈Case〉 의료관광 비자 필요 문의

Patient: Hello.

MTC: Good morning. DEF Medical Travel Agency.

This is Lee speaking.

What can I do for you?

Patient: I am interested in a plastic surgery (procedure) in Korea.

How can I get the medical VISA?

MTC: If you submit the required information and documents to me, on behalf of you, I will fill out the VISA application form on the webpage of the Immigration Office.

Korean government has already authorized us to facilitate the VISA process for the sake of patient's convenience.

After your VISA application is approved, a VISA reference number code will be sent to me.

As soon as I receive the reference number by cellular phone or e-mail, I will let you know it.

When you visit Korean Embassy or Consulate in China, you just present the code. It will facilitate the process of getting VISA from Korean Embassy or Consulate in China.

1.2 공항영접 비용 및 방법 문의

How much do you charge for (the) airport pick up service?

There is 110,000 Korean Won charge for airport pick up service. 110,000 Korean Won is roughly equal to USD 100(one hundred US Dollars).

There is an extra charge for airport pick up service.

Airport pick up service is available for an additional[13] charge.

There will be an additional pick up charge of USD 100.

■ 〈Case〉 공항 영접비용 문의

Patient: How much do you charge for (the) airport pick up service?

MTC(Staff): It is USD 60 per person.

Patient: How can I recognize you?

MTC: I will hold a paging board with your name on. You can easily notice(find) me.

■ 〈Case〉 공항 영접신원 확인방법

Patient: How should I identify myself when I get to the airport? How can I recognize(find) you?

MTC(Staff): Airport pickup service will be arranged by us.

The staff from ABC Hospital will hold up a paging board with your name on and wear identification card on the neck.

■ 〈Case〉 공항 영접비용 및 차량종류 문의

Patient: Is there an extra[14] charge for airport pick up service?

MTC(Staff): We offer the pick up service between the airport and ABC hospital.

About price, it depends on the number of clients.

How many members are expected to visit Korea with you?

---

13) additional: 추가의
14) extra: 별도의

Patient: My wife(husband) will accompany[15] me.

I will go to Korea with my wife. Just two of us.

MTC: What kind of vehicles do you want?

Ambulance, van or automobile?

The fare is different depending on the type of vehicles.

Patient: Van is OK with me.

1.3 공항 영접

Welcome to Korea.

My name is Gil Dong Hong.

I am from ABC Hospital.

1.3.1 의료관광객 환영

■ 〈Case〉 의료관광객 확인, 명함 전달, 차량으로 이동, 병원까지 차량이동 소요시간 문의

MTC(Staff): Nice to meet you.

I am Lee from ABC Medical Travel Agency.

I hope that you will have a good time with us.

Patient: It's a pleasure to meet you.

MTC: This is my business card.

(명함을 전달하면서)

Patient: Thank you.

MTC: This is my cellular phone number.

(핸드폰 번호를 가리키면서)

I will be accompanying you all the time[16] during your stay in Korea.

First of all, I will guide you to the hotel right away.

---

15) accompany: 동행하다. 동반하다.
16) all the time: 항상

16

Please come this way.

Patient: OK

MTC: Please get on the mini-bus.

Now, the mini-bus will start toward ABC Hospital.

(버스 출발)

Patient: How long does it take?

MTC: To (get to) DEF hospital, it will take about one hour and a half.

Patient: I see.

MTC: When you arrive at the hospital, you are required to fill out the preliminary medical check form.

Also please be very detailed with your information.

After that, you are supposed to go into the consultation[17] room and get examined.

Patient: I got it.

■ 〈Case〉 의료관광객 환영, 방문 소감

MTC(Staff): I am very glad to meet you.

I am Lee from ABC Medical Travel Agency.

Patient: Glad to meet you.

MTC: Is this your first time in Seoul(Busan, Daegu, Daejeon, Jeju)?[18]

Patient: Yes, this is my first time.[19]

MTC: Please enjoy the view of Korea through the window until we arrive at the hospital.

What is your first impression of Seoul(Busan, Daegu, Daejeon, Jeju)?

Patient: It is beautiful.

■ 〈Case〉 의료관광객 확인, 명함전달, 대기차량으로 이동, 차량이동 소요시간 문의

MTC(Staff): Good morning. This is Kim from ABC Hospital.

Here is my business card.

---

17) consultation room: 상담실, 진료실
18) = Is this your first visit to Seoul(Busan)?
19) No, this is my second visit to Seoul. : 두 번째 방문의 경우

(명함을 전해주면서)

Patient: Nice to meet you.

It is so nice of you to come and meet me at the airport.

MTC: Welcome to Korea.

We have a mini-bus waiting outside.

Is this all your luggage?

Let me help you carry your luggage.

Patient: Thank you.

MTC: You are welcome.

(수하물을 들어주면서)

Did you have a nice flight?

Patient: Yes, it was a quite pleasant flight.

MTC: Is this your first visit to Korea?

Patient: Yes, it is.

I feel jet-lagged a little.

MTC: I am sorry to hear that.

As soon as we get to the hospital, you can take a rest.

I have arranged a consultation with the doctor tomorrow morning 10 o'clock.

Patient: How long is the drive to the hospital? (How long does it take to the hospital by car?)

MTC: It will take about 10 minutes to the hospital.

Let me point out some interesting sights on our way to the hospital.

Patient: OK.

■ 자기소개의 주의사항

① 명찰을 전해 주면서 자기소개

② 억양은 부드럽게 한다.

③ 상대방과의 eye-contact

④ 영어는 세계 공용어이므로 지나친 미국식 발음을 자제한다.

⑤ 해당 국가의 모국어로 간단한 인사말을 하면서 환영의 뜻을 전한다.

■ 명함에 대한 인식차이

① 서양에서 명함이 자신을 알리는 도구이며, 회사에 대한 정보는 상대적으로 중요하지 않다. 따라서 동양에서는 회사의 로고와 회사명이 눈에 띄게 크게 만들지만, 서양의 경우 회사 로고는 우측이나 좌측 상단에 작게 들어가고 본인의 이름이 크게 들어간다.

② 서양에서는 비즈니스용과 사교용(Calling Card)을 나누어서 다니기도 한다.

③ 서양에서는 개인의 직책이 여러 개일 경우 중요한 것 1~2개만 적는다. 너무 많이 적으면 자신을 과시한다고 생각한다.

④ 인도와 중남미에서는 명함에 학위를 표시하는 경향이 있다.

⑤ 중국은 번영을 바라는 의미에서 명함의 글자에 황금색을 쓰기도 한다.

⑥ 명함은 아랫사람이 윗사람에게, 나이 어린 사람이 많은 사람에게, 방문객이 직원에게 먼저 주는 것은 동·서양이 동일하다.

⑦ 명함을 상대방이 읽을 수 있는 방향으로 전달한다.

⑧ 서양은 처음 본 사람에게 명함을 내밀지 않으며, 충분히 애기하고 나서 연락처가 필요하다 싶으면 그때 명함을 꺼낸다.

⑦ 오른손으로 명함을 주고받으며, 장갑을 끼고 주고받아도 무례한 행위가 아니다.

⑧ 일본의 경우, 명함의 예절은 매우 중요하다. 명함에 존경과 경외심을 담아서 취급해야 된다. 명함을 항상 두 손으로 주고받아야만 된다. 명함을 받은 후 2~3초간 명함을 읽어야만 한다. 그리고 상대방의 이름과 소속부서, 직책을 따라 읽어야만 한다. 어떻게 읽어야 할지 모른다면 반드시 상대방에게 물어보아야 한다. 미팅이 끝날 때까지 명함을 주머니에 넣으면 안 된다. 명함을 테이블에 가지런히 놓는다. 상대방의 이름이 생각나지 않아서 명함을 몇 차례 힐끗 보는 것도 실례이다. 따라서 명함을 받으면 암기하듯 읽을 필요가 있는 것이다. 명함에 뭔가를 메모하는 것도 피해야 된다. 이는 상대방의 얼굴에 낙서를 하는 것과 동일하다.

1.3.2 이동

여기서는 공항 로비를 출발하여 Shuttle Bus / 차량을 이용해서 숙박장소까지 이동하는 동안 어떤 대화를 하면 좋을까?

1.3.2.1 이동전 인원 및 수하물 확인

① 수하물의 분실에 유의하다.

② 출발 전에 최종적으로 인원을 점검한다.

③ 이동후의 일정에 대해서 간략하게 브리핑한다.

■ 〈Case〉 단체 의료관광객 출발 전 공지사항 전달

MTC(Staff): How many people are there in your group?[20]

Patient: Nine people including me. We are all here.

MTC: Shall we leave and take the mini-bus?

Come this way please.

Please don't leave any luggage behind.[21]

May I help you with your luggage[22]?

Patient: Thank you.

How far is the hotel from the airport?

MTC: It will take about one hour and 30 minutes to the hotel by this bus[23].

The hotel is not far from the airport.

The airport is about 25 miles[24] away from downtown.

20) = How many members do you have in your group?
21) Please don't leave any luggage left behind.
    = Please take all the belongs you have.
22) = May I help you with your baggage?
23) It will take us an hour to get to the hotel.
    = It will take an hour for us to get to the hotel.
    * It takes + 사람 + 시간 + to ~
    It takes + 시간 + for + 목적격 + to ~: 사람이 ~하는데 얼마의 시간이 걸리다.
    How long does it take to ~ ?: ~하는데 얼마나 걸립니까?
    A: How long does it take to go home?
    B: It take me an hour(to go home)
24) 1mile = 1.609km
    5miles = 8.045km
    25miles = 40.23km

Right after you get out of the airport terminal building, there is a six-lane road.

We have to cross the road to get to the parking lot.

(주차장 도착 후)

MTC: Please get on the bus.

Patient: Thank you.

MTC: You are welcome.

■ 〈Case〉 단체 의료관광객 출발 전 공지사항 전달

MTC(Staff): Ladies and gentlemen.

Please gather around the banner(placard). We are leaving for GHI hotel you are going to stay while you are in Seoul(Busan).

Please take all the luggage you have[25].

Patient: How long does it take from here to the hotel?

MTC: It will take about 30 minutes by bus. The mini-bus is waiting for us outside the airport building.

Please come this way.

Let me help you with your bag.

Patient: Thank you.

MTC: There are a lot of top doctors and surgeons[26] with relevant international experience in Korea.

They are worth trusting.

Patient: That's why I came to Korea.

MTC: I will do my best for you to enjoy the excellent quality of medical service and care.[27]

Patient: Thank you.

---

25) Please take all the luggage(baggage) you have
   = Please take all the belongs you have
26) surgeon specialist: 전문의
   eye specialist: 안과 전문의
   cancer specialist: 암 전문의
27) I will do my best for you to enjoy the excellent quality of medical service and care.
   = I will do my best for the excellent quality of medical service and medical care.

MTC: If you have any inconvenience during your stay in Korea, please do not hesitate to call me.[28]

This is my name(business) card.

Patient: Thank you.

MTC: You are welcome.

1.3.3.2 공항로비에서 차량으로 이동

이동시 가벼운 마음으로 선택할 수 있는 대화 내용은 주로 날씨, 여정, 가족관련 사항 등이다.

(1) 날씨

• 〈Case〉기후

MTC(Staff): What is the weather like in U.S.A(Canada) at this time of the year?

Patient: It is very cold.

• 〈Case〉기후

MTC(Staff): How do you like the weather in Korea?

Patient: It is wonderful.

(2) 여정

• 〈Case〉비행여정

MTC(Staff): Did you enjoy the flight from U.S.A(Japan) to Seoul(Busan)?

Patient: Yes, I did.

• 〈Case〉비행여정

MTC(Staff): How was the trip?

Patient: It was wonderful.

• 〈Case〉기내음식

MTC(Staff): How was the meal service of OPQ Airlines?

Patient: It was great.

Especially I enjoyed Korean meal.

---

28) please do not hesitate to call me.

= please feel free to call me.

= please do not hesitate to contact me.

22

MTC: I am glad to hear that.

(3) 일정

• 〈Case〉 일정

MTC(Staff): Is this your first visit to Korea.

Patient: Yes it is.

MTC: You are scheduled to visit Gyungju(Busan) after the plastic surgery

It is a kind of open air museum.

(4) 취미

• 〈Case〉 취미생활

MTC(Staff): What is your hobby.

Do you enjoy playing golf?

Patient: Yes, I do.

MTC: Well, there are many outstanding golf courses near[29] Seoul(Busan).

It takes only 40 minutes from Seoul(Busan) by car.

Patient: It sounds great.

(5) 의료관광

• 〈Case〉 의료관광 정보

MTC(Staff): How did you find information about ABC Hospital?

Patient: One of my friends recommended ABC Hospital to me.

My friend had a spine surgery done(performed) there.

1.3.3.3 보행시 및 탑승시 예절

1.3.3.3.1 보행시 예절

• 왼쪽에서 한발 앞서서 안내한다.

• 방향을 바꾸는 경우 손으로 방향을 미리 알려준다.

• ① 1순위 자리, ② 2순위 자리, ③ 3순위 자리, ④ 4순위 자리

↑ ②① (의료관광객 1, 의료관광코디네이터 2)

---

29) We want to find a house nearer the station.: 역에 더 가까운 집을 찾기 원한다.

a nearby village: 바로 이웃마을

↑ ③①② (의료관광객과 동행자 1.2, 의료관광코디네이터 3)

↑ ④③②① (의료관광객과 동행자 1.2.3, 의료관광코디네이터 4)

↑ ① (의료관광객과 동행자 1, 의료관광코디네이터 2)

②

↑ ② (의료관광객과 동행자 1.2, 의료관광코디네이터 3)

①

③

1.3.3.3.2 자동차 승차시의 예절

① 상위자가 마지막에 타고, 먼저 내리는 경우와 상위자가 먼저 타고 먼저 내리는 경우[30]가 있다.

② 프랑스에서는 상위자가 먼저 타고 먼저 내린다.

① ③ ② ④ Driver	의료관광코디네이터 ④

1.3.3.3.3 승강기 승차시의 예절

① 운전요원이 있는 경우: 상위자가 먼저 타고 먼저 내린다.

먼저 탑승하도록 요청할 때의 표현: After you. ['먼저 타시라'는 의미에서 손을 앞으로 내밀면서]

② 운전요원이 없는 경우: 안내자가 먼저 타고 문의 "OPEN"장치를 누르고 있거나 문이 갑자기 닫히지 않도록 손으로 문을 잡는다.

③ 엘리베이터 조작버튼 앞이 낮은 자리이고, 대각선 뒤쪽 방향이 가장 상석이 된다.

④ 엘리베이터 내에서는 큰소리로 떠들거나 전화통화를 하지 않는다.

⑤ 내릴 때는 고객이 먼저 내린다.

① ③ ② ④ Button	의료관광코디네이터 ④

---

30) 하위자는 자동차를 뒤로 돌아 반대편 문으로 승하차한다.

1.3.3.4 차량 출발 전 간단한 소개

■ 〈Case〉 의료관광코디네이터 및 병원에 대한 간단한 소개

MTC(Staff): Welcome to Seoul(Busan).

My name is Hong Gil Dong[31].

I am a staff from DEF Medical Tour Agency.

My primary[32] job is to help you (to) feel comfortable and confident while you are in Seoul(Busan).

I believe the ABC Hospital will provide you with the quality of service you deserve.[33]

We will meet quite often during your stay in Korea.

If you need my help, please don't hesitate to ask me[34]. I will sit on the first chair in this bus.

I hope you enjoy your staying in Seoul(Busan).

Patient: Thanks for your kindness.

■ 〈Case〉 의료관광코디네이터 및 병원에 대한 간단한 소개

MTC(Staff): Ladies and gentlemen. Welcome to Seoul(Busan).

I am glad to meet you.

I am going to escort you to GHI Hotel.

You are scheduled to stay for 7 days and 6 nights in Seoul(Busan).

ABC Hospital will meet your standards and expectations for medical cares. A dedicated and experienced medical team is ready for your

---

31) 영어로 된 별명을 하나 가지고 있으면 외국인이 쉽게 기억할 수 있다.

My English nick name is James.

영어 이름을 어떻게 만들 수 있을까?

www.babynames.com에서 쉽게 찾을 수 있다.

32) primary: 주요한

primary duty: 주요 의무

33) I believe the hospital will provide you with the quality of service you deserve.

= I believe the hospital will provide you with the excellent quality of medical care.

34) please don't hesitate to ask me

= please feel free to ask me

medical operations.[35)]

Please feel at home while you are in Seoul(Busan).

If you have any inconvenience, please let me know.

Patient: Thank you.

MTC: You are more than welcome.

1.3.3.5 공항에서 호텔로 이동

• 장거리에서 온 경우 공항에서 바로 병원으로 안내하는 것은 피해야 한다. 장시간의 비행으로 심신이 피로한 사람을 이끌고 바로 업무협의를 한다는 것은 무리다. 호텔로 가서 복장을 갈아입은 후 또는 다음 날부터 공식일정을 시작하는 것이 좋다.

• 공항에서 호텔로 가는 동안의 대화는 주로 일정, 가벼운 개인적인 내용의 사항이 바람직하다.

1.3.3.5.1 공항에서 호텔로 모시고 가는 동안의 대화

① 비행시간이 출발 국가와의 거리에 따라서 다르다. 미국, 캐나다는 11~12시간의 장시간 비행으로 피곤하므로 상황을 판단하여 대화를 유도한다. 서비스는 상대방의 마음을 잘 읽어서 정신적 · 육체적으로 편하게 해주는 것이 서비스이다. 따라서 만약 탑승 후 약 5분 정도

경과하여 탑승자의 표정을 보았을 때, 탑승자들이 피곤해 보이는 모습이면, 조용히 목적지까지 가는 것이 현명하다. 그러나 탑승자들이 호기심 가득찬 눈으로 창밖을 보고 있으면 준비한 자료를 읽거나 미리 암기한 내용을 전달하도록 한다.

② 공적인 내용의 대화와 사적인 내용의 대화중에서 가능하면 공적인 대화를 중심으로 말을 풀어나간다.

③ 결혼, 이혼에 대한 질문은 피한다.

(예) Are you married? (×)

---

35) A dedicated and experienced medical team is ready for your medical operations.
   = A good and experienced medical team is ready for your medical surgery.
   = A world-famous and experienced medical team is ready for your medical operations.

④ 종교에 대한 질문은 피한다.

    (예) Are you a christian? (×)

         Do you believe in christianity? (×)

⑤ 날씬하다 등 신체에 대한 대화도 피한다.

    (예) You look so sexy. (×)

1.3.3.5.2 대화거리의 준비

① 국제의료관광코디네이터가 좋아하는 것에 관해서 질문하면 좋은 대화가 될 수 있다.

    (예) What do you usually do on weekends?

        I play bowling with my wife and children.

    (예) Do you like mountain-climbing?

        I sometimes enjoy climbing mountains on weekends.

② 의료관광객의 지역, 기후, 위치, 자랑거리 등에 대해서 인터넷에서 미리 정보수집한다.

③ 취미가 독서 [http://www.amazon.com: 각종 저서에 대한 줄거리 요약 등의 자료를 얻을 수 있다. 취미가 동반자 행사와 관련 있으면 적극적으로 대화를 유도한다.

④ 해외여행의 경험을 이야기한다.

⑤ 수술 일정에 대한 대화를 한다.

⑥ 주변의 시설물, 주변의 경관, 건물, 공단, 시설에 대한 설명한다. 공항에서 호텔로 오는 동안의 코스를 사전 답사한 후, 주요 시설물에 대한 영문소개를 준비한다. (한국관광공사의 홈페이지 http://www.knto.or.kr를 방문하면 한국에 대해서 영어로 소개된 자료를 구할 수 있다.)

⑦ 간단한 대화도 분위기를 부드럽게 하는데 도움이 된다.

1.3.3.6 이동 중 한국에 대해 소개

한국에 대해서 소개하고 싶을 때는 유창한 영어로 소개할 수 없다면 가장 좋으나, 만약 시간적인 여유가 부족하거나 경험이 부족한 경우 아래의 참고자료를 읽고 필요한 부분을 발췌한 후 컴퓨터로 입력해서 보기 좋게 프린트해서 나눠주는 방법도 있다.

① 한국의 안내책자

② 영자 신문[객실에 비치]

1.4 호텔 도착

특급 호텔의 경우, 투숙객의 국기가 게양되어 있도록 사전에 확인하고 조처한다.

■ 〈Case〉 호텔 도착 안내

MTC(Staff): Here we are.

This is DEF Hotel.

Let us get off the bus.

Watch out your steps.

Please come this way.

Watch out the revolving door[36].

Patient: Thank you.

MTC: You are welcome.

■ 〈Case〉 호텔 도착 안내

MTC(Staff): Here we are.

Watch out the steps, please.

This is DEF Hotel.

Please get off here.

Patient: OK.

MTC: Let us wait until your luggage is unloaded.(Let us wait until the driver takes out all the luggage from the bus.)

■ 〈Case〉 호텔 도착 안내

MTC(Staff): Here we are.

Please watch out the steps.

(수하물을 꺼낸 후)

MTC: I will take your luggage(baggage) for you.

Patient: Thank you.

---

36) revolving door: 회전문

MTC: You are welcome.

Please come this way.

1.5 호텔 숙박 체크인

■ 〈Case〉 체크인

MTC(Staff): Your room is reserved.(Your room has already been reserved.)

Patient: Thank you.

MTC: Just a minute, please.

(체크인 종료 후)

MTC: Here is your room key. It is on the 17 floor.[37]

The bellman will escort you to the room.

■ 〈Case〉 체크인

MTC(Staff): A double room is reserved for you.

Patient: OK.

MTC: I will get the room key.

Just a second please.

(체크인 종료 후)

MTC: Here is your room key.

Patient: Thank you.

1.6 호텔 체크인 종료 후

■ 호텔에서의 주의사항

① 객실은 개인공간이므로 객실 안까지 따라 들어가는 것보다는 객실 밖에서 또는 로비에서 대화를 마치고 헤어지는 것이 바람직하다.

---

37) 중국인은 8자와 9주가 들어간 객실 번호를 선호한다. (예) 808호, 909호

② 객실 안에서 술을 함께 마시는 것은 피한다.

③ 여성이 혼자 있는 객실에는 절대로 들어가지 않는다.

④ 호텔은 City, 복도는 Road, 객실은 House의 개념으로 보아야 한다.

⑤ 큰소리로 말하지 않는다.

⑥ 호텔에서는 아무리 급하더라도 절대로 뛰지 않는다.

■ 〈Case〉 작별인사

MTC(Staff): Please unpack[38] your luggage in the room and have a good sleep[39].

Patient: Thank you.

MTC: See you at 10:00 am tomorrow morning in the lobby.

Patient: In the lobby 10:00 am.

MTC: Good night.

I will be waiting for you in the lobby tomorrow morning.

I will wear a blue cap with the name of ABC Hospital on.

You can easily recognize me.

Patient: See you tomorrow.

■ 〈Case〉 다음날 일정에 대한 확인

MTC(Staff): Tomorrow morning you are supposed to meet Dr. Lee at DEF Clinic.

Let me check your schedule.

(일정표를 확인하면서)

You are scheduled to meet him(her) at 11:00 am.

Patient: 11:00 am?

MTC: Yes.

I will give you a ride to his(her) office(clinic). It takes about 10 minutes by car from the hotel to his(her) clinic.[40]

I will be here by 10:20 am

Patient: 10:20. See you then.

---

38) unpack: 짐을 풀다.

39) = have a deep sleep

40) It takes about 10 minutes by car from the hotel to his clinic.

= It will take about 10 minutes by car from the hotel to his clinic.

MTC: See you tomorrow. Have a good sleep.

■ 〈Case〉 일정 확인 후에 헤어지는 인사

MTC(Staff): Tomorrow morning, there will be a meeting with the doctor.

I hope you have a good sleep.

Patient: Thank you.

MTC: See you tomorrow morning at 10:00 in the lobby.

Patient: I'll show up at the appointed time tomorrow morning.[41]

1.7 관광일정 안내 및 지역 소개

■ 〈Case〉 관광지 안내

Patient: This is my second visit to Korea.

I am interested in Korean culture. Can you recommend[42] some places worth[43] visiting?

MTC(Staff): Where did you visit in your first visit to Korea?

Patient: Gyungbok royal palace.

MTC: Gyungbok palace is a wonderful place to visit.

There are Art museum as well as Folklore museum in this city.

And you can also visit the temples and some temples in Korea provide a temple stay program for people from overseas.

---

41) I'll show up at the appointed time tomorrow morning.

= I'll be here at 10:00 am.

42) recommend: 추천하다.

43) worth + ing

This book is worth reading.

= It is worth while to read this book.

worth, near, opposite, like 등의 형용사는 목적어를 취하며 전치사로 볼 수도 있다.

* My house is near the lake.

* They are opposite each other.

* They are very like each other.

■ 〈Case〉 관광일정 안내

Patient: Are there any sightseeing tours in the afternoon?

MTC(Staff): Yes, there are some city tours.

It will start in one hour and the bus will pick you up in front of the hotel(hospital).

■ 〈Case〉

Patient: Are there any special tour program tomorrow?

MTC(Staff): All the participants(guests) have the

option of going on a tour of Seoul(Busan) or a tour of Folk Village. You will be able to know more about Korean cultures if you participate in the tour of Folk Village.

We will provide you with a bus service back to the hotel at a pre-scheduled[44] time.

■ 〈Case〉 관광안내 브로셔 전달

Patient: Do you have travel brochures about local scenic spots and places of historic interest?

MTC(Staff): Yes, we do. Here you are.

Besides this, English brochures about local history and sports are also available.

If you need more detailed travel brochures, please feel free to ask me.

■ 〈Case〉 차량 안내

• 병원과 호텔에는 많은 차량이 정차해 있으므로 쉽게 찾을 수 있도록 차량번호, 차량 색상을 알려주는 것이 효과적이다.

• 차량의 측면과 유리 앞면에 의료관광 프로그램 이름을 표기할 때, Medical이란 단어 보다는 Healthcare란 단어가 더 바람직하다. Medical은 왠지 환자라는 느낌이 더 강하다.

Patient: Where is the pick-up point[45]?

MTC(Staff): Just in front of the hotel.

---

44) pre-scheduled: 예정된
45) pick-up point: 탑승장소

Patient: But there are many buses, so I cannot figure out which one is the shuttle
bus for the tour.

MTC: The green-colored bus with the red-line in the middle. Bus number is 9185.

Patient: Thank you.

MTC: You are welcome.

■ 〈Case〉 병원 및 호텔 주변식당 안내

• 병원 퇴원 후 및 호텔 숙박 중 호텔 근처의 식당을 이용할 경우, 어떤 종류의 음식
을 주의해야 하는지 의사와 먼저 상의를 해야만 한다. 병원과 호텔 근처의 식당을
안내할 때는 직접 위생상태 등을 확인한 곳을 추천하도록 한다.

Patient: Would you please recommend[46] a good restaurant not far from the
hotel(hospital)?

MTC(Staff): Sure.

Look to the right hand side in front of the hotel, you will find a
five-story[47] blue building.

On the 3rd floor there is a nice Korean traditional restaurant.

The foods at the restaurants are very delicious.

Patient: Your information would be very useful.

Thank you.

MTC: You are welcome.

■ 〈Case〉 병원 및 호텔 주변 쇼핑안내

참가자들도 의료서비스 전·후에 시간이 나면 관광
객들과 마찬가지로 쇼핑을 즐기기도 한다.

Patient: Excuse me. Can you recommend a good
shopping area?

MTC(Staff): There are many fine department stores

---

46) recommend: 추천하다.
   Can you recommend a good dictionary to me?: 나에게 좋은 사전을 추천해 줄 수 있습니까?
   They recommended her as a good lawyer.: 그들은 그녀를 훌륭한 변호사로 추천했다.

47) a five-story building = a building of five stories: 5층 건물
   five stories of high: 5층 높이

downtown Seoul(Busan), but I'd like to recommend Itaewon(Seomyun).

Patient: Is it far from here?

MTC: No, it will just take 20 minutes from here by taxi.

The taxi fare will be about 5,000 Won, equal to USD 4.

Patient: Can I go there by subway or by bus?

MTC: You can use the shuttle bus.

It runs every thirty minutes in front of this hotel.[48]

Patient: Thank you very much.

MTC: You are welcome.

1.8 사건 · 사고

■ 〈Case〉 교통 혼잡으로 약속시간 지연

MTC(Nurse): This is ABC Clinic.

Nurse Kim speaking.

What can I do for you?

Patient: I am caught in a traffic jam.

I might be (able to be) late for the appointment.

MTC: May I have your name?

Patient: My name is Susie Maria Hans.

MTC: Your appointment is scheduled for(at) 10:30.

I will postpone your appointment to 11:20 am.

Would that be OK with you?

Patient: Thanks.

I will be there before 11:10.

---

48) =The shuttle bus runs between this hotel and Itaewon at thirty minutes interval on the course.

■ 〈Case〉 교통 혼잡

MTC(Staff): This is ABC Clinic.

Nurse Lee speaking.

How can I help you?

Patient: The bus(taxi) is caught in the traffic jam.

Patient: I wonder if we might be late for the appointment.

MTC: The bus(taxi) will arrive at the hospital in 20 minutes.

We won't be late for the consultation[49] with the doctor because we left the hotel 20 minutes earlier before the consultation schedule.

Patient: I see.

■ 〈Case〉 분실사고

• 개인물품 분실사고: 보험처리가 가능하도록 협조
• 도난신고: 경찰서로부터 도난사고 증빙서류 발급

Patient: Excuse me.

MTC(Staff): Yes. What can I do for you?

Patient: I've lost my shoulder bag this morning.

MTC: I am sorry to hear that. Have you checked your room?

Patient: Yes. I've already looked all over the room.

It seems to me that I've lost it at the coffee shop.

MTC: Then, we'd better check there first.

Patient: I've already been there, but they didn't find it.

MTC: Could you give me some detailed information on it? Color and shape.

Patient: Sure, it's a black bag of Channel.

■ 〈Case〉 분실사고

MTC(Police Officer): May I have your name, please?

Patient: It's Maria Smith.

MTC: Where are you from?

Patient: From U.S.A.

---

49) consultation: 상담, 진료

MTC: Would you please fill out this "Lost Property Report[50]"?

Patient: Sure. Here you are.

MTC: Thank you. Please don't worry.

We'll do our utmost to find your shoulder bag.

■ 〈Case〉 분실 사고

Patient: Excuse me. I left my bag in a bus.

MTC(Staff): When did you take the bus?

Patient: I guess it was about 10 o'clock and the bus was bound[51] for Itaewon.

MTC: Will you tell me what your bag looks like?

Patient: It was made of black leather and it has gold fitting on the handle.

MTC: How large is it?

Patient: It's about briefcase size.

MTC: I'll ask about your bag right now. Just a minute, please.

(잠시 후)

MTC: I am sorry but they have no information about your bag so far. If they find it, they will give you a call.

1.9 관광일정 변경

■ 〈Case〉 의료관광객 건강관리 때문에 관광일정 변경

MTC(Staff): The doctor says that there is a possibility of complications[52] including infection[53] or a reaction to the anesthesia[54], if you take a long trip.

---

50) Lost Property Report: 분실신고서
51) bound: ~행의, ~에 가려고
    Where are you bound?: 어디에 가십니까?
    The ship is bound for New York.: 그 배는 뉴욕행이다.
52) complications: 부작용

Patient: I see.

MTC: You were scheduled to visit Gyungju city, but you are forced to change the schedule according to the advise of the surgeon.

The doctor is one of the most qualified surgeon in Korea, so that we have to accept this advise and follow his(her) instructions[55].

Patient: Okay. Then, what is the best choice?

MTC: We are going to visit the most famous tourist spots near Seoul(Busan).

Patient: Good.

MTC: Thanks you for your understanding.

■ 〈Case〉 의료관광객 건강관리 때문에 관광일정 변경

MTC(Staff): I am afraid that the doctor says that there might be a possibility of complications[56], if you take a trip.

Patient: I am listening.

MTC: So, we have no choice but to change our schedule.

You are scheduled to visit Gyungju city, but you have to cancel the schedule according to the advice of the doctor. He(She) is a world-famous doctor, so that we have to accept his(her) advise.

Patient: Okay. Then, what shall I do?

MTC: You had better stay at the room in the hotel(hospital) or take a city tour of Seoul(Busan, Daegu, Daejeon, Jeju).

Patient: I understand.

MTC: Thank you very much for your understanding.

Patient: In this case, can I get a refund for that portion of the uncompleted trip?

MTC: I am afraid that I can not answer that question right now.

---

53) infection: 감염
54) anesthesia: 마취
55) instruction: 지시사항
56) complications: 부작용

I will ask my boss and let you know what I can do about that.

Patient: Okay.

(다음 날)

 MTC: The company has decided to refund the portion of the uncompleted trip. The amount of refund will be about USD 30.

Patient: Thank you.

 MTC: You are welcome.

1.10 의료관광통역 비용

A translator will be offered at an extra charge.

What language is more convenient for you?

Superior quality translation service will be offered at affordable[57] rates.

A top quality English to Korean and Korean to English translation service will be offered.

■ 〈Case〉 의료관광통역 문의

Patient: Do you have a translation service?

MTC(Staff): Yes, a translation service is available upon request. What language can you speak?

Patient: My mother tongue is Japanese.

 MTC: Japanese translators are ready for you.

It will cost you 110,000 Korean Won per hour, equal to USD 100 based on the currency rate of USD to Korean Won. As of today, one dollar is worth about 1100 Korean Won.

■ 〈Case〉 의료관광통역 문의

Patient: Is English translation service available at ABC Hospital?

---

57) affordable: 저렴한, 알맞은

MTC(Staff): Yes, ABC Hospital has English translators.

Patient: What days do you have an English translator available?

My best time is Tuesday 16th after lunch time.

MTC: English translators are working every day.

Patient: Then, I'd like you to book[58] the translation service for me, please.

■ 〈Case〉 의료관광통역 문의

Patient: Do you have English translators in your clinic for foreign patients?

MTC(Nurse): Yes, we have an English translator.

ABC Hospital thinks highly of a language bridge[59] between patients and doctors.

■ 〈Case〉 영어 이외의 의료관광통역 문의

MTC(Nurse): Do you need an interpreter?

Patient: Yes.

MTC: What kind of language interpreters do you want?

Patient: Chinese.

MTC: I will arrange a Chinese interpreter for you.

Patient: Thanks a lot.

■ 〈Case〉 영어 이외의 의료관광통역 문의

Patient: I can speak in English, but Arabic is more comfortable because my mother tongue is Arabic.

MTC(Staff): Arabic translation is not available, but I can call the Arabic translator if you tell me your expected visit time.

---

58) = make a reservation for the translation service

59) language bridge: 언어 가교

language barrier: 언어장벽

I am sorry for your inconvenience.

■ 〈Case〉 영어 이외의 의료관광통역 문의

Patient: I can speak English a little.

Do you have a Thai translator?

MTC(Staff): If you need a Thai translation, we can prepare it.

Please let me know the expected time of your arrival, I will find a Thai translator.

It takes a little time (for us) to find a Thai translator, so please inform us of your expected arrival date at least two weeks in advance.

Patient: OK. I will let you know my flight schedule at least two weeks before I visit Korea.

■ 〈Case〉 영어 이외의 의료관광통역 문의

Patient: I am not fluent in English.

Do you have a Japanese interpretor?

MTC(Staff): If you need a Japanese interpretor, we can arrange it.

Please inform me of the exact expected time of your arrival, I will find a Japanese interpreter.

■ 〈Case〉 영어 통역 전화연결

Patient: Do you have someone who can speak English?

MTC(Staff): I am afraid that my English is not good.

I will have someone who can interpret in English on the phone when I call you back. It'll be a three-way conversation.

Chapter 2

의료관광객 병원예약 · 입원 서비스

2.1 예약

병원예약은 입국 전에도 이루어진다. 의료관광 비자가 필요한 경우 사증발급 인정서를 발급받기 위해서 의료관광객으로부터 의료관광비(진료비)의 일부를 미리 입금받을 필요가 있다.

I need to make an appointment.

I need to see the doctor.

When is the doctor free?

If it is all right, I would like to visit your clinic next Friday.

I'd like to call on you next Monday.

Do you think the doctor could squeeze(fit) me in tomorrow?

I need to make an appointment for my husband.

My child needs to come in for a check-up.

The doctor wants to see you again in two weeks.

Would Monday be all right?

When can I speak with the doctor?

What time are visiting hours?

What time will be convenient?

When is it convenient for you to visit?

Will you please make an appointment for me at 10:30 in the morning.

What is your schedule for the next week?

What day suits you best?

Which day and what time is good for you?

January the 3rd is okay with you?

We're running an hour behind schedule.

Dr. Kim is away. Instead of Dr. Kim, you'll be seeing Dr. Hong.

May I have your telephone number? I'll call you back.

Let me call you back later.

I will call you again in 20 minutes.

Let me call you back in 20 minutes.

■ 〈Case〉 병원예약

Patient: Hello.

MTC(Nurse): Good morning. ABC Hospital.

This is Nurse Lee speaking.

How may I help you?

Patient: I want to visit ABC Hospital on Monday.

MTC: May I have your name, please?

Patient: My name is Susie Maria Hans.

I have a toothache.

MTC: Is 2:00 pm OK with you?

Patient: That time is most convenient for me.

MTC: In the meantime, if you have any question, please feel free to contact me or you can leave your questions at the comments in the homepage of ABC Hospital.

On the right hand top side of the web page of ABC Hospital, there is a Q&A.

Patient: Would you tell me your e-mail address?

■ 〈Case〉 병원예약

Patient: Hello.

MTC(Nurse): Good afternoon. ABC Hospital.

This is Nurse Park speaking.

How can I help you?

Patient: I happened to read your webpage and I am interested in finding out more information about your medical service and the price.

I'd like to find out more information about the skin whitening program at your clinic.

MTC: I am proud to tell you that ABC Hospital is world-famous for skin care programs.

Patient: I am glad to hear that.

Can I make an appointment this coming Friday?

MTC: Friday is available.

■ 〈Case〉 병원예약

Patient: Hello.

MTC(Nurse): Good morning. ABC Hospital.

This is Nurse Park speaking.

How may I help you?

Patient: I'd like to make an appointment to see a doctor.

MTC: What's the problem?

Patient: I've been sick for over a week.

My head hurts and I keep coughing and sneezing[1].

I feel horrible.

MTC: I see.

You can make an appointment to see Dr. Kim on Thursday.

MTC: Well, he(she) might be able to fit you in this afternoon at 3:00.

Patient: Thanks a lot. 3:00 pm is fine.

---

1) sneeze: 재채기

MTC: Have you visited us before?

Patient: No, this is my first time.

MTC: OK.

Make sure you bring your health insurance I.D.

■ 〈Case〉 병원예약

Patient: Hello.

MTC(Nurse): Good afternoon. ABC Hospital.

This is Nurse Kim speaking.

How can(may) I help you?

Patient: I want to make an appointment the doctor.

MTC: When do you want to make an appointment?

Patient: I'd like to see a doctor on Thursday afternoon.

MTC: Your appointment is made this coming Thursday 3:00 pm.

Would that time be all right with you?

Patient: Sure.

MTC: If you want to reschedule or cancel the appointment, please give us a call.

Patient: Thanks. I'll see you then.

■ 〈Case〉 병원예약

Patient: Hello.

MTC(Nurse): Good morning. ABC Clinic.

This is Nurse Lee speaking.

How may I help you?

Patient: Can I make an appointment this afternoon?

MTC: There is no opening for Dr. Park this afternoon.

10:00 am tomorrow morning is available.

Patient: Then, I want to visit 10:00 am tomorrow morning.

MTC: May I have your name, please?

Patient: My name is Susie Maria Hans.

MTC: If you want to reschedule or cancel the appointment, please give us a call.

■ 〈Case〉 병원예약

Patient: Hello.

MTC(Nurse): Good morning. ABC Hospital.

This is Nurse Park speaking.

How may(can) I help you?

Patient: May I make an appointment with the doctor?

MTC: Is this a routine check up or for some other reasons?

Patient: I have a severe headache.

MTC: Dr. Park is available at 10:00 am.

Will that be a good time?

Patient: Yes, 10:00 am will be fine.

■ 〈Case〉 당일 병원예약

MTC: What is your name?

Patient: Susie Maria Hans.

MTC(Nurse): Doctor Lee's Office.

Nurse Park speaking.

How can I help you?

Patient: I need to make an appointment with Dr. Lee.

MTC: What is your name, please?

Patient: Susie Maria.

MTC: Okay Susie Maria.

Hold one moment while I find your Hospital ID.

(확인 후)

Thanks for waiting.(I am sorry to have kept you waiting)

Now, what do you need to see the doctor about?

Patient: Well, I have been fighting a cold for more than a week, and I think I might have a chest infection or something.

My cough is getting worse each day.

MTC: Doctor Lee is off tomorrow.

Do you think you can wait until Wednesday?

Patient: I am really hoping to get in today or tomorrow in case I need some antibiotics.

Maybe I will have to go to the walk-in-clinic instead.

MTC: Actually, we have a cancellation for 2:00 pm today.

Patient: It is almost 1:00 pm already.

I think I can make it if I leave right now.

MTC: We are running a bit behind schedule, so you can probably count on seeing the doctor around 2:30.

Patient: That is great.

Thanks for fitting me in.

MTC: No problem.

We will see you in an hour or so.

■ 〈Case〉 병원예약

Patient: Hello.

MTC(Nurse): Good afternoon. ABC Clinic.

This is Nurse Kim speaking.

How may I help you?

Patient: I would like to make an appointment with Dr. Lee 10 o'clock tomorrow morning.

MTC: I am afraid 10 o'clock is filled, but we have 3:00 pm open.

Will you take it?

Patient: Ok, I will take it

■ 〈Case〉 병원예약 및 이름 철자 확인방법

Dentist(Nurse): Good morning, Dr. Lee's office.

This is Nurse Lee speaking.

How may I help you today?

Patient: Good morning, I'd like to schedule a check-up.

MTC: I'd be happy to do that for you.

Have you been in to see Dr. Lee before?

Patient: Yes, I have.

My last check-up was six months ago.

MTC: Great.

Can I get your name, please?

Patient: My name is Susie Maria.

MTC: Thank you Susie Maria.

Which dentist did you see on your last check-up?

Patient: I'm not sure, really.

The doctor looked like he was at his forties[2].

MTC: That's OK.

Let me check your ID.

Oh, the doctor you met the other day was Dr. Lee.

Patient: Yes, that's right.

MTC: OK.

Dr. Lee has time next Friday in the morning.

Patient: That's not good.

I've got to work.

How about the week after that?

MTC: Yes, Dr. Lee will be available the week after the next.

Would you like to suggest a time?

Patient: Does he have anything open in the afternoon?

MTC: Yes, we could fit[3] you in on Thursday, January 14th at 2:30 in the afternoon.

Patient: Great. That'll work.

MTC: OK, thank you for calling.

We'll see you at 2:30 pm on the 14th of January.

Patient: Thank you. Good bye.

MTC: Goodbye.

---

2) be at his/her forties: 40대

3) we could fit you in = we could squeeze you in

만약 E-mail 주소가 세계적으로 유명한 yahoo 또는 hotmail이 아닌 경우, 그 부분도 전화상으로 불러주어야 하므로 불편함이 있을 수 있다. 따라서 의료관광코디네이터는 E-mail주소를 yahoo 또는 hotmail.com으로 갖고 있는 것이 바람직하다.

Character	Telephony	Character	Telephony
A	Alpha	N	November
B	Bravo	O	Oscar
C	Charlie	P	Papa
D	Delta	Q	Quebec
E	Echo	R	Romeo
F	Foxtrot, Fox	S	Sierra
G	Golf	T	Tango
H	Hotel	U	Uniform
I	India	V	Victor
J	Juliet	W	Whiskey
K	Kilo	X	Xray
L	Lima	Y	Yankee
M	Mike	Z	Zulu

■ 〈Case〉 병원 당일예약 및 방문

Patient: Hello.

MTC(Nurse): Doctor Kim's Clinic.

This is Nurse Lee speaking.

How may I help you?

Patient: I need to make an appointment with Dr. Kim.

MTC: Do you know your Insurance ID number?

Patient: I am afraid that I do not know. It is at home and I'm at work right now.

MTC: No problem. What's your name, please?

Patient: Susie Maria Hans.

MTC: Okay. Hold one moment please while I find your Insurance ID number.

Patient: Sure.

MTC: Thanks for waiting. Now, what do you need to see the doctor about?

Patient: I've been fighting a cold for more than a week, and I think I might have a chest infection[4] or something.

My cough is getting worse day by day.

MTC: Doctor Kim is off tomorrow. Do you think you can wait until the day after tomorrow?

Patient: Oh, I was really hoping to get in today or tomorrow in case I need some antibiotics[5].

MTC: Actually, we had a cancellation for 2:00 pm today if you can get away from the office.

Patient: It is almost 1:00 pm already.

I think I can make it if I leave the office right now.

MTC: We're running a bit behind schedule, so you can probably count on seeing the doctor around 2:30 pm.

Patient: That's great. Thanks for fitting me in.

MTC: No problem.

We'll see you in an hour or so.

■ 〈Case〉 재방문객 병원예약

Patient: Hello.

MTC(Nurse): Good morning. ABC Hospital.

This is Nurse Lee speaking.

How may I help you?

Patient: I'd like to make an appointment for my first visit.

What is the earliest available day and time?

MTC: The earliest available day would be on Friday, June 21st.

Would you like to come in 10:00 am on Friday?

---

4) infection: 감염
5) antibiotics: 항생제

Patient: Is there any other time available on that day?

I'd like to come in the later afternoon.

MTC: OK. I made an appointment for you at 3:00 pm on the 21st of June.

May I have your name?

Patient: My name is Susie Maria Han.

MTC: Thank you.

See you then.

■ 〈Case〉 상담 후 병원예약

Patient: Hello.

MTC(Nurse): Good morning. ABC Hospital.

This is Nurse Lee speaking.

How may I help you?

Patient: I have been suffering from high blood pressure and diabetes[6] for the last 10 years.

MTC: When will you be able to come to Korea?

Patient: As soon as I can make an appointment.

MTC: Do you have passport and Medical VISA?

Patient: Yes, I do.

MTC: I have to consider the possibility of an angina[7].

If you are feeling a chest pain with on going high blood pressure and diabetes, we need exam for both angina problem.

Do you understand everything that I've explained so far?

Patient: What is an angina?

MTC: It would not be 100% accurate to explain what is wrong with you without looking at the medical chart or other records.

Angina is chest pain that is the result of inadequate oxygen supply to the heart muscle.

---

6) diabetes: 당뇨병
7) angina: 협심증

In order to give you a precise consultation, we need to look at the records and proper tests are needed.

Patient: Is it OK for me to send you the necessary documents via E-mail?

MTC: It is OK.

I will make an appointment with the cardiologist.

Dr. Lee is a heart problem specialist.

Patient: I still don't understand you clearly, because of all the medical terminology[8]. They are too hard to comprehend.

MTC: Then I will send you the information via E-mail as well.

You can always contact us by telephone or E-mail so don't hesitate to contact us if you have any question.

Patient: Thank you.

I am a bit relieved.

MTC: You might need to consider staying for 3 to 4 days in Korea due to further examinations if they are needed.

For example, we might perform an exercise tolerance test and echocardiography[9]. Another test is examing coronary artery[10] closely, there is a test called angiocardiography[11] and there is a possibility that we might be conducting

---

8) terminology: 전문용어
   medical terminology: 의료전문용어
   = medical jargon
   = medical vocabulary
9) echocardiography: 심장 초음파검사

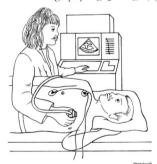

Wendolyn Hill

10) coronary artery: 관상동맥
11) angiocardiography: 심혈관조영술

that test as well.

Do you need further explanation?

Patient: When can I see the doctor?

MTC: If you like, I can made an appointment with the doctor for January 21st Monday at 9 am.

Please do not feel burdened by the arrangement of the appointment.

You can cancel at anytime and it is better to make an appointment now rather than not being able to do so late?

Would you like me to make that appointment?

■ 〈Case〉 추가 예약 불가

Patient: I want to see Dr. Lee today.

MTC(Nurse/Receptionist): Do you have an appointment with him?

Patient: No, but it is my day off and I want to see him for my check-up.

MTC: I am sorry, but Dr. Lee's schedule is completed booked for today.

2.2 예약변경

I am calling you to ask if you could postpone my appointment with you, which is scheduled for next Monday morning.

I want to change my appointment from Monday to Friday.

I want to change my appointment from 10:00 am to 3:00 pm.

■ 〈Case〉 예약변경

Patient: May I change my appointment?

MTC(Nurse): When is your previous[12] appointment?

When is your reservation date?

Patient: It's at 10 o'clock on September 5th.

---

12) previous: 이전의, 먼저의

I want to change the time to 2 o'clock on the same day.

MTC: Alright, Your appointment has been changed to September 5th at 2:00 pm.

■ 〈Case〉 예약변경

Patient: I made an appointment with Dr. Lee, however, I need to reschedule my appointment.

MTC(Nurse): What date is your previous appointment?

Patient: September 5th, but I want to reschedule it to 2 o'clock on September 11th.

MTC: I am afraid that Dr. Lee is not available at that time.

Can you make it at 4:30 instead?

Patient: OK, I will.

■ 〈Case〉 예약변경

Patient: I need to change my previous appointment on November 9th 3:00 pm, because my plane is arriving at Incheon Airport on November 9th at 4:00 pm. Do you think I will arrive at the clinic on time on November 9th before it closes or should I make an appointment for November 10th instead?

MTC(Nurse): You had better postpone the appointment to November 10th.

■ 〈Case〉 예약변경

Patient: I would like to postpone my appointment with Dr. Lee.

MTC(Staff): What is the best time to visit Dr. Lee's office.

Patient: I wonder if Dr. Lee is available at 2:00 pm on Friday.

MTC: Let me check the schedule.

(스케줄 확인 후)

MTC: 2:00 pm on Friday is possible.

Patient: OK. I will see the doctor then.

MTC: Your appointment with the doctor is confirmed.

See you at 2:00 pm on Friday.

2.3 예약취소

I'll call you if there are any cancellations. I will call you if I am forced to cancel my reservation

I am afraid the doctor(Dr. Kim) is not available on Friday, because he(she) will attend a conference at that time.

I am sorry but I have to cancel my appointment with you, which is scheduled for next Monday morning.

■ 〈Case〉 예약취소

Patient: I want to cancel my previous appointment.

MTC(Nurse): When is your appointment?

Patient: It is at 10 o'clock on September 5th.

MTC: I see. I will cancel it for you. What is the reason for the cancelation?

Patient: I have a meeting at work.

2.4 병원 도착 및 예약확인

Did you make a reservation?

May I have your name?

Did you bring the insurance card?

■ 〈Case〉 예약확인 방법

Patient: How should I identify myself when I get to the hospital?

Should I print out the form that shows when my appointment is?(Should I print out the form with my appointment?)

MTC(Staff): Your reservation is reserved and just tell me your name.

■ 〈Case〉 예약확인

Patient: I am here to see a doctor.

MTC(Staff): Have you made an appointment?

Patient: Yes, I called earlier for the appointment.

MTC: May I have your name?

Patient: I am Susie Maria Hans.

MTC: Susie Maria Hans.

Welcome to ABC Hospital.

Have you ever been here before?(Have you ever visited this clinic before?)

Patient: No. This is my first visit here.

MTC: Then, could you please fill out this medical questionnaire with your name, address, and phone number.

Do you have international medical insurance?

Patient: Yes, I am insured by traveler's medical insurance.

MTC: That sounds good. What seems to be the problem today?

Patient: I have a bad ear pain.

MTC: That's too bad.

Please fill out this medical questionnaire[13], please.

Sit down and wait until I call your name.

■ 〈Case〉 예약확인

Patient: I would like to make an appointment with the doctor, but I have some problem.

MTC(Nurse): What kind of problem do you have?

Patient: I've been sick for over a week. (It has been more than a week since I was sick.)

My head hurts and I keep coughing.

MTC: Do you want to postpone[14] the appointment with the doctor?

Patient: I wonder if my condition has nothing to do with the cosmetic surgery.

MTC: It does not matter.

---

13) medical questionnaire: 문진표
14) postpone: 연기하다.

Patient: Then, can I make an appointment to see the doctor this coming Friday. Is the doctor available this coming Friday?

MTC: The doctor might be able to fit you in at 2:30 pm on Friday.

Patient: OK, thanks.

2:30 pm is fine.

Patient: Do I need to take any special precautions[15] before and after the botox treatment?

MTC: You are required not to apply make up[16] for 12 hours afterwards.

You must not drink anything too hot or too cold if you have a lip treatment.

You should use a perfume-free[17] moisturizer if you have any dry skin.

■ 〈Case〉 예약확인

MTC(Nurse): Good morning. How may I help you?

Patient: Yes, I'd like to see a doctor, please.

MTC: Did you make a reservation?

Patient: No, I did not.

MTC: Are you insured?

Patient: No, I am not.

MTC: May I see your passport?

Patient: Here it is.

(여권을 보여주면서)

MTC: Thank you.

If you are not insured, then you have to pay in cash or by credit card.

■ 〈Case〉 예약확인

MTC(Nurse): How may I help you?

Is this your first visit to ABC Hospital?

Patient: Yes, it is.

MTC: Did you make a reservation?

---

15) precaution: 주의사항
16) make up: 화장
17) perfume-free: 향수 없는

Patient: No, I didn't.

MTC: Do you have your insurance card with you?(Do you bring the insurance card?)

Patient: Here it is.

(보험카드 확인 후 되돌려준다.)

MTC: Please fill out this medical questionnaire.

(문진표 작성 후)

Patient: Here you are.

MTC: Thank you.

As this is your first consultation[18], please go to the counter.

■ 〈Case〉 예약확인, 문진표 작성

Patient: Good morning.

MTC(Nurse): Good morning. How may I help you?

Patient: I made a reservation yesterday.

MTC: May I have your name?

Patient: I'm Susie Maria Hans.

MTC: Do you have your health insurance card with you?

Patient: No, I don't. I am not insured.

MTC: If you are not insured, you will have to pay the full fee in cash.

Patient: I see.

MTC: Please fill out the consultation form[19].

(문진표를 전달하면서)

Patient: Here it is.

(문진표를 작성 후 돌려주면서)

MTC: Thank you.

Please go to the counter on the 6th floor.

Patient: OK

MTC: Please put your consultation form in the box at the counter.

Wait on the chair until the nurse calls your name.

---

18) consultation: 상담
19) consultation form + medical questionnaire: 문진표

■ 〈Case〉 예약확인 및 진료대기

MTC(Nurse): Good morning. How may(can) I help you?

Patient: Yes, I'd like to see a doctor, please.

MTC: May I have your name?

Patient: I'm Susie Maria.

MTC: Have you ever been here before?

(Have you ever visited this clinic before?)

Patient: No, I have not.

MTC: Did you make a reservation?

Patient: No, I did not.

MTC: Are you insured?

Patient: Here is the insurance card.

(보험카드 받으면서)

MTC: Thank you.

One moment, please.

Thank you for waiting.(I am sorry to have kept you waiting.)

Here you are.

(보험카드를 되돌려주면서)

MTC: Would you like to have a seat over there and wait for a few minutes until I call your name, please?

Patient: Thank you.

해외 동포가 거소신고를 하였거나 90일 이상 체류하는 외국인은 국민건강보험에 가입이 가능하다.

국민건강보험에 가입한 해외 동포 및 외국인은 의료관광객으로 분류하지 않는다.

■ 〈Case〉 예약확인

MTC(Staff): Here we are. This is ABC Hospital.

I will help you with your check in procedure.

Patient: Thank you.

MTC(Nurse): Welcome to ABC Hospital.

Did you make a reservation?

Patient: Yes, I did.

MTC: May I have your name, please?

Patient: Susie Maria Hans.

MTC: Let me check your name in(on) the list.

OK. Here it is.

MTC: Let me help you with your admission procedure.

We have the room ready.

Your room(ward) number is 567 on the fifth floor.

Patient: OK.

MTC: Would you please fill out the admission form.

Patient: OK. Here you are.

MTC: Thank you.

Let me show you to your room(bed).

Patient: Thank you.

■ 〈Case〉 예약확인

(병원에 도착하면서)

MTC(Nurse): Here we are.

Please get off the mini-bus.

Watch out the steps.

Please come in this way.

Patient: It is a big hospital.

MTC: Yes, this is a newly built hospital.

Patient: I see.

MTC: Please sit here.

First, fill in this medical questionnaire in detail.

Patient: Do I have to answer all the questions?

MTC: Yes, that is right.

If you are done, please submit it to me and wait here.

You are supposed to go into the consultation room[20] in order.

■ 〈Case〉 이름확인 후 진료실 안내

MTC(Nurse): Good morning. May I help you?

Patient: Good morning. My name is Susie Maria Hans.

I have an appointment with Dr. Kim at 10 o'clock today.

MTC: Would you please write down your name, please[21]?

Patient: OK.

Here it is.

MTC: One moment, please.

(의료관광객 이름을 찾은 후)

MTC: Thank you for waiting.

Doctor Kim is expecting you.

Please take the elevator on your right hand side to the 6th floor.

Dr. Kim's office is on the left hand side.

Patient: Thank you.

MTC: Do you want me to assist you?

Patient: Yes, please.

MTC: OK. Please follow me.

Patient: Thank you.

2.5 병원등록 및 예진

구 분	내 용
예약	전화・홈페이지・팩스 등을 통한 예약 예약 없는 직접 방문
방문(등록)	예약자 확인 등록(병원카드 발급)
예진(문진)	문진표를 통해 환자의 가족력, 병력, 현재상태를 확인 예진을 통해 호소증상별 상담
진료(진찰)	문진표를 토대로 진료상담 진료 후 추가조사가 필요하면 실시
처방	처방전 발급

---

20) consultation room: 상담실
21) 외국인의 이름을 정확히 알아들을 수 없다면, 이름을 종이에 적도록 요구한다.

■ 〈Case〉 미예약 방문객의 진료상담

Patient: I want to see Dr. Lee today.

MTC(Receptionist): Do you have an appointment with the doctor?

Patient: No, but it is my day off and I want to see the doctor for my check-up.

MTC: I am sorry, but Dr. Lee's schedule is completely booked for today.

Instead of Dr. Lee, Dr. Park is available.

Dr. Park is also trained in America.

I do not hesitate to recommend the doctor to you.

Patient: OK.

■ 〈Case〉 병원등록 확인

(병원 등록카드 가입 신청서를 전달하면서)

MTC(Nurse): Would you write down your name and your phone number on this paper?

Patient: Here you are.

(작성 후)

MTC: Wait for a minute

Please be seated here and wait until your name is called.

(의료관광객 이름 호명)

MTC: Come in, please.

■ 〈Case〉 병원등록 확인

Patient: My right hand hurts.

I need you to fill out this medical questionnaire.

MTC(Receptionist): What is your medical record number?

Patient: It is 123-456-7890

MTC: And your home address?

Patient: 203-1 Irvine, California, 92620

MTC: Your home phone number?

Patient: 714-345-6789

MTC: Very well, wait until the nurse calls your name.

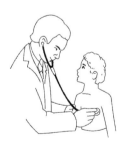

■ 〈Case〉 병원등록 확인

MTC(Staff): You need to register.

Please fill out the admission form.

Patient: OK.

(작성 후)

Patient: Here it is.

MTC: The nurse will call your name as soon as the admission procedure is completed.

■ 〈Case〉 병원등록 확인

MTC(Staff): Good morning.

Patient: Good morning.

MTC: Please fill out the admission form.

(병원등록 카드 신청서를 전달하면서)

Patient: OK.

(작성 후)

Patient: Here you are.

MTC: You will get basic tests and screening.

The doctor might ask you more precise tests after you consult with the doctor.

Please take a seat and wait until the nurse calls your name.

■ 〈Case〉 병원등록 확인

MTC(Doctor): Are you allergic to any medication?

Patient: I am allergic to nuts.

MTC: Do you have any family history of cancer, diabetes[22], or heart attack?

Patient: I don't think so.

MTC: Are you pregnant?

Patient: Yes

MTC: When is due date?

---

22) diabetes: 당뇨병

Patient: Probably May 25th.

MTC: OK, We are done.

Please sign at(on) the bottom line.

■ 〈Case〉 병원등록 확인

Patient: I have an appointment at 10 o'clock.

MTC(Nurse): Have you seen Dr. Lee before?

Patient: No, Today is my first appointment with him(her).

MTC: Please fill out this medical questionnaire and return it when you're finished.

Patient: I am not familiar with this medical questionnaire.

So can you help me fill it out?

MTC: Let's start now. What is your last name?

Patient: Hans.

MTC: What is your own name?

Patient: Susie Maria.

MTC: What is your date of birth?

Patient: January, 1st 1975.

MTC: What is your current address?

Patient: 4001 W.Garden Grove Blvd. Orange, California

MTC: What is your home telephone Number?

Patient: 714-750-4256

MTC: What is your marital status?

Patient: I am married with one child.

MTC: What is your occupation?

Patient: I am a teacher.

■ 〈Case〉 병원등록 확인

MTC(Nurse): I am going to ask you about your medical history. Are you currently taking any drugs or medication?

Patient: No.

MTC: Do you exercise regularly?

Patient: Not really, but I walk around the park a few times a week.

MTC: Have you been under physicians care during the past 5 years?

Patient: Yes, I was treated pneumonia[23] six months ago.

MTC: Do you smoke?

Patient: Yes, I smoke 2 cigarettes a day.

MTC: How long have you been smoking?

Patient: For 2 years.

2.6 비용 납부

■ 〈Case〉 의료비 납부

MTC(Staff): How may I help you?

Patient: I called yesterday for an appointment with Dr. Lee.

MTC: Have you ever been this clinic before?

Patient: This is my first time visit here.

MTC: Are you insured?

Patient: I am insured by traveler's medical insurance.

MTC: May I see your insurance card?(Do you bring the insurance card?)

Patient: Here you are.

(건강보험증을 전달하면서)

MTC: Just a moment, please.

■ 〈Case〉 의료비 납부

MTC(Staff): What kind of insurance do you have?

Patient: I have Blue Cross Blue Shield Insurance.

MTC: What are your insurance policy numbers and patient Id numbers?

Patient: Policy Number is A12340 and my Id Number is 1234.

MTC: Let me calculate your medical expense.

---

23) pneumonia: 폐렴

Your medical expenses are 660,000 Korean Won, equal to USD 600.
As of today, one dollar is worth about 1100 Korean Won, based on the
currency rate of American dollar to Korean Won.

Patient: How can I pay the expenses.

MTC: You can pay in cash or by credit card.

Patient: Do you accept American express.

MTC: American Express is acceptable.

Patient: Here you are.

(신용카드를 전달하면서)

MTC: Please sign at the bottom.

(서명 후)

MTC: Here is your receipt.

(영수증을 전달하면서)

- ■ 〈Case〉 의료비 납부

MTC(Staff): Are you insured?

Patient: No, I am not.

MTC: Then you have to pay in cash[24] in advance.

Patient: How can I pay it?

MTC: You can pay by cash or bank credit card Visa or Master.

Patient: I will pay by Master card.

- ■ 〈Case〉 의료비 납부

MTC(Staff): Hello, how can I help you?

Patient: I've got an appointment with Dr. Hong.

MTC: Are you Ms(Mr.) Kennedy?

Patient: Yes, I am. I have an appointment at 10.

MTC: We just need to fill in some information for our files.

Could you fill out these forms?

Patient: Certainly.

---

24) pay in cash: 현금으로 지불하다.

= pay by cash

(작성 중)

Patient: What's this medical questionnaire for?

MTC: It's a form informing us of your physical condition as well as your previous diseases.

Patient: Is that really necessary?

MTC: I'm afraid it is. Could you also sign that form?

Patient: OK, there you go. Here's my insurance provider's card.

■ 〈Case〉 의료비 납부

MTC(Staff): Are you insured?

Patient: I am insured by traveler's medical insurance.

MTC: Did you bring your insurance information?

Patient: Yes I did.

Here's my insurance card.

(신용카드 전달하면서)

MTC: Thank you.

You can take a seat right over there.

I will be with you shortly.

Patient: Thank you.

MTC: Here is your insurance card.

■ 〈Case〉 의료비 납부

MTC(Staff): Are you insured?

Patient: I don't have insurance.

MTC: How do you want to pay the medical service?

Will you pay in cash or by credit card?

Patient: By credit card.

MTC: May I have your credit card?

I need your credit card number and expiration date?

Patient: Here you are.

(신용카드 전달하면서)

MTC: Thank you.

■ 〈Case〉 의료비 납부 오류 의심

MTC(Staff): How can I help you today?[25]

Patient: I just received this bill.

There are a lot of charges.

Can you tell me what they are?

I am very worried.

Please check if I had paid everything.

MTC: There are four charges for services provided on September 23 and September 30.

■ 〈Case〉 의료비 납부 오류

Patient: I still don't understand why there are so many charges.

MTC(Staff): I need to call the billing office to clarify the charges.

Please wait a few seconds.

(확인 후)

MTC: There must have been a mistake.

The staff will correct errors and reissue the billing documents.

MTC(Staff): Please accept my apologies for mistakes.

■ 〈Case〉 의료비 납부

MTC(Staff): What can I do for you?

Patient: Yes, I'm here to see the doctor.

MTC: OK. Do you have an appointment?

Patient: I do. My name is John Kennedy.

MTC: Good morning Mr. Kennedy.

We spoke on the phone.

You're here to see the doctor because of your shoulder, right?

Patient: That's right.

It's been aching for days.

MTC: OK. Did you bring your insurance information?

---

25) = How may I help you today?

Patient: Yes I did.

Here's my card.

(보험증을 제시하면서)

MTC: Thank you.

You can take a seat right over there.

She should be with you shortly.

Patient: Thank you.

■ 〈Case〉 의료비 납부

Patient: I need a medical check up.

MTC(Staff): There are two kinds of medical check up packages.

Here is the brochure showing information on medical check up packages.

Patient: Thank you.

What is the difference between Package A and Package B.

MTC: Package A includes general health check-up, physical evaluation, physician's examination, blood test, and electrocardiogram.

Package B includes endoscopy and colonoscopy in addition to Package A.

Patient: Can I have one item among Package B?

MTC: Which one do you want to choose?

Patient: I need an endoscopy.

MTC: I understand.

Then, here is the list of tests you need.

(건강검진 항목을 보여주면서)

Would you please reconfirm the list.

An endoscopy has been newly added.

Patient: I see.

How much is the cost?

MTC: The total comes to 200 American dollars.

How would like to pay?

Patient: Do you accept VISA card?

MTC: Yes, we do.

Patient: Here you are.

(신용카드를 전달하면서)

MTC: Would you sign at the bottom?

(영수증에 서명 후)

MTC: Here is the receipt.

Patient: Thank you.

2.7 입원

Will I have to be hospitalized?

Please use the nurse call if you have any trouble.

Will it take long?

I think it will take about a week.

Will I be able to get well soon?

Do I have to come to the hospital everyday?

Wouldn't it be all right to recuperate[26] at home?

Isn't there any good medicine for it?

■ 〈Case〉 추가조사를 위한 입원

MTC(Doctor): The X-ray results shows that there a black shadow on your head.

You need further examination.

Patient: What kind of examination do I need?

MTC: MRI scan is necessary to get precise diagnosis[27] and treatment.

Patient: Do I need to be hospitalized?

MTC: Yes, you have to fill in this admission form.

(입원신청서를 전달하면서)

MRI scan is scheduled for tomorrow morning.

---

26) recuperate: 회복하다.
27) diagnosis: 진단, 진찰

■ 〈Case〉 추가조사를 위한 입원

MTC(Doctor): You need to be hospitalized for the further evaluation.

Patient: Is there something wrong with me?

MTC: I am afraid to say that but your examination result is not good.
The result is saying that there is something wrong with your body.

Patient: I cannot be hospitalized because I have a baby at home.

MTC: It's too complicated to treat you if you're not admitted and being an outpatient.

Patient: How long should I stay in the hospital?

MTC: You need to take about two weeks off your work.

Patient: How do I get through the admission procedure?

■ 〈Case〉 추가조사를 위한 입원

MTC(Doctor): You need to be hospitalized to undergo a more detailed physical examination.

Patient: I understand.
How long should I be hospitalized?

MTC: I am not sure but you will stay for about a week.

Patient: Then, I should postpone my flight back to U.S.A.

2.8 병원입원 중 서비스

■ 〈Case〉 회복

MTC(Doctor): Are you awake?
Can you recognize me?

Patient: Is the surgery over?

MTC: Yes, it is.

The operation went smoothly.

You are now in the recovery room[28].

Patient: I feel a little dizzy.

MTC: It is because of the anesthesia[29].

The stitches[30] will be taken out in a couple of days.

You may stay in the hospital up to five days.

■ 〈Case〉 회복실

Patient: I wonder if my surgery is going to prevent me from going back to my normal daily lives.

MTC(Doctor): You are absolutely certain to do your normal daily lives.

Patient: I am happy to hear that.

Is there anything I have to be cautious about?

MTC: You need more exercise.

■ 〈Case〉 회진

MTC(Doctor): Good morning.

Patient: Good morning.

MTC: I am Dr. Lee, the physician on duty today.

It is nice to meet you.

Patient: Nice to meet you.

MTC: Is everything OK in the room(ward)?

Patient: Yes.

MTC(Doctor): How are you feeling today?

Patient: I am feeling much better.

MTC: Your surgery is successful.

You have a full recovery.[31]

---

28) recovery room: 회복실
29) anesthesia: 마취제
30) stitch: 실
31) You have a full recovery.: 완전히 회복되었다.

Patient: I am glad to hear that.

MTC: You will be discharged from the hospital soon.

■ 〈Case〉 중환자실 환자 병문안

MTC(Nurse): What can I do for you?

Patient's Husband: I would like to meet my wife.

MTC: I am afraid visiting hours are over, sir.

Patient's Husband: My wife is in the room(ward) 354.

MTC: Sorry, you will have to come back in the morning.

Patient's Husband: And leave her all alone overnight?

MTC: I am afraid that is the policy, sir.

Patient's Husband: Surely you can make an exception?

What if she needs me in the night?

MTC: Don't worry, we will look after her.

What she really needs is her rest.

Patient's Husband: Some of her friends want to see her, too.

When can they come?

MTC: Visiting hours are from 9 to 11 in the morning and 4 to 7 in the evening, but I am afraid while your wife is on bed rest the doctor has requested that only immediate family members come in to see her.

Patient's Husband: Can't her friends even stop by to bring her flowers?

MTC: Flowers are not permitted in this ward.

We just can't risk any germs that might come in with them.

Patient's Husband: Well, I guess it is all in the best interest.

MTC: Thanks for understanding.

Now, I am going to bring your wife her dinner.

Patient's Husband: I really hate to leave her, but that is probably a good idea.

MTC: She is in good hands here.

I will tell her you were here and that you will see her in the morning.

You have a quick recovery.: 빨리 회복되었다.

2.9 재방문 예약

■ 〈Case〉재방문

MTC(Nurse): OK. You are all done here.

Patient: That was quick.

MTC: You'll need to sign your name right here.

Patient: OK. Can I pay with my credit card?

MTC: Of course. First let me see your insurance card.

Patient: Here it is.

(신용카드 전달하면서)

MTC: Thank you.

Will you be wanting to reschedule another visit?

Patient: I suppose I should.

When would be a good time?

MTC: I recommend you visit me every six months.

How about in February? The 23rd?

Patient: That sounds good.

I'll mark the date on my calendar.

Please call to remind me, Okay?

Chapter 3

의료관광객 문진 및 증상 표현

3.1 병원 소개

- 〈Case〉 의사 소개

MTC(Doctor): Good morning.

Please, come in

Take a seat.

Patient: Thank you.

MTC: I am Dr. Kim.

I'm not fluent in English, so I apologize[1] if I have to ask you to repeat anything. And please stop me if there's anything you don't understand.

Patient: OK.

- 〈Case〉 병원 소개

MTC(Nurse): What is your impression of ABC Hospital?

Patient: The hospital looks ultramodern.

MTC: ABC Hospital is well known for the extraordinary[2] healthcare.

---

1) apologize: 사과하다.
2) extraordinary: 대단한, 특별한

■ 〈Case〉 병실 소개

MTC(Nurse): This is your room(ward).

The nurse's section is just on the left hand side of the elevator.

Patient: I see.

MTC: This is your bed. The head of the bed can be raised by pushing this button.

(버튼을 가르키면서)

Patient: I understand.

MTC: On the panel there are light switches and a nurse's call button.

Patient: I see.

■ 〈Case〉 병원 느낌

MTC(Nurse): How do you like ABC Hospital?

Patient: It is very comfortable and clean.

MTC: ABC Hospital is famous for its low ratios[3] of staffs to patients, highly educated physicians and clinical staffs, and the latest[4] in medical technology.

■ 〈Case〉 병원 느낌

MTC(Nurse): What is your impression of ABC Hospital?

Patient: The hospital looks nice and clean.

MTC: ABC Hospital is proud of its quality and highly advanced medical and nursing care service to patients.[5]

■ 〈Case〉 병원 느낌

MTC(Nurse): What do you think of ABC Hospital?

---

3) ratio: 비율
4) latest: 최신의 것
   combine the latest in medical technology with personalized care
5) The ABC Hospital is proud of its quality and highly advanced medical and nursing care service to Patients.
   = The ABC Hospital is proud of its clinical excellence and Patient service.
   = The ABC Hospital is proud of its outstanding nursing care and Patient-centered facilities.

Patient: ABC Hospital has superb patient facilities.

MTC(Nurse): ABC Hospital is well known for its high quality services in cardiology[6] and cardiac surgery.

■ 〈Case〉 병실 소개

MTC(Nurse): Please come in.

This is your bed.

This is the safety box.

This is the closet.

This is the refrigerator.

This is the toilet.(This is the rest room.)

If you press this blue button, the head of the bed will be raised.

This red button is the emergency call button.

If you press this black button, you can turn off the lights.

Patient: Thank you.

3.2   국제의료관광코디네이터의 자기소개

■ 〈Case〉 자기소개

MTC(Nurse): Good morning. I am Gil Dong Hong. I am a medical tour coordinator of ABC Hospital.

From now on, I will assist you until you leave Korea.

Patient: Glad to meet you.

■ 〈Case〉 자기소개

MTC(Nurse): This is my name card.

(명함을 전달하면서)

My cellular phone is written on this card.

---

6) cardiology: 심장병

If you have any question, please feel free to contact me at anytime.

Patient: Thank you.

3.3 의료서비스 일정 확인

■ 〈Case〉 다음 날 일정 소개

MTC(Staff): The nurse will come tomorrow morning 9:30 and she will take your medical history.

Patient: OK.

MTC: After the nurse takes your medical history, you will go through a physical check-up.

This is the routine procedure of this clinic.

Patient: I see.

3.4 대기

■ 〈Case〉 진료대기

주의: 동남아에서 온 의료관광객에게 찬 음료는 매우 성의 없는 접대로 인식된다. 의료관광코디네이터는 언어적인 능력뿐만 아니라 문화적 차이도 이해할 필요가 있다.

MTC(Staff): May I take your coat.

Patient: Oh, thank you very much for your kindness.

MTC: You are welcome.

Did you eat or drink anything?

You must refrain[7] from drinking anything for at least 8 hours before the medical check-up.

----

7) refrain: 자제하다, 삼가다

Patient: I did not drink water nor eat food since last night.

MTC: OK.

■ 〈Case〉 진료대기 중 음료서비스 제공

주의: 건강검진의 경우는 검사 전에 물 한 모금
도 마실 수 없으며, 껌조차도 금지되어 있
다. 의료관광객에게 어떤 음료를 제공할 수
있는지 의사에게 문의하고, 진료서비스에
영향을 미치지 않는 음료서비스 종류를 결
정한다.

감기약은 카페인을 함유하고 있으므로 커
피, 초콜릿, 콜라와 함께 복용하면 카페인
섭취량이 갑자기 증가해서 두근거림과 불
면증 등 카페인 부작용을 일으킬 수 있다. 우유나 유제품의 칼슘성분은 테프
라사이클린 등 일부 항생제나 항진균제 성분과 결합해 체내 흡수를 방해해서
약효를 떨어뜨릴 수 있다.

MTC(Staff): Would you care for something to drink?

Patient: Yes, coffee, please. Thank you.

MTC: How do you like your coffee?

Patient: With cream and sugar, please.

MTC: One moment, please.

Here you are.

Patient: Thank you.

MTC: You're welcome.

■ 〈Case〉 진료대기 중 음료서비스 제공

MTC(Staff): Would you like to have a cup of coffee while you're waiting?

Patient: No, thanks

MTC: May I give you something to read before the consultation with the
doctor?

Patient: Thank you.

MTC: You are welcome.

Here you are.

■ 〈Case〉 진료대기

MTC(Nurse): Please sit down and wait until 1 call your name.

Patient: I am afraid my English is not so good.

MTC: Don't worry.

In this hospital we have medical interpreters for patients from overseas.

I will get you somebody who speaks Russian well for you.

■ 〈Case〉 진료대기

MTC(Nurse): Please wait here till you are called.

Patient: I see.

MTC: When you are called, please go to the room.

Patient: Thank you.

(대기한다.)

MTC: Will you be able to wait a little longer?

Patient: Why?

MTC: Many patients are waiting.

Please wait here for about 10 more minutes.

Patient: OK.

■ 〈Case〉 진료대기

MTC(Nurse): When you are called, you can meet the doctor.

Please tell us if you feel sick while you are waiting.

Patient: OK.

MTC: Please come in.

Please be seated.

■ 〈Case〉 진료대기

MTC(Nurse): Please make yourself comfortable.

Dr. Kim will be with you in a few minutes.

Patient: OK

  MTC: Wait here until the nurse calls your name.

(간호사 호출)

      Now the nurse calls your name.

      Would you come this way, please?

Patient: Thank you.

■ 〈Case〉 진료대기 장소로 이동

MTC(Nurse): The orthopedics[8]' office is located upstairs.

      I'll take you up to Dr. Kim's office.

      This way, please.

Patient: Thank you.

  MTC: Would you get on the elevator, please?

Patient: Thank you.

  MTC: Would you step out, please?

■ 〈Case〉 진료대기 동안의 대화거리

MTC(Staff): This hospital is famous for the operation.

Patient: I am happy to hear that.

  MTC: I think it is because there are a lot of highly trained and skilled doctors.

Patient: I think so, too.

■ 〈Case〉 진료대기 중 간단한 대화거리

MTC(Nurse): The doctor will be here in a moment.

      On the basis of first come, first served, the earlier patients check in, the earlier they can meet the doctor.

Patient: I understand.

  MTC: What is your first impression of Seoul(Busan)?

Patient: It is a beautiful city.

  MTC: This is the first visit to Seoul(Busan)?

Patient: No, this is my second visit.

---

8) orthopedics: 정형외과

MTC: Is there any place you want to visit Seoul(Busan) during your stay?

Patient: I want to go to Gangnam street.

■ 〈Case〉 진료대기 중 간단한 대화거리

MTC(Staff): The weather is very agreeable[9], isn't it?

Patient: Yes, it is fine today.

MTC: What are your hobbies?

Patient: My only hobby is playing golf. What are yours?

MTC: I like golf, too.

I know there is a fine golf course near this hotel.

How about playing golf with me after the medical checkup?

Patient: It is great.

Then I will go with my wife.

MTC: It will be my pleasure.

■ 〈Case〉 진료대기 중 간단한 대화거리

MTC(Nurse): What is your first impression of ABC Hospital.

Patient: It is wonderful.

MTC: This hospital is the best of the best for your medical surgery.

It is well known for its superior quality treatment.

Patient: I feel more comfortable to hear that.

■ 〈Case〉 진료대기 중 화장실 이용

Patient: Excuse me. I'm trying to find the ladies' room.

MTC(Staff): Go straight down the hall and turn right at the corner.

Patient: Thank you.

MTC: You're welcome.

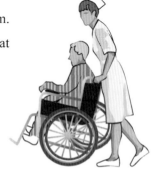

9) agreeable: 알맞은

3.5 증상 설명

3.5.1 문진표 작성

병원을 찾은 고객과의 첫인사

Good morning.

How may I help you?

What can I do for you.

Welcome to ABC Hospital.

What is the problem?

What brought you here today.

What's the problem with you?

■ 〈Case〉 문진표 작성

MTC(Nurse): May I have your name, please?

Patient: John Kennedy.

MTC: You are arranged to get a medical check-up.

This is the medical check-up questionnaire. Please fill out this questionnaire.

(문진표 작성 후)

Patient: Here is the completed form.

MTC: OK.

You can select one of the various screening packages.

Patient: What kind of screening packages do you have?

MTC: From the basic medical check-up to the most comprehensive medical screening.

Patient: Can I have a brochure?

MTC: Sure. Here you are. This is the brochure.

Patient: Thank you.

(병원 브로셔를 전달하면서)

MTC: While you read, if you have any questions, feel free to ask me.

Patient: OK.

3.5.2 의료관광 통역 녹음

「의료법」 제19조(비밀 누설 금지)에서 "의료인은 이 법이나 다른 법령에 특별히 규정된 경우 외에는 의료·조산 또는 간호를 하면서 알게 된 다른 사람의 비밀을 누설하거나 발표하지 못한다"고 규정하고 있다.

의료관광코디네이터는 의료인이 아니지만, 「의료법」 제19조에 의거 의료관광객의 정보를 다른 사람에게 누설하지 못한다.

의료관광코디네이터가 의료통역의 잘못 여부를 재확인하기 위해서 의료관광객과의 대화내용, 통화내용을 녹음한다면 법적으로 어떤 문제가 있을까?

의료관광객의 동의 없이 대화내용을 녹음하는 경우, 법적으로 어떤 문제가 있을까?

① 법적으로 형사처벌 가능성
② 녹음된 내용이 법정에서 증거자료의 능력 여부

「통신비밀보호법」[10] 제3조 및 제14조 제1항에서는 "누구든지 공개되지 아니한 타인 간의 대화를 녹음하거나 전자장치 또는 기계적 수단을 이용하여 청취할 수 없다"고 정하고 있다.

즉 '공개된 타인간의 대화' 또는 '공개된 당사자 간의 대화' 또는 '공개되지 아니한 당사자 간의 대화'는 금지대상이 아니다.

따라서 의료관광코디네이터와 환자, 그리고 의료관광코디네이터와 의사·간호사 등 의료진과의 대화 내용을 제3의 타인이 녹음·청취한다면 처벌대상이지만, 의료관광코디네이터가 당사자가 되어 상대방과의 대화내용을 몰래 녹음하였다면 처벌되지 않는다.

---

10) 「통신비밀보호법」 제3조(통신 및 대화비밀의 보호) ① 누구든지 이 법과 형사소송법 또는 군사법원법의 규정에 의하지 아니하고는 우편물의 검열·전기통신의 감청 또는 통신사실 확인자료의 제공을 하거나 공개되지 아니한 타인 간의 대화를 녹음 또는 청취하지 못한다. 다만, 다음 각호의 경우에는 당해 법률이 정하는 바에 의한다.
　1. 환부 우편물 등의 처리(폭발물 등 우편금제품이 들어 있다고 의심되는 소포우편물)
　2. 수출입 우편물에 대한 검사
　3. 구속 또는 복역 중인 사람에 대한 통신
　4. 파산선고를 받은 자에 대한 통신
　5. 혼신제거 등을 위한 전파감시
「통신비밀보호법」 제14조 (타인의 대화비밀 침해금지) ① 누구든지 공개되지 아니한 타인 간의 대화를 녹음하거나 전자장치 또는 기계적 수단을 이용하여 청취할 수 없다.

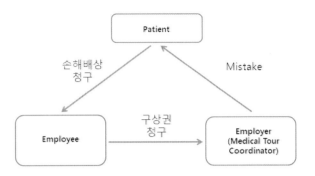

결론적으로, 자신이 상대방과의 이해관계에 있어 그 사실을 확인하기 위해 몰래 녹음한다는 것은 형법상 일종의 자력구제행위 노력, 정당방위 행위로 볼 수 있다.

의료관광객의 동의를 구한 후에 녹음하는 경우

■ 〈Case〉 녹음 동의 후 녹음

MTC(Nurse): This is the recorder.

(녹음기를 보여주면서)

I am going to record conversation between you and me(between patients, doctors, and nurses).

I will double check if I make a mistake or not when I play the recorded conversation.

Without your permission[11], I will not use the recorded conversation for any other purpose.

If you disagree with recording conversation or if you feel uncomfortable, I will not record conversation between you and me.

---

11) permission: 허락

■ 〈Case〉 녹음 동의 후 녹음

MTC(Doctor): This is the recorder.

Your answers will be recorded in the recorder, however, the hospital will use that information only for the medical examination and the recorded files will be destroyed after a certain period of time.

Without your permission, any information about you will not be revealed.

Patient: I think it might be useful to me as well.

3.6 건강검진

3.6.1 통증

3.6.1.1 통증정도

How will you describe your pain? Burning, cramping, dull or sharp, pressure like, pulsating, piercing?

Can you rate your pain on a scale of 1 to 10?

Can you rate your pain on a scale from 1 to 10? 1 is no pain at all and 10 is the worst pain you have had.

Can you rate your pain on a scale from 1 to 10 with 1 being no pain and 10 being the worst pain you have ever felt.

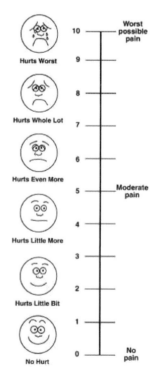

■ 〈Case〉 통증정도

MTC(Nurse): On a scale of 1 to 10, how severe is your pain?

Patient: Five.

■ 〈Case〉 통증정도

MTC(Doctor): How is your pain?

Patient: I have a mild pain nowadays.

■ 〈Case〉 통증정도

MTC(Doctor) Can you describe your pain to me?

Patient: The pain is getting worse.

■ 〈Case〉 통증정도

MTC(Nurse): Can you rate your pain on a scale from 1 to 10?

Patient: Six

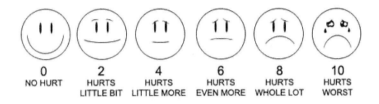

MTC(Nurse): On a scale of one to ten, how would you rate them?

Patient: Five

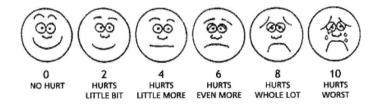

■ 〈Case〉 통증정도

MTC(Doctor): Can you give me a number to describe how bad the pain is?

Patient: Seven

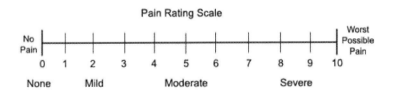

■ 〈Case〉 통증정도

MTC(Doctor): Let me ask it another way.

How bad is the pain? Is it mild? Moderate? Or really painful?
Please indicate the degree of your pain.

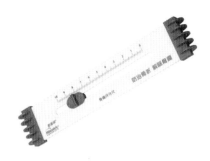

3.6.1.2 통증부위

Would you please show me the exact location of your pain?
Does the pain travel anywhere else?
Do you have a pain in one or both feet?
What part of the foot hurts?
Does the pain move from joint to joint, or does it always occur in the same place?
Did the pain begin suddenly or slowly?
Do you have numbness in your toes?

■ 〈Case〉 통증부위

MTC(Doctor): Where do you have a pain?
Patient: I have throbbing[12] pain in my knees.

■ 〈Case〉 통증부위

MTC(Doctor): Where does it hurt?
Patient: It is just below my right ribs.

■ 〈Case〉 통증부위

MTC(Doctor): In what part of your body do you feel a pain?
Patient: I feel a pain in the right side of my lower abdomen.

---

12) throbbing pain: 욱신거리는 고통

■ 〈Case〉 통증부위

MTC(Doctor): Does the pain moves to some other places?

Patient: Yes, It moves to my shoulder and right upper arm.

■ 〈Case〉 통증부위

MTC(Doctor): Where is it sore?

Patient: I have splitting[13] headache on the left side of my head.

3.6.1.3 통증기간

The pain is worse at night.

When did the pain start first?

Was the pain sudden or gradual?

How long have you been feeling this way?

Have you had chest pain this week?

Have you had a stomachache today?

Is the pain continuous or does it come and go?

How long does the pain last each day?

■ 〈Case〉 통증시기

MTC(Doctor): When do you usually feel the pain?

Patient: It is usually at night.

■ 〈Case〉 통증시기

MTC(Doctor): When do you feel more pain? In the morning or in the evening?

Patient: In the morning.

■ 〈Case〉 통증기간

MTC(Doctor): How long have you had pain?

Patient: I have had it for a couple of weeks.

■ 〈Case〉 통증기간

---

13) splitting headache: 머리가 쪼개지는 듯한 두통

MTC(Doctor): How long has the pain been bothering you?

Patient: Maybe for a few months.

■ 〈Case〉 통증기간

MTC(Doctor): How many days have you had the pain?

Patient: I have had the pain for about 2 days.

■ 〈Case〉 통증기간

MTC(Doctor): How long does the pain tend to last?

Patient: I had a back pain probably over the past 2 years.

■ 〈Case〉 통증기간

MTC(Doctor): How often do you have a shoulder pain?

Patient: I have it several times a day.

3.6.1.4. 통증원인

What is the cause of the pain in my left stomach?

What is causing the pain from your back and down your legs?

What were you doing when the pain started?

Do you remember anything which could be responsible for the pain?

How did the pain progress?

Did the pain get better or did the pain become worse?

Is the pain constant or does the pain come and go?

How often does the pain happen?

How many episodes per day do you have pains?

It is hard to pinpoint the cause of the pain.

3.6.2 머리

■ 수면부족, 불면증

Do you sleep well?

I could not have sufficient[14] sleep.

I can't sleep at night.

I've been suffering from insomnia[15].

I'm suffering from insomnia.

I spent a sleepless night.

I frequently wake up in the middle of the night.

I'm a light sleeper.

My nerves get so excited that I can't sleep well.

I can not sleep with any noise.

I can not get to sleep because I can feel everything moving slightly.

■ 〈Case〉 수면부족

Patient: I have not been sleeping well these days.

MTC(Doctor): How has your pattern of sleep changed?

Patient: I usually go to sleep around 11:00 pm, but recently I cannot get to sleep until 2:00 or 3:00 am in the morning even if I lie down.

■ 〈Case〉 수면부족

Patient: I can not sleep at night.

MTC(Doctor): I'm going to give you a prescription[16] for some medicines to help you get a better night's sleep.

Patient: Thank you.

MTC: Here you are.

You can take this prescription to any pharmacy.

---

14) sufficient: 충분한
15) insomnia: 불면증
16) prescription: 처방전

Patient: How often should I take the medicine?

　MTC: Just take one pill about 30 minutes before you go to bed.

Patient: How long should I take them?

　MTC: The prescription is for thirty days. If you're not sleeping well after thirty days, please come back again.

Patient: Is there anything else I can do to help me sleep at night?

　MTC: Don't worry so much about things at work.

■ 〈Case〉 수면부족

Patient: I can not sleep at night.

　　　　 Even sleeping pills[17] do not work.

MTC(Doctor): A brain scan is necessary for the accurate diagnosis.

■ 악몽

I woke up in the middle of night because of a nightmare[18].

I woke up from a nightmare.

I have nightmares.

I can not sleep due to constant nightmares.

I am scared to go to sleep because of nightmares.

I am afraid to fall asleep because of nightmares.

■ 〈Case〉 악몽

Patient: I have experienced an increasing number of nightmares for about a month.

MTC(Doctor): You should not eat anything after six in the evening. You had better have a nice hot bath to relax your body.

---

17) sleeping pill: 수면제
18) nightmare: 악몽

■ 무기력 및 피로

When do you feel low?

I'm feeling low.

I feel down all the time.

I'm not feeling well.

I don't feel well.

I feel tired and I don't want to do anything.

I have absolutely no energy.

It's hard to point to something in particular, but I get tired easily and I feel languid[19].

I feel weak.

I have a tired feeling.

I get tired easily these days.

I seem to be a little tired.

I'm utterly[20] tired of life.

I'm dead tired.

I feel dead tired.

I have a heavy feeling.

I want to relieve my fatigue[21].

■ 〈Case〉 무기력

Patient: I feel often fatigued.

MTC(Doctor): Do you have breakfast?

Patient: I sometimes skip breakfast.

MTC: When you woke up, you must check if your blood sugar[22] level is OK.

You must have a proper breakfast before you start your daily life.

Skipping breakfast drains[23] your energy, contributing to the fatigue problem.

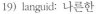

19) languid: 나른한
20) utterly: 완전히
21) fatigue: 피로
22) blood sugar: 혈당
23) drain: 소모시키다, 빼앗다

It is important to eat nutritiously[24] at every meal, especially focus on breakfast.

Patient: I understand.

MTC: What is your job?

Patient: I am involved in the computer science.

MTC: Do you get a lot of stress from your work?

Patient: Yes, I do.

MTC: When you are under stress, breathing becomes more shallow[25].

You had better take 5 to 10 deep breaths when you feel stressed and fatigued.

■ 〈Case〉 무기력

Patient: I seem to have no energy.

MTC(Doctor): Do you drink water a lot?

Patient: No, I don't think so.

MTC: Dehydration[26] can cause you to feel very tired or fatigued.

You must drink 8 glasses of water every day.

Patient: I see.

MTC: How many hours do you sleep?

Patient: I could not sleep well.

MTC: OK, here is a tip.

Go to bed at the same time each night, get up at the same time each day.

You establish a habit so that your body will recognize it's time to sleep.

Take warm bath before bed or read a book before you go to bed.

■ 〈Case〉 무기력

Patient: I don't feel too well.

MTC(Doctor): Can you describe your symptoms to me?

---

24) nutritiously: 영양분이 되게
25) shallow: 얇은
26) dehydration: 탈수, 건조, 탈수증

Patient: Well, lately I've been feeling extremely tired.

I have no appetite and my throat is always dry.

MTC: For how long have you felt this way?

Patient: It started about two weeks ago, but it's gradually gotten worse.

MTC: Do you take any medications?

Let me take your temperature.

It is normal.

Patient: Sometimes I take aspirin.

■ 정서불안

Panic Disorder: 공황장애

Depressive Disorder: 우울증

Bipolar Disorder: 조울증(양극성 장애)

Sleep disorder: 수면장애

Hyperkinetic Disorder: 과잉운동성 장애

ADHD(Attention Deficit Hyperkinetic Disorder): 주의력결핍 과잉행동장애

I have hallucinations[27].

I've developed auditory hallucinations[28].

Delusions[29] badly haunt me.

I have no confidence[30] in myself.

Everything disgusts me.

I find everything just too troublesome.

I feel scared.

I feel nervous and afraid.

When I sleep, I do not want to wake up, even though I do wake up. I try to sleep again.

---

27) hallucination: 환각, 환영
28) hallucination: 환상, 환각
    auditory hallucination: 환청
29) delusion: 망상
30) confidence: 자신감 = a sense of confidence

■ 〈Case〉 정서불안

MTC(Doctor): What can I do for you today?

Patient: I often get terribly anxious.

MTC: How do you feel when the anxiety hits you?

Patient: When the feeling is really strong, I want to commit suicide.

■ 〈Case〉 정서불안

Patient: Nowadays I cannot sleep well.

Last night I could not sleep for an hour.

MTC(Doctor): What makes you sleepless?

Patient: Nowadays I feel fatigued and powerless.

MTC: How many times do you fall in depression a day?

Patient: When I do my office work, I feel good.

But when I am alone at home, I feel anxiety[31] for no reason.

MTC: I need to run[32] some tests on you for more precise diagnosis.

■ 〈Case〉 정서불안

Patient: I sometimes feel terribly depressed[33].

MTC(Doctor): When do you feel it particularly?

Patient: When it is a rainy or cloudy day, I get particularly depressed.

MTC: Do you sleep well?

Patient: I go to sleep at night normally, but the sleep seems relatively shallow and then I wake up early in the morning.

---

31) feel + 명사 : feel pain
   feel + 형용사 : feel nauseous
32) run a medical test : 검사를 하다.
   = perform a medical test
   = conduct a medical test
   = take a medical test
   need a medical test : 검사가 필요하다.
   pass a medical test : 검사를 통과하다.
33) depress: 우울하게 하다.

- 〈Case〉 정서불안

Patient: I am really scared.

I have been feeling scared and weird for a few weeks.

I am scared because I am afraid I am suffering from some illness.

MTC(Doctor): You need to undergo psychological[34] tests.

Please answer the questionnaires.

- 조울증 및 우울증

I had a mixed feeling of joy and sorrow.

I am suffering from manic depression[35].

Although I don't suffer from manic depression, I have battled anxiety disorder

When do you feel depressed?

I feel sad.

I am in deep grief[36].

I feel melancholic[37].

I feel dismal[38].

I feel blue.

I feel depressed[39].

Rainy weather always depresses me.

I feel hopeless.

I always have an uneasy feeling.

I can't regain vitality[40].

I can't get enthusiastic about my daily life.

My situation is desperate[41].

Everything seems pointless and useless to me.

---

34) psychological: 심리의, 정신의
35) manic depression: 조울증
36) grief: 슬픔
37) melancholic: 불안한
38) dismal: 우울한
39) depressed: 우울한, 의기소침한
40) vitality: 활기, 활력
41) desperate: 자포자기의, 절망적

I'm very pessimistic[42] about the world.

I have a dreadful feeling[43].

It's hard for me to go on.

I'm fretful.[44]

I've become fretful and irritated[45].

I feel irritated about what I'm doing.

I feel impatient[46].

I feel spiteful[47] and hateful about everything.

I'm disgusted[48].

I feel gloomy. I know there is something wrong, but I do not know what it is.

I feel out of sorts[49].

I am frustrated[50].

I have an uncomfortable feeling.

I'm always moody[51].

I feel I'm under a curse[52].

I suspect that people are saying bad things about me behind my back.

I can't even talk with people.

I'm always tense[53].

I feel like someone is blaming me.

---

42) pessimistic: 염세적인, 비관적인
43) a dreadful feeling: 두려운 마음
44) fretful: 안달하는, 초조해 하는
45) irritated: 안달이 난, 속이 탄
46) impatient: 참을성 없는
47) spiteful: 악의적인, 앙심을 품은
48) disgusted: 정떨어지는
49) out of sorts: 기분이 언짢은, 기운이 없는
50) frustrated: 낙담한, 욕구불만의
51) moody: 시무룩한, 변덕스러운, 기분이 언짢은
52) under curse: 저주받은
53) tense: 긴장한

■ 〈Case〉조울증

Patient: I do not have many friends.

MTC(Doctor): What makes you think in that way?

Patient: I do not socialize because I am afraid of judgement.

I am really sensitive to it.

I do not want my life waisted on my bed.

MTC: It sounds like you are isolated[54].

You must make an effort to try to get outside yourself by becoming involved with many people.

■ 분노

I easily fly into a rage[55].

I am quick-tempered[56].

I've become short-tempered recently.

I've lost much of my patience.

■ 〈Case〉분노

Patient: I get angry easily.

I understand getting angry too easily increases stress levels and negatively impacts my relationship with family and friends.

How can I get rid of my anger?

MTC(Doctor): Most short-tempered people look for the same high standards and perfectionism[57] in others.

Let me test your anger level.

Please answer this questionnaire.

---

54) isolated: 외톨이가 된
55) fly into a range: 격분하다. = fly into a fury
56) quick-tempered: 성급한, 걸핏하면 화내는 = short-tempered
57) perfectionism: 완벽주의

■ 건망증

I'm absent-minded[58].

I always feel hazy and fuzzy[59].

I've become forgetful very often.

I am forgetful very often.

I have a short memory.

■ 〈Case〉 건망증

MTC(Doctor): I am going to ask you few questions to assess[60] your attention
and memory.

Patient: OK.

MTC: Could you tell me your full name?

What is the date today?

Can you tell me what city are we in?

Where are you now?

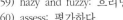

■ 〈Case〉 건망증

Patient: I have become forgetful these days.

MTC(Doctor): Do you remember when it started?

Patient: I cannot say when it started exactly.

MTC: Can you remember how you came here today?

■ 〈Case〉 건망증

Patient: I easily forget things I do or I have done.

MTC(Doctor): Do you often forget why you went to somewhere or did something?

Patient: I sometimes forget what I am looking for while I am looking for it.

MTC: You need to undergo a mental test, a blood test and even a brain scan.

---

58) absent-minded: 멍한, 얼빠진
59) hazy and fuzzy: 흐리멍덩한
60) assess: 평가하다.

■ 치매

My mother is suffering from dementia[61].

My husband has been diagnosed[62] with dementia.

■ 〈Case〉 치매

MTC(Doctor): Please say these words: boat, school, universe.

Patient: Boat, school, universe.

MTC: Now spell the word "Pencil" backwards for me, please?

Can you close your eyes and put your hands together and bring them on to your belly and then on to your forehead.

I want you to recall the 3 words that I told you few minutes ago.

■ 〈Case〉 치매

MTC(Doctor): Can you copy the drawing?

(그림을 보여주면서)

Patient: OK.

(그림을 그린 후)

Patient: Here you are.

MTC: Thank you.

Could you close your eyes and tell me where I touch you?

Patient: You touched my nose.

■ 〈Case〉 치매

MTC(Doctor): I am going to place my finger on your nose.

Please touch your nose.

Now, do the same while I move my finger in different positions.

Patient: OK.

■ 중풍(뇌졸중)

MTC(Doctor): Hold my hands tight.

---

61) dementia: 치매
62) diagnose: 진단하다.

OK. Don't let me go.

Relax.

Make a fist.

Don't let me open.

Relax.

Bring your arms in front.

Patient: Stretch my arms forward?

MTC: Yes, right.

Palms[63] up.

Don't let me push you down.

Now palms down.

Don't let me push you up.

Push your legs forward against my resistance.

■ 〈Case〉 중풍(뇌졸중)

MTC(Doctor): Please stand still with feet together and open your arms aside.

Close your eyes and balance yourself.

Patient: It is hard to keep balance.

MTC: Don't worry.

I will be behind you in case you need some assistance.

■ 〈Case〉 중풍(뇌졸중)

Patient: I sometimes feel dizzy.

MTC(Doctor): Now I am going to press on some areas on your face to examine your sinuses[64].

Please let me know if you feel a pain.

Patient: OK.

■ 〈Case〉 중풍(뇌졸중)

Patient: I sometimes feel nauseous[65].

---

63) palm: 손바닥
64) sinus: 구부러짐, 우묵 들어간 부분

MTC(Doctor): I am going to take this gauze pad and touch some places on your face with it.

Please close your eyes.

Do you feel this?

Patient: Yes, I do.

MTC: Did it feel similar or not?

Smile for me, please.

Could you frown[66] for me?

■ 두통

Do you have a severe headache?

My head feels heavy.

Blood rushes to my head.

I have a headache.

I feel a pain the back of my head.

I have a terrible headache.

I have a throbbing headache.

I have a chronic[67] headache.

I have a smarting pain[68] in the back of my head.

This part of my head particularly aches.

There is a throbbing pain in my temples[69].

My temples hurt when I cough.

I have a splitting headache[70].

I can't stand this headache.

I have a slight headache.

65) nauseous: 구역질하는
66) frown: 언짢은 얼굴
   frown line: 미간의 주름
67) chronic: 만성의
68) smarting pain: 콕콕 쑤시는 고통
69) temple: 관자놀이
70) splitting headache: 머리가 쪼개질 것 같다.

■ ⟨Case⟩ 두통

Patient: I have a headache.

MTC(Doctor): Have you had any other symptoms with your headache?

Patient: I sometimes feel dizzy.

■ ⟨Case⟩ 두통

Patient: I have a splitting headache.

MTC(Doctor): Do you have any other accompanying symptoms?

Patient: I feel dizzy.

MTC: When do you have the headache and dizziness?

Patient: When I walk up stairs.

■ ⟨Case⟩ 두통

Patient: I have a headache.

MTC(Doctor): Do you take any medicine for the headache?

Patient: Aspirin.

MTC: Does the aspirin help?

Patient: I don't think so.

MTC: You might have to take an MRI scan.

■ ⟨Case⟩ 두통

Patient: Nowadays I cannot sleep well.

Last night I could not sleep for an hour.

MTC(Doctor): What's the reason for that?

(What makes you sleepless?)

Patient: I think I became old nowadays.

I feel fatigued and powerless.

MTC: How many times do you fall in depression[71] a day?

Patient: When I do exercise or jogging, I feel good.

But when I am alone at home feel anxiety.

---

71) depression: 우울

MTC: Let's us run some tests on you for more precise diagnosis[72].

You'll have x-ray, blood and urine tests. Go down stairs to get X-ray shot first.(Go down stairs to have X-ray taken first)

■ 〈Case〉 두통

MTC(Doctor): Please urinate in this bottle and bring it back here.

That's all you need to do today.

Patient: OK. I will be right back.

Here it is.

MTC: All right.

You have to come back here next week to see your results.

Patient: OK. Thank you a lot.

■ 〈Case〉 두통

Patient: I couldn't sleep last night because of a terrible headache.

MTC(Doctor): What kind of pain is it?

When did it start?

Patient: It is a throbbing pain.

It started yesterday afternoon.

■ 〈Case〉 두통

MTC(Doctor): How are you today?

Patient: Not too good.

MTC: What is the matter?

Patient: I have a high fever and a terrible headache.

MTC: Let me take your temperature first.

■ 편두통

I have a migraine[73].

---

72) diagnosis: 진단

precise diagnosis: 정확한 진단

73) migraine: 편두통

편두통: 머리의 한 쪽에 나타나는 두통을 가리키며, 통증이 일정시간 지속되고, 구토 및 빛이나 소

I have a mild migraine, but it persists.

I always suffer from the migraine.

- ■ 〈Case〉 편두통

MTC(Doctor): I'm afraid to say that, but your examination
result is not good statement.

Patient: What's wrong?

(What's the matter with my test result?)

MTC: Our MRI finding shows herniated disc in your back.

Although it probably needs a further evaluation to see what's going on
in your body, you seem to have herniated disc in your back.

Patient: Does that serious disease?

MTC: No, if you get a surgery done(performed) you'll be fine.

However, you need to be hospitalized.

Patient: Is the operation hurt?

MTC: No, you're going to be under the anesthesia[74].

You won't feel any pain at all.

Don't worry about that.

- ■ 〈Case〉 편두통

Patient: I have been having a slight stomachache recently.

MTC(Doctor): Is the pain related to meals?

Patient: I feel the pain when I am hungry.

MTC: Do you drink or smoke?

Patient: I don't smoke, but I drink almost a bottle of beer everyday.

MTC: Let us do an X-ray examination of the digestive tract[75].

리 공포증이 나타나는 특징이 있다.

74) anesthesia: 마취제

75) tract: 관

digestive tract: 소화관

■ 어지럼증 및 현기증

When do you feel dizzy?

I feel dizzy.

My head is swimming[76].

I have dizzy spells[77].

■ 〈Case〉 현기증

Patient: I sometimes feel dizzy.

MTC(Doctor): Do you remember when the dizziness began?

Patient: I don't know exactly, but it seems to have begun a couple of days ago.

MTC: When exactly do you feel dizzy?

Patient: After a bath, I often feel dizzy.

MTC: Do you take any medicines such as antihypertensive[78] agents[79]?

Patient: No, I haven't been taking any medicines recently.

■ 〈Case〉 현기증

Patient: I took the pills that the doctor prescribed for me and I feel sick.

MTC(Nurse): What do you mean by sick?

Give me your symptoms.(Please explain your symptoms in detail.)

Patient: I feel dizzy, weak and tired all the time.

MTC: These are all side effects of the medication that you are taking.

■ 〈Case〉 현기증

Patient: For three weeks, I had been feeling very dizzy and very nauseous[80].

MTC(Doctor): What do you do when you feel dizzy?

Patient: When I am feeling dizzy, I lie down until dizziness is gone.

---

76) My head is swimming: 현기증 나다, 머리에 쥐가 나다
77) have dizzy spells: 어지럽다
78) hypertensive: 고혈압의
    antihypertensive agents: 혈압강하제 = antihypertensive drug
    hypotensive: 저혈압의
79) agent: 약품, 약제
    oxidizing agent: 산화제(산소를 주는 역할을 한다)
80) nauseous: 메스꺼운, 욕지기나는

MTC: Drinking water can sometimes help when you are feeling dizzy.

Studies show that dizziness is often caused by dehydration[81].

I will do a MRI scan to see if you have internal bleeding[82].

■ 머리 상처

I had a head injury in an accident.

I'm afraid there is internal bleeding in your head.

■ 빈혈

Do you have anemia[83]?

I suffer from a bad case of anemia.

Yesterday I collapsed from anemia.

■ 〈Case〉 빈혈

Patient: I had a severe dizziness.

MTC(Doctor): How long have you been having the dizziness?

Patient: About a couple of days.

MTC: Has the dizziness been steady?

Patient: No. The dizziness comes and goes.

MTC: You seem to have anemia.

You need to do a blood test.

■ 〈Case〉 빈혈

MTC(Doctor): Do you feel nauseous[84]?

Patient: Yes, I do.

MTC: How many times have you thrown up?

Patient: I have vomited about 4 times for the last 2 days.

MTC: Have you had other prominent symptoms besides that?

---

81) dehydration: 탈수
82) internal bleeding: 내출혈
83) anemia: 빈혈
84) nauseous: 구역질나는
　　feel nauseous
　　= have nausea

Patient: I've been losing my appetite a lot.

MTC: Although you'll need more precise examinations, you seem to have anemia.

■ 고혈압

Do I have a high blood pressure?

Your blood pressure is too high.

Your blood pressure is not at dangerous levels.

Your blood pressure is 120 over 80.

Your blood pressure is normal.

Your blood pressure is at a healthy level.

■ 〈Case〉 고혈압

MTC(Doctor): Do you have high blood pressure?

Patient: I have no idea.

MTC: I will check your blood pressure and pulse.

I think you have the symptoms of hypertension[85].

■ 저혈압

I have low blood pressure.

I have hypotension[86].

■ 음주 및 숙취

Do you drink alcohol often?

How often and how much do you drink alcohol?

How much alcohol do you drink every week?

Is it all right to drink?

Are you addicted to alcohol?

I am addicted to drinking alcohol.

You will gain weight from drinking alcohol.

I was once told by a doctor to stop drinking alcohol.

---

85) hypertension: 고혈압
86) hypotension: 저혈압

I want to stop drinking alcohol.

I have a hangover[87].

I'm suffering from a bad hangover.

I feel sick due to drinking last night.

This is the first time I have ever felt like this.

- 〈Case〉 숙취

MTC(Doctor): How often do you have a hangover?

Patient: I think I drink alcohol a lot.

MTC: Drinking alcohol is not good for health when you get addicted[88] to it.

- 흡연

Do you smoke frequently?

How many cigarettes do you smoke a day?

- 〈Case〉 흡연

MTC(Doctor): How many packs of cigarettes do you smoke every day?

Patient: I am a heavy smoker.

MTC: How many years have you smoked?

Patient: For about 10 years.

MTC: Smoking is not good for your health.

It ruins your lungs and can give you cancer.

3.6.3 눈

- 시력저하

My eyes are dimmed[89].

My eyesight is failing.

My eyesight is getting bad.

My eyesight is getting worse.

---

87) hangover: 숙취
88) addicted: 중독되어 있는
89) dimmed: 흐릿한

My eyesight is getting worse each year.

My eyesight seems to be gradually worsening.

■ 〈Case〉 시력저하

MTC(Doctor): How are you feeling?

Patient: Not too well.

My eyesight is falling down these days.

MTC: Let me check your eyes.

■ 안과질환

My eyes are itchy[90].

My eyes itch.

My eyes are sore.

My eyes are strained[91].

My eyes smart[92].

My eyes feel hot.

I have a pricking[93] pain in my left eye.

There's a throbbing pain in my right eye.

My eyes hurt so much that I can't keep them open.

My eyes hurt.

My eyes are painful.

My eyes feel sandy.

My eyes feel irritated[94]

I get a headache when I wear my glasses.

I see things in double.

Things look distorted[95].

Things look double.

---

90) itchy: 가려운
91) strained: 압박감의
92) smart: 욱신거리다
93) pricking: 따끔하게 찌르는
94) irritated: 염증을 일으키고 있는, 따끔따끔한, 벌겋게 된
95) distorted: 왜곡된

Things appear blindingly[96] bright and tears come out of my eyes.

The image of something like a rainbow appears in my eyes.

■ 〈Case〉 눈질환

MTC(Doctor): How are you feeling today?

Patient: Not too well.

　MTC: What is the matter?

Patient: I can't see object clearly.

　MTC: Let us examine your eyes[97].

■ 〈Case〉 눈질환

MTC(Doctor): Please look ahead.

　　　　　I am going to shine this penlight on your eyes.

Patient: OK.

　MTC: Please continue to look ahead, as I shine this light from the side.

■ 〈Case〉 눈질환

Patient: I cannot see things clearly.

MTC(Doctor): I'd like you to follow my finger with your

　　　　　eyes only.

　　　　　Please do not move your head.

　　　　　Follow it out here.

(손가락을 움직이면서)

　　　　　Here.

　　　　　Now, I want you to watch my finger carefully.

　　　　　I go very close.

　　　　　Don't close your eyes.

■ 〈Case〉 눈질환

Patient: I see things in double.

---

96) blindingly: 아주, 극도로

97) Let me examine your eyes.

　= Let me take a look at your eyes.

MTC(Doctor): Could you look to a fixed point on the wall?

I am going to check inside your eyes.

■ 〈Case〉 눈질환

MTC(Doctor): Could you please cover your right eye with your right hand.

Patient: OK.

MTC: Can you see my finger moving?

Patient: Yes.

MTC: Can you see this? What about this?

Patient: I can see it.

■ 〈Case〉 눈질환

Patient: My eyes get tired easily and I sometimes get headache.

MTC(Doctor): Let me see your eyes.

It may be glaucoma[98].

I'd like to do some further tests.

■ 눈 충혈

My eyes are red and painful.

My eyes are red.

My eyes are bloodshot[99].

■ 〈Case〉 눈 충혈

Patient: My eyes are red and painful.

MTC(Doctor): Let me check your eyes.

Can you look up for me, please?

Look down, please.

■ 눈피로

I've been staying up late and my eyes have been bleary[100].

---

98) glaucoma: 녹내장
   cataract: 백내장
99) bloodshot: 충혈된

When I look at close things, my eyes get tired.

My eyes get tired.

My eyes feel tired.

■ 〈Case〉 눈피로

Patient: What seems to be the problem?

MTC(Doctor): My eyes are very tired and I sometime have headaches.

Patient: Does your work strain[101] your eyes?

MTC: I do computer work at the office.

Patient: Do you have a regular life style?

MTC: No, I don't.

Patient: Do you sleep well?

MTC: No, I don't. I sometimes suffer from insomnia[102].

■ 원시 · 근시 · 난시

I am far-sighted[103].

You are near-sighted[104].

I think I am short-sighted.

I can see near very good but I can not see things far away.

I seem to have astigmatism[105].

I have bad eye-sight.

Lately I'm losing my eyesight.

Everything looks blurred.

My vision is blurred[106].

---

100) bleary: 흐릿한
101) strain: 긴장시키다
102) insomnia: 불면증
103) far-sighted: 원시의
104) near-sighted: 근시의
  근시: 안구의 길이가 길어서 망막 위에 맺혀야 하는 초점이 망막의 앞에 맺히는 경우로 먼 곳을 바라볼 때 물체의 상이 잘 안 보이고 가까운 곳이 잘 보이는 눈을 말한다.
105) astigmatism: 난시
106) blurred: 흐릿해진, 선명하지 않은

- 〈Case〉 시력저하

    Patient: Recently I cannot see well when I look at something far away.

    MTC(Doctor): Do you have headache or nausea[107]?

    Patient: I sometimes feel headache, but it is not serious.

    MTC: Have you ever had any eye trouble?

    Patient: No, nothing particular.

    MTC: I will give you some eye tests and check your ocular tension.

- 색맹

    I seem to be color-blind.

    I can't tell one color from another.

    The colors of things seem to be different.

3.6.4 코

- 감기

    I have a cold and sneeze[108] a lot.

    I have a cold.

    I have a head cold[109].

    I was in bed with a cold for a couple of days.

    I caught a cold.

    I am not feeling well. I am afraid I caught a cold.

    I have a slight cold.

    I have a mild cold.

    I have a bad cold.

    I think I've caught a cold from someone.

- 코감기

    I have a bad cold with a runny nose.

    I have a runny nose.

---

107) nausea: 욕지기, 뱃멀미, 구역질
108) sneeze: 재채기하다
109) head cold: 코감기

My nose is terribly stuffy[110].

My nose is stuffed up[111].

My nose tickles[112] and I sneeze[113].

My nose is always stuffed up. I have to blow it all the time.

My nose is dry and cannot smell.

My nose throbs[114].

When I blow my nose, my ears squeak[115].

There is a dull pain in my nose.

The inside of my nose feels itchy[116].

- ■ 〈Case〉 코감기

Patient: I have been sneezing[117] a lot and I have a runny nose.

MTC(Doctor): When did it start?

Patient: It started a few days ago.

It happens mostly in the spring.

The symptoms are really bad this year.

MTC: Do you have any other symptoms?

Do your eyes get itchy or anything?

Patient: Sometimes my eyelids are puffy[118] or my nose get stopped up.

- ■ 〈Case〉 코감기

Patient: Every year around this time I start sneezing and my nose runs.

MTC(Doctor): Do you have any other symptoms?

Patient: I feel a little tired.

My eyes itch.

---

110) stuffy: 답답한, 숨막히는
111) stuffed up: 코가 막힌
112) tickle: 간질이다
113) sneeze: 재채기하다
114) throb: 욱신거리다
115) squeak: 찍찍거리다
116) itchy: 가려운, 근질근질한
117) sneeze: 재채기하다
118) puffy: 부푼

■ 〈Case〉 코감기

Patient: I have a sore throat and my nose is stopped up.

MTC(Doctor): I think you caught a cold.

I will give you a prescription for medications.

Please take this medicine to prevent secondary infection[119].

■ 〈Case〉 코감기

Patient: I have a runny nose.

MTC(Doctor): I am going to lift the tip of your nose to check inside.

Could you open your mouth for me, please?

Stick out your tongue.

Move it side to side.

Now, I am going to place this tongue depressor.

Say Ah.

Patient: Ah.

MTC: You can put your tongue back.

■ 〈Case〉 코감기

Patient: I need some medicine for the flue.

MTC(Nurse): What are your symptoms[120]?

Patient: I have a fever and a runny nose[121].

And also, I have this nasty cough and keep

spitting up phlegm[122] too bad.

MTC: You have to consult a doctor[123].

Patient: Thank you.

MTC: You have to take a rest for the time being.

Patient: Thank you very much.

---

119) infection: 감염
120) symptoms: 증상
121) a runny nose: 콧물
122) phlegm: 가래
123) consult a doctor: 의사의 진료를 받다

MTC: You're welcome.

■ 기침

I have dry coughs[124].

I choke when I cough.

I can't stop coughing once it starts.

I cough and get short of breath.

I have a cough and a sore throat.

I have coughing and phlegm all the time.

I have a terrible dry cough.

When I suddenly start coughing, it does not stop.

■ 〈Case〉 기침

Patient: I have a mild cold.

    I am pregnant.

    Is it OK to take cold medicine?[125]

MTC(Doctor): Please try to get plenty of rest and sleep as much as you can with head slightly raised so the nose mucus does not drip down to make you cough.

■ 〈Case〉 기침

Patient: I have a terrible dry cough.

MTC(Doctor): How long have you been suffering a cough.

Patient: It has been two weeks.

    I have gone to clinics three times.

    I have taken antibiotics[126] and cough medicine.

MTC: It is not unusual to suddenly become allergic to something.

---

124) cough: 기침
125) Cold medicine: 감기약 = a medicine for cold
126) antibiotics: 항생제

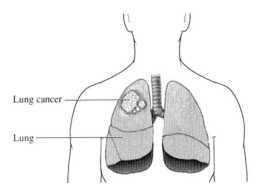

■ 〈Case〉 기침

Patient: I'm feeling ill.

I've got quite a bad cough, but I don't seem to have a fever.

MTC(Doctor): How long have you had these symptoms?

Patient: Oh, I've had the cough for two weeks, but feeling ill just these past few days.

MTC: Are you having any other problems?

Patient: I've got a headache.

I've also had a little bit of diarrhea[127].

MTC: Do you produce any phlegm[128] when coughing?

Patient: Sometimes, but it's usually pretty dry.

MTC: Do you smoke?

Patient: Yes, a few cigarettes a day.

MTC: How many cigarettes do you smoke a day?

Patient: I smoke no more than half a pack of cigarettes a day.

Can I get cancer for smoking half a pack of cigarettes a day?

MTC: Yes, it is possible.

People can get cancer whether they smoke or not.

However, smoking increases the risk of lung cancer by a huge percentage.

Patient: I had better quit smoking.

MTC: How about allergies? Do you have any allergies?

127) diarrhea: 설사
128) phlegm: 담, 가래

Patient: Not that I'm aware of.

MTC: Does your head feel stuffy?

Patient: Yes, for the past few days.

MTC: Now let's have a look. Could you please open your mouth and say 'Ah?'

Patient: Ah.

■ 독감

I have a flue[129].

You have a seasonal influenza[130].

I have a touch of the flu.

You got a flue epidemic[131].

■ 〈Case〉 독감

Patient: After I got the flue shot, it began having headache.

MTC(Doctor): Where does your head hurt? All over? Any specific place?

Patient: My forehead.

Above the eyebrows.

MTC: How painful is it?

On a scale of 1 to 10, with 1 being very mild pain and 10 being the worst possible pain, how would you rate it?

Patient: 8 to 9.

■ 〈Case〉 독감

Patient: I've had flu-like symptoms over a month.

MTC(Nurse): Do you have any pre-existing diseases?

Patient: I have diabetes.

MTC: How do you control your diabetes[132]?

Patient: I'm controlling it with diet and exercise.

---

129) flu: 유행성 감기, 독감
130) seasonal influenza: 계절 독감
131) epidemic: 유행성
     a flue epidemic: 유행성 독감
132) diabetes: 당뇨병

MTC: Alright, the doctor will be here soon.

Patient: Thanks.

■ 〈Case〉 독감

Patient: I've had flu-like symptoms with headache, runny nose, sneezing[133] and a light cough.

I sometimes can not breathe well.

MTC(Doctor): I'll check your through.

Please, open your mouth and stick on your tongue.

I'll check your lungs, take a deep breath and hold breath.

■ 〈Case〉 독감

Patient: I feel a pain in the throat.

MTC(Doctor): Let me check your throat.

The back of your throat is swollen and red.

You may have some slight pain in the throat when you swallow.

■ 코골이

He snores[134] terribly in his sleep.

What can I do to stop snoring?

I have a bad habit of snoring while I sleep.

■ 〈Case〉 코골이

Patient: I developed really bad snoring.

I have tried an anti-snoring pill, but no results.

Do I need nose surgery to solve this?

MTC(Doctor): Sleep study should be done to diagnose the problem.

There are several treatment options including weight loss.

■ 코피

I have a nose bleed.

133) sneeze: 재채기하다
134) snore: 코골다.

I have a severe nose bleed.

There is blood in my nasal discharge[135].

I have a nose bleed every morning.

My nose often bleeds.

■ 〈Case〉 코피

Patient: I have had several nose bleeds[136] recently.

MTC(Doctor): When do you get these nose bleeds.

Patient: Whenever I blow my nose.

MTC: Have you ever had this problem before?

Patient: No, never.

That is why I came here today, because I am anxious about it.

3.6.5 입

■ 구취

I suffer from bad mouth smell.

I suffer from halitosis[137].

My mouth has a bad smell.

My breath smells bad.

I have foul[138] breath.

■ 구강질병

My mouth is dry.

My mouth feels dry and rough.

My mouth forms a lot of saliva[139] and feels very hot inside.

I have an inflammation[140] in my mouth.

---

135) nasal discharge: 콧물
136) nosebleed: 코피
137) halitosis: 구취, 입냄새
138) foul: 악취가 나는
139) saliva: 침, 타액
140) inflammation: 염증

I have a small canker[141] in my mouth.

There are several round specks[142] in my mouth.

There is a swelling in my mouth.

3.6.6 혀 및 치아

■ 혀질환

I have a swollen tongue.

I have a rough tongue.

I have a painful tongue.

I have a white furry tongue.

■ 〈Case〉 혀질환

Patient: I have a swollen tongue.

MTC(Doctor): Do you feel a pain in the throat?

Patient: Yes, I do.

MTC: A swollen tongue and sore throat can be caused by an allergic reaction.

Let us run an allergic test.

■ 입술질환

My lips are dry and rough.

My lips ache when I open my mouth.

It's difficult to open my mouth.

I have some kind of sore on both corners of my mouth.

■ 치아질환

Do you have a toothache?

I have a toothache.

The tooth smarts[143] when I eat something cold.

---

141) canker: 아구창

아구창: 혀 및 구강 내벽에 생기는 염증을 말한다.

142) speck: 반점

143) smart: 욱신거리다, 시리다

I have a piercing pain[144] when I eat something sour.

When I eat sweet things I feel pains in my teeth.

I can't chew my food well because of a toothache.

One of my teeth in the back hurts.

I have a throbbing[145] toothache.

I have a tooth with throbbing pain.

My teeth in the back hurts so much I can't sleep at night.

My teeth in the back hurts so much I can't stand it any longer.

I think I have pyorrhea[146].

I want to have the tooth treated.

My teeth feel loose and I have difficulty chewing.

My wisdom teeth seem to be budding[147] and it has been hurting me.

■ 〈Case〉 치아질환

MTC(Doctor): I'll be cleaning your teeth today.

Patient: Dr. Hong has just filled two cavities[148].

    Why do I need a cleaning?

MTC: Well, we have to make get your teeth and gums[149]

    clean and disease free.

Patient: I guess that makes sense.

MTC: Oral health leads to trouble-free teeth.

    I'll start off by removing plaque[150].

    Please lean back and open wide.

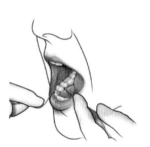

Patient: OK, I hope it's not too bad.

MTC: Everybody gets plaque, even if they floss regularly.

    That's why it's important to come in twice a year for check-ups.

---

144) piercing pain: 꿰뚫는 듯한 고통
145) throbbing pain: 욱신거리는 아픔
146) pyorrhea: 치조 농루(잇몸에서 피가 나고 고름이 남)
147) budding: 싹트기 시작하는
148) cavaty: 충치
149) gum: 잇몸
150) plaque: 치석

Please take a drink and rinse.

Patient: Ah, that's better.

MTC: Now, let me give your teeth a final flossing[151].

Patient: What type of floss tape do you recommend?

MTC: Personally, I like the flat tape.

It's easier to get between the teeth.

Patient: OK, I'll remember that the next time I buy floss.

How often should I floss?

MTC: Everyday or twice a day if possible!

Some people like to floss after every meal, but that's not absolutely necessary.

(치아치료 후)

Patient: I feel much better.

Thank you.

MTC: My pleasure.

Have a pleasant day, and remember to floss every day or at least once a day!

- 〈Case〉 치아질환

Patient: I have an appointment with Dr. Hong at 11:30.

MTC(Nurse): Good morning, can I have your name, please?

Patient: Yes, it's Susie Maria Hans.

MTC: Yes, Mrs. Susie Maria Hans.

Is this the first time you've seen Dr. Hong?

Patient: No, I had my teeth cleaned and checked last year.

MTC: OK, just a moment, I'll get your chart.

Patient: I changed my insurance. Here's my new provider card.

MTC: Thank you. Is there anything in particular you'd like the dentist to check today?

Patient: Well, yes. I've been having some gum pain recently.

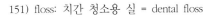

151) floss: 치간 청소용 실 = dental floss

MTC: Alright, I'll make a note of that.

Patient: And I'd like to have my teeth cleaned as well.

MTC: Of course.

That'll be part of today's dental hygiene.

Patient: Oh, yes, of course.

MTC: Please have a seat and the Dr. Hong will be with you momentarily.

Patient: Thank you.

MTC: You're quite welcome

■ 〈Case〉 치아질환

Patient: My right(left) side teeth are chilled.

MTC(Doctor): Since when did it begin?

Patient: It began long ago.

MTC: Then, let's take an X-ray.

Patient: Okay, I see.

MTC: Do you get scalings regularly?

Patient: No, I have never done it.

MTC: Really? It would be good to do a scaling this time.

Patient: Okay.

MTC: You also have a cavity[152].

Why don't you have a cavity treatment along with the scaling?

■ 〈Case〉 치아질환

MTC(Doctor): What's your name?

Patient: My name is Susie Maria.

MTC: How old are you?

Patient: I am thirty five years old.

MTC: When were you born?[153]

MTC: Do you have allergic reactions to any medications?

---

152) cavity: 충치
153) = When is your birthday?
= What is your date of birth?

Patient: No, I don't.

MTC: Where does it hurt? / Would you describe your symptoms, please?

Patient: I have a throbing pain in the teeth.

MTC: Which tooth is hurting right now.[154]

Patient: The tooth in the back.

MTC: When did you start feeling pain?

Does it hurt after you eat or drink?

Patient: Since last night.

MTC: Does it hurt here?

Patient: Yes, it does.

MTC: Would you please wait for a moment?

(잠시 후)

MTC: Please, come here[155].

Let me take an X-ray.[156]

- **잇몸질환**

My gums bleed whenever I bite (into) an apple.

My gums are swollen and they bleed when I brush my teeth.

My gums are so swollen that I can't eat.

Blood and pus[157] discharge from my gums.

- **〈Case〉 잇몸질환**

Patient: My right(left) side teeth are chilled.

MTC(Doctor): Since when did it begin?

Patient: It began long ago.

MTC: Then, let's take an X-ray.

Patient: Okay, I see.

---

154) = Which tooth is painful?

155) = Please follow me.

156) = I'll take an X-ray.

157) pus: 고름

■ 〈Case〉 잇몸질환

MTC(Doctor): Do you get scaling regularly?

Patient: No, I have never done it.

MTC: Really? It would be good to do a scaling this time.

Patient: Okay.

MTC: You also have a cavity.

Why don't you have a cavity treatment along with the scaling?

How often should I have my teeth scaled?

I would like to have my teeth scaled.

Do I need to have my teeth scaled regularly?

■ 〈Case〉 스케일링

Patient: Is scaling not good as it grinds off part of the tooth?

MTC(Doctor): Scaling is a treatment used to remove plaque and calculus stuck to teeth, and it does not cause any damage to your teeth.

When the calculus is removed, inflammation of the gums caused by the calculus, which shrinks the gums and exposes the roots of teeth.

This may cause teeth to hurt when drinking cold water, but you should recover from this effect within several days.

■ 의치

I want to have a false tooth[158] put in.

Please fix my artificial teeth.

I need to have two teeth implanted.

You should go through one more surgery to have a tooth implanted.

■ 〈Case〉 임플란트

Patient: Is an implant painful?

MTC(Doctor): In general, an implant is administered under local anesthesia[159].

---

158) false teeth: 의치, 틀니 = denture
159) local anesthesia: 부분 마취

As it is carried out under anesthesia, patients will experience absolutely no pain.

Pain may be experienced after coming out of the anesthetic, but this can be easily remedied by taking an ordinary pain killer[160].

The pain is less than the pain experienced when pulling out a wisdom tooth.

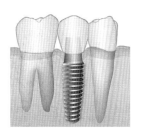

- 치아부상

One of my front teeth is chipped[161].

One of my back teeth has broken off.

- 발치

I want to have this tooth pulled out.

I want to extract[162] the tooth.

You must have your wisdom teeth removed.

- 치아 흔들림

It feels like my teeth are shaky.

I have a tender tooth[163].

I have a loose tooth[164].

- 치아 기형

I have a crooked[165] teeth.

- 치석

Please remove the cigarette stains from my teeth.

I would like to remove the nicotine stains from my teeth.

---

160) pain killer: 마취제
161) chip: 깨지다, 빠지다
162) extract: 추출하다
163) a tender tooth: 만지면 이가 아프다
164) have a loose teeth: 치아가 흔들리다
165) crooked: 기형의, 비뚤어진

I have a lot of tartar[166] on my teeth.

I'd like to have my teeth cleaned.

I want to get rid of plaque[167] on my teeth.

■ 충치

I have a cavity in my tooth and it's very painful.

You have three decayed[168] teeth.

The filling of the tooth cavity[169] fell out.

I want to get my teeth cleaned.

You have two cavities.

■ 〈Case〉 충치

Patient: I've been having some gum pain recently.

MTC(Doctor): Let me take a look at your teeth.

Please open your mouth.

(치아검사 후)

MTC: Well, there is some inflammation[170] of the gums[171].

It looks like you may have a few cavities as well.

Patient: That's not good news.

MTC: There are just two superficial[172] cavities.

We need to take X-rays to identify the depth of tooth decay.

Patient: I see.

MTC: Here, put on this protective[173] apron.

Patient: OK.

---

166) tartar: 치석
167) plaque: 치석
168) decay: 썩다
169) cavity: 충치
170) inflammation: 염증
171) gum: 잇몸
172) superficial: 표면적인
173) protective: 보호하는

(X-Ray 촬영 후)

MTC: I don't see any evidence of further decay.

3.6.7 귀

■ 귀질환

I have a severe earache.

I have a throbbing pain in my ear.

I have an ear infection[174].

I have a very bad earache after swimming.

I have a pain in the ear.

My left ear tingles[175].

My ear hurts terribly when I touch it.

My ear especially hurts when I chew.

Both ears hurts so much that I can't stand it.

■ 〈Case〉 귀질환

Patient: I feel a pain in the ear.

MTC(Doctor): I am going to check your ears.

Let me pull your ear first.

Do you feel any pain?

Patient: I feel pain inside the ear.

MTC: Let me check inside.

Now let me check the other ear.

Your inner ear[176] seems to be infected.

The inside ear looks red and swollen.

---

174) infection: 감염, 전염
175) tingle: 따끔거리다
176) pinna: 귓바퀴
   cochlea: 달팽이관
   malleus: 추골
   incus: 침골
   stapes: 등골
   tympanic membrane: 고막

■ 〈Case〉 귀질환

Patient: I have a slight pain and a feeling of obstruction[177] in the inner ear.

MTC(Doctor): I suspect your ear is infected[178].

■ 귀지

I want to clear my ear wax.

I have unusual amount of dark colored ear wax in one ear.

■ 〈Case〉 귀지

Patient: My ears have been clogged up with wax.

MTC(Doctor): A certain amount of wax in the ears is normal.

Your ear canals do not need to be wax free.

Let me check the inside of your ears.

I am going to widen your ear canals to get rid of ear wax.

■ 귀고름

Pus[179] is coming out of my ear.

Mucus[180] is coming out of my ear.

It's difficult even to drink water and the pain goes as far as my ears.

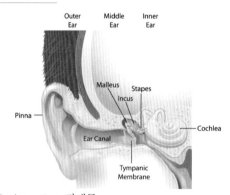

177) obstruction: 장애물
178) infected: 감염된
179) pus: 고름
180) mucus: 진액

■ 청력저하

I am hard of hearing.

I am deaf in one ear.

I'm a little hard of hearing these days.

It's difficult to catch what people say.

My ears feel plugged up[181] and I can only hear myself when I'm
speaking very loudly.

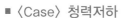

■ 〈Case〉 청력저하

MTC(Doctor): I'm a little hard of hearing these days.

Patient: Now, I am going to strike this tuning fork on my hand and place it on
the back of your ear.

Can you hear this?

■ 이명

What are the causes of ringing in the ear?

I have a ringing in my ears.

I have been hearing a beeping sound from my left ear for about a week.

Why do I hear a beep sound in my ear?

I always hear a beeping sound in my ear.

My ears ring.

I hear a sound as if something is rolling around in one of my ears.

My ears have suddenly started to hum[182].

I feel irritated because my ears are always ringing.

I heard a low humming[183] in my ears.

---

181) plugged up: 막힌
182) hum: 웅웅거리다
183) humming: 윙윙거리는

3.6.8 목

■ 갑상선

〈case〉 갑상선

MTC(Doctor): I am going to check if you have swollen thyroid glands[184].

　　　　　　Pleased let me know if you have any discomfort.

Patient: OK.

　MTC: Please take a deep breath.

　　　In.

　　　Out.

　　　I am going to touch your neck when you swallow your saliva.[185]

Patient: OK

　MTC: Please swallow your salvia now.

■ 목통증

I strained[186] my neck and can't move my head.

My neck is so stiff that I can't move.

I got a crick[187] in my neck while sleeping.

I have a sharp pain if I try to turn my head. I was wondering if something may be wrong with the neck bones.

My neck is so painful that I can't turn it.

My neck snapped[188] when I suddenly put on the brakes.

I have a hard lump[189] in my neck.

I have a ringworm[190] or fungus[191] infection on my neck.

---

184) thyroid gland: 갑상샘
185) saliva: 타액
186) strain: 긴장시키다
187) crick: 근육 경련
188) snap: 탁 부러지다
189) lump: 혹, 덩어리
190) ringworm: 백선, 동전 버짐, 도장부스럼
　　 백선: 효모나 사상균과 유사한 미생물인 곰팡이에 의한 피부감염이다. 백선은 거의 모든 부위에 생길 수 있으나 사타구니, 발가락 사이, 비만인 사람은 피부가 접히는 부위 등에 잘 생긴다.
191) fungus: 곰팡이

■ 목구멍 통증

My throat is swollen. It's difficult to talk.

Do you have a sore throat?

I got sore throat as well, and I can not even talk.

I have a sore throat.

I have an irritated throat.

My throat hurts when I swallow.

I think my tonsils[192] are swollen.

I have a rough throat.

The back of my throat is itchy and ticklish[193].

My throat hurts and feels unpleasant.

■ 〈Case〉 목구멍 통증

Patient: I have a sore throat and my nose is stopped up.

MTC: I think you caught a cold.

Please take this medicine to prevent secondary infection.

MTC: How are you feeling today?

Patient: I have a bad sore throat.

MTC: When did it start?

Patient: Three days ago.

MTC: Do you have any other symptoms?

Patient: I have a slight fever.

MTC: Okay. I will have to look at your throat.

192) tonsil: 편도선

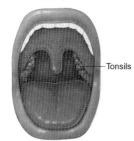

193) ticklish: 까다로운

(목 검사)

        I am going to give you a prescription for an antibiotic.

Patient: How often should I take it?

  MTC: Take a pill three times a day for seven days.

        You will probably start to feel better in a couple of days.

Patient: Thank you.

■ 〈Case〉 목통증

Patient: Every morning I wake up the first thing I get is a stiff neck.

MTC(Doctor): Do you have any other symptoms?

Patient: I have a sharp headache on the right side on my head throughout the whole morning up until noon.

  MTC: When you turn your neck, do you feel more pain?

Patient: Yes, I do

  MTC: You should get an X-ray.

■ 〈Case〉 목통증

Patient: I have a severe pain in the neck.

        I feel muscle weakness in my arms.

MTC(Doctor): I need to take an X ray of your neck.

(X-레이 촬영 후)

  MTC: The X Ray shows that your neck bone is straight.

        Originally, the neck bone is a form of C.

■ 가래

I cough up phlegm[194].

I bring up phlegm.

I cough up thin sputum[195].

I cough up thick sputum.

---

194) phlegm: 가래
    가래는 기도로부터 배출되어 뱉어내는 담을 말한다. 객담이라고도 한다.
195) sputum: 가래

I cough up bloody phlegm.

I feel like sputum is sticking in my throat.

I get phlegm in my throat and have difficulty breathing.

I have a long lasting productive cough[196].

Have you ever coughed up phlegm?

I have a productive cough[197]

When I cough, I have sputum[198].

■ 〈Case〉 가래

Patient: I cough up phlegm[199].

MTC(Doctor): When you are sick, white blood cells fight the infection.

Many of these white blood cells die and are expelled from the body through mucus[200].

Patient: I see.

MTC: It is good to cough up phlegm.

It is bad to ingest it because it is excrete from our body system.

■ 쉰 목소리

I have a hoarse[201] cough.

My voice gets hoarse[202].

For the past few days I've been hoarse.

If I speak for any length of time, I get hoarse.

If I talk too much or speak in a loud voice, I get hoarse.

---

196) productive cough: 객담을 동반하는 기침
non-productive cough: 객담을 동반하지 않는 마른기침
197) productive cough: 객담을 동반하는 기침
non-productive cough: 객담을 동반하지 않는 마른기침
198) sputum: 가래, 침, 타액
199) phlegm: 가래, 담
200) mucus: 콧물
201) hoarse: 쉰 목소리의
202) hoarse: 쉰

■ 목 이물감

It feels as if something were in my throat.

I cannot remove the fishbone stuck in my throat.

I have an uncomfortable feeling deep in my throat.

It feels as if food is stuck in my throat.

■ 〈Case〉 목 이물감

Patient: When I swallow, I feel something like a small object in the throat on the right side.

MTC(Nurse): Let me check your throat.

■ 갈증

I'm always thirsty.

I feel dry in my mouth.

My throat feels completely dried out.

I have a dry mouth.

■ 〈Case〉 갈증

Patient: I feel dry in my mouth.

I feel thirsty all the time.

MTC(Doctor): Let me check your mouth.

Please open your mouth and say "Ah"

■ 구토

Do you feel nauseous[203]?

I am nauseous and have chest pain also.

I have nausea.

I throw up all I eat.

Just a while ago I vomited everything I had eaten.

I suddenly felt like vomiting.

I feel like vomiting.

---

203) nauseous: 구역질나는

138

I have absolutely no energy and I feel like vomiting.

■ 〈Case〉 구토

Patient: I was nauseous up to throat.

I was throwing up but nothing came out.

MTC(Doctor): I will check your throat through a laryngoscope[204]).

■ 〈Case〉 구토

Patient: For the past 4 to 5 days, I suddenly feel like I need to throw up.

MTC(Doctor): Do you have an upset stomach?

Patient: No, I don't.

It is just like the feeling you get when are about to puke.

MTC: You need an MRI scan.

The MRI scan will help me to plan appropriate treatment.

Patient: I see

■ 〈Case〉 구토

Patient: I sometimes vomit with blood.

MTC(Doctor): What color was the blood?

Is it bright red or dark red?

Patient: It looked dark red.

MTC: Do you vomit with food?

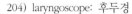

204) laryngoscope: 후두경

Patient: No.

MTC: Do you cough up blood?

Patient: No.

MTC: How many times have you thrown up?

Patient: I have vomited about four times for the last two weeks.

■ 〈Case〉 구토

Patient: After lunch, I threw up everything I had for lunch.

MTC(Doctor): What did you have for lunch.

Patient: I had Korean meal.

■ 혈토

I vomited blood.

I found vomit with blood in it.

I had a sharp pain and then I coughed up some blood.

■ 〈Case〉 혈토

Patient: For the first time I vomited blood.

MTC(Doctor): If you vomit bright red blood, it is a sign of bleeding in the throat or stomach.

■ 아침 구토증상

I have terrible morning sickness[205].

Isn't there any medicine for morning sickness?

3.6.9 복부

■ 복통

I have a terrible pain in the stomach.

I have a stomachache.

---

205) morning sickness: 아침의 구역질, 아침의 구토증

■ 〈Case〉 복통

MTC(Doctor): Let me palpate[206] your belly to examine it.
Please turn your head to the other side and cough for me.

(기침한다.)

MTC: Now please let me listen your belly.
I need to press lightly on your stomach area.
I need to press a little more deeply now.
Any tenderness here[207]?
I know it feels a little uncomfortable, but if you feel pain please let me know.
Take a deep breath.

■ 〈Case〉 복통

Patient: Hello, Doctor.

MTC(Doctor): Hello, how can I help you?

Patient: Actually, since last two days I am having a stomach pain.

MTC: Tell me where exactly the pain is?

Patient: It is somewhat near the lower abdomen.

MTC: Is it a severe pain or just a light pain?

Patient: I can't say.
Sometimes it is severe and sometimes mild.

MTC: What have you eaten two days before?

Patient: I went to a wedding party and there we had dinner.

MTC: Do you feel like eating anything?

Patient: No.

MTC: It is minor stomach infection[208].
I'm giving you medicine's for 5 days and you will feel better.

Patient: Thank You.

---

206) palpate: 만져보다
207) Any tenderness here?
    = Any pain here?
208) infection: 감염

■ 〈Case〉 복통

Patient: I have a stomachache.

MTC(Doctor): Did you have anything strange around that time?

Patient: I had a Japanese food at a restaurant in Seoul(Busan).

Do you think I could have picked something up?

MTC: It's possible.

■ 〈Case〉 복통

Patient: I am suffering from a bad stomachache, and I'd like to have a doctor examine me.

MTC(Nurse): Oh, I see.

I'll call the doctor immediately.

Patient: Yes, please.

MTC(Doctor): Good evening.

Let me check your temperature. In the meanwhile, you can tell me briefly your condition.

Patient: It was nine o'clock in the evening after dinner, I first felt a little pain and tightening of stomach.

MTC(Doctor): When did you have dinner?

Patient: Seven o'clock.

I took some pills thinking that it'd relieve[209] the pain, but it's getting worse and worse.

Now I feel a sharp pain in the lower right side of my bowel[210].

MTC(Doctor): I'll give you a shot.

This will ease[211] your pain temporarily.

Patient: Thank you very much.

---

209) relieve the pain: 고통을 덜다

No words will relieve my sorrow.: 어떤 위안의 말도 나의 슬픔에 위로가 되지 않는다.

210) bowel: 창자, 내장

have loose bowels: 설사를 하다

211) ease: 완화하다

ease pain: 고통을 덜다

- ⟨Case⟩ 복통

  Patient: My stomach stings.

  MTC(Doctor): Is the pain dull or sharp?

  Patient: I have a sharp pain in the stomach.

  MTC: How long have you had the pain?

  Patient: Since a couple of days.

  MTC: Did you have to vomit?

  Patient: No, I didn't.

  MTC: I will order the blood test and X-ray.

- ⟨Case⟩ 복통

  Patient: I am sick.

  MTC(Doctor): Where does it hurt?

  Patient: My stomach hurts.

  MTC: What kind of pain do you have?

  Patient: I have a burning pain in my stomach.

- ⟨Case⟩ 복통

  Patient: I have a stomachache.(I feel a pain in the stomach.)

  MTC(Doctor): What's the pain like?[212]

  Patient: I feel like my stomach muscles are going to split.

  It is especially painful when I sneeze[213] or cough.

- ⟨Case⟩ 복통

  Patient: I have a stomachache.

  MTC(Doctor): How does it hurt?

  Patient: I feel a sharp pain.

  MTC: When did the pain start?

  Patient: Since a couple of days.

---

212) Can you describe the pain?
   What kind of pain is it?
213) sneeze: 재채기하다

MTC: Where is painful?

Patient: Since a couple of days.

MTC: Where is painful?

Patient: Just below the rib cage, on the left hand side.

■ 〈Case〉 복통

Patient: My stomach hurts.

MTC(Doctor): How long have you had the pain?

Patient: Two days.

MTC: What kind of pain is it?

Sharp? Constant?214)

What does it feel like?

Patient: The pain in the stomach is especially severe when the stomach is empty

■ 〈Case〉 복통

Patient: I have a stomachache.

MTC(Doctor): Do you have any other symptoms with your stomachache?

Patient: I feel nauseous215).

■ 〈Case〉 복통

Patient: My stomach hurts.

MTC(Doctor): Let me examine you. Please lie down there.

How long has your stomach been hurting?

Patient: A couple of days.

MTC: Do you feel bloated after a heavy, fatty, or greasy meal?

Patient: Yes, a little bit.

MTC: May I listen to your chest?

Please roll up your shirt.

Please take a deep breath.

Now breathe out.

214) constant: 지속적인
215) nauseous: 구역질하는

Do you feel any pain when I palpate[216] your stomach?

Patient: No, I don't.

MTC: Have you ever vomited blood?

Patient: No, I haven't.

MTC: Based on your symptoms and the physical examination, you may have a mild stomach ulcer.

I will write a prescription for some medicine to cure your stomach ulcer.

■ 〈Case〉 복통

Patient: I've been feeling very weak and sleepy all the time.

Then, I started getting stomach aches and feeling dizzy.

MTC(Doctor): When did this start?

Patient: The stomachaches recently started about three days.

No, a week ago.

But it's been more than a couple of weeks that I've been feeling weak.

It's been quite awhile.

MTC: Do you have any thoughts as to why this might be happening?

Patient: Not really.

■ 〈Case〉 복통

Patient: Since my stomach is feeling better, do you think I can drink alcohol again?

MTC(Doctor): Perhaps. But the heartburn[217] may come back if you do that.

You could try drinking small amounts and cut back if it causes problems.

Try taking a couple of antacids[218] before you drink and eat some food along with the alcohol.

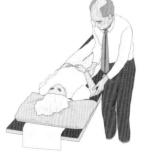

---

216) palpate: 만져보다
217) heartburn: 속쓰림
218) antacids: 산을 중화하는, 제산제

■ 〈Case〉 복통

Patient: I have had stomach pains, nausea[219], diarrhea[220], and lack of appetite for a week.

I feel very weak because I have not been able to eat for the last few days.

MTC(Doctor): Have you been out of the country recently, or have you eaten any foods that you think could have made you sick?

■ 식욕

How is your appetite?

I have a poor appetite.

I have little appetite.

I have lost my appetite.

I have no appetite.

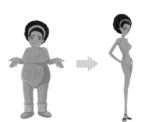

My appetite usually falls in the summer because of the hot temperature.

I usually lose my appetite in the summer under the influence of the hot temperature.

I don't have much of an appetite.

I have a very large appetite.

A little exercise will give you an appetite.

I have absolutely no appetite.

I have no energy nor appetite.

Have you had any significant change in your weight recently?

Have you had any change in your appetite?

■ 〈Case〉 식욕부진

Patient: I have had a poor appetite for the past month.

MTC(Doctor): How about your stomach?

Are you nauseated[221]?

---

219) nausea: 메스꺼움
220) diarrhea: 설사
221) nauseate: 구역질나게 하다
　　Are you nauseated?
　　= Do you feel nauseated?

Patient: No nausea, but I have a heavy feeling in my stomach.

That is why my appetite is gone.

MTC: How about your weight?

Patient: I have lost 2 Kilos in the last month.[222]

MTC: Let's do an X-ray examination of your stomach.

■ 〈Case〉 식욕부진

MTC(Doctor): How is your appetite.

Patient: These days I don't have any appetite.

■ 복통

Do you have a pain in the stomach?

I have stomach cramps[223].

I have heartburn[224].

My stomach stings.

My stomach twinges[225].

My stomach tingles[226].

I have a squeezing pain in the stomach.

I have a biting pain in my stomach.

Whenever my stomach is empty, it begins to hurt.

Before meals, my stomach feels heavy and there is a burning sensation.

My stomach aches after meals.

Every time I drink something alcoholic, I have a stomachache the next morning.

I have a pain in the lower abdomen.

I don't feel well in my stomach.

I suffer from a chronic upset stomach.

Even though I haven't had anything to eat since morning, my stomach feels

---

222) I have lost 2 kilos in the last month.

= I have lost 4.4 pounds in the last month.

223) stomach cramps: 위경련

224) heartburn: 속쓰림

225) twinge: 쑤시듯이 아프다

226) tingle: 따끔따끔 아프다

heavy and I have no appetite.

The pain has gone but my stomach still feels heavy.

I feel a pressing in my stomach.

The majority of people lose their appetite in the summer.

I have a sharp griping[227] pain in the side of my abdomen[228].

At first there was a pain on the right side of my abdomen, but then my chest, shoulders, and my back began to ache.

There is a continuous pain in the left side of my abdomen.

The right-hand side of my abdomen suddenly begins to hurt sometimes.

I suddenly got a pain on the right-hand side of my abdomen.

I have a burning pain on the right side of my abdomen.

■ 〈Case〉 갈비뼈 부분의 통증 및 간 질환

Patient: I feel a severe pain in the ribs.

MTC(Doctor): I am going to press on the right side below your ribs to feel your liver.

Please take a deep breath.

In.

Out.

I am going to press on the left side of your belly.

Please take a deep breath.

Let me know if it hurts.

I need to press in on your stomach area.

Tell me if it hurts more when I press in or let go.

---

227) I have a griping pain in the bowels: 장을 쥐어짜는 고통을 느끼다
228) abdomen: 복부

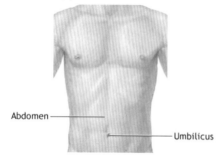

Abdomen ———

——— Umbilicus

■ 〈Case〉 간 질환

Patient: I feel tired all over my body and I don't have any appetite.

MTC(Doctor): You don't look very well.

   Please lie down on the bed.

   I will check your abdomen.

(검사 후)

MTC: The liver is swollen as I thought.

   It might be hepatitis.

   How much alcohol do you drink a week?

Patient: I drink about two bottles of Soju twice a week.

MTC: First of all, let us have a blood test.

■ 〈Case〉 복부 위의 통증

Patient: I have a pain a little bit above the stomach after meals.

MTC: Do you eat at irregular time?

Patient: I have to meet customers very often so I often eat out.

MTC: Do you smoke?

Patient: Yes, I smoke approximately 10 cigarettes.

MTC: It may be a stomach ulcer.

   Let us have a upper gastrointestinal X-ray exam to check it.

■ 〈Case〉 복부통증

Patient: My stomach hurts.

MTC(Doctor): How is your appetite?

Patient: None, I don't have any appetite?

MTC: Let me examine you.

   Please lie down there.

   How long has your stomach been hurting?

Patient: A couple of days.

MTC: Do you feel bloated after a heavy, fatty, or greasy meal?

Patient: No, I can't say I do.

MTC: OK. May I listen to your chest?

Please take a deep breath for me.

Now exhale.

That's good. Do you feel any pain when I palpate your stomach?

Patient: No, I don't.

MTC: Have you ever vomited any blood?

Patient: No.

MTC: Based on your symptoms and the physical examination, you may have a mild stomach ulcer.

It is probably causing your stomachache.

I will write a prescription for some medicine.

I will help you get rid of the pain.

■ 〈Case〉 복부통증

Patient: The right side of my stomach started to really hurt last night.

MTC(Doctor): How is it now?

Do you feel nauseated?

Patient: I am nauseated.

MTC: What did you have for dinner last night?

■ 〈Case〉 복부통증

Patient: I have a severe pain in the stomach.

MTC(Doctor): How long have you been having this pain?

Patient: It started in June.

My stomach hurts after some meals, but not always.

MTC: You should have come in earlier.

Let's get to the bottom of this.

Have you changed your eating habits during this period?

Patient: No, not really.

Well, that's not true. I'm eating the same foods, but less.

You know, the pain seems to come and go.

MTC: How strong is the pain exactly?

On a scale of one to ten, how would you describe the intensity of the pain?

Patient: Well, I'd say the pain is about a two on a scale of one to ten.

Like I say, it's not really bad. It just keeps coming back.

■ 〈Case〉 복부통증

Patient: I feel pain in the abdomen.

MTC(Doctor): How long does the pain last when you get it?

Patient: It comes and goes. I sometimes hardly feel anything.

Other times, it can last up to half an hour or more.

MTC: Is there a type of food that seems to cause stronger pain than other types?

Patient: Heavy foods like steak usually brings on pains.

I've been trying to avoid those.

MTC: Does the pain travel to any other parts of your body-chest, shoulder or back?

Or does the pain remain around the stomach area.

Patient: No, it just hurts here.

■ 〈Case〉 구토 및 위산역류 확인

MTC(Doctor): Have you thrown up?

Patient: No, I haven't.

MTC: Do the stomach acids come up?

Patient: Yes, a little.

■ 더부룩함

I feel bulged[229] in the stomach.

I feel bloated after eating too much dessert.

My stomach rumbles[230].

I feel as if I have a bulging, stuffed stomach.

My stomach feels uncomfortably heavy.

You can hardly call it pain, but I feel a kind of pressure around the right upper

---

229) bulge: 볼록하다
230) rumble: 꾸르륵 소리 나다

area of my abdomen.

I feel pumped up in the lower abdomen.

3.6.10 가슴 및 피부

■ 호흡곤란

Is it hard to breathe?

I feel as if it is hard to breathe.

I feel short of breath after each meal.

I get out of breath when I walk a little.

I feel as if it is hard to breathe.

I have a heavy feeling in my chest.

I get out of breath when I walk stairs.

Are you short of breath after mild exercise?

I have difficulty in breathing.

Please take a deep breath.

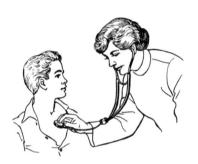

■ 〈Case〉 호흡상태 확인

MTC(Doctor): Could you cross your arms in front?

Please say 99 every time I place my hands.

Patient: 99.

■ 〈Case〉 호흡상태 확인

Patient: I feel heavy in the chest.(I feel a pressure in the chest.)

MTC(Doctor): I am going to listen to your lungs.

Please open your mouth and take a deep breath.

In and out through your mouth.

In.

Out.

Now breath normally.

I am going to press on some areas on your chest to feel your heart impulse.

■ 〈Case〉 호흡곤란

Patient: I have been wheezing[231] since last week.

MTC(Doctor): Do you have any idea what is causing it?

Patient: I caught a cold and it has been hard to breathe ever since.

I start to get these attack at night and I cannot sleep because it is so hard to breathe.

MTC: There is a strong possibility that you have asthma.

Have you ever had any allergies in the past?

■ 심장통증

I feel the chest pain when I move the shoulders.

I feel the chest pain from inside.

I sometime feel a palpitation[232].

Do you feel palpitations after exercise or intense[233] emotion or stress?

I feel as if I have a convulsion[234] in my heart.

I have a heart disease.

My heart skips beats.

There is an occasional pause in my pulse.

My heart goes pit-a-pat[235].

You are weak-hearted.

■ 〈Case〉 심장통증

Patient: I have severe a chest pain.

MTC(Doctor): How long have you had the chest pain?

Patient: For a couple of days.

MTC: Is this the first time you have had the chest pain?

---

231) wheeze: 헐떡거리다, 가쁜 숨을 내쉬다
232) palpitation: 두근거림
233) intense: 격렬한
234) convulsion: 경련
235) pit-a-pat: 두근두근, 펄떡거리는

Patient: I sometimes have chest pains.

MTC: When do you feel the chest pain?

Patient: Especially when I climb stairs[236].

MTC: How long does the chest pain last?

Patient: A couple of minutes.

MTC: What do you usually do when you have chest pain?

Patient: I take a rest or I have some painkillers[237].

MTC: Let me check your blood pressure.

Please roll up your sleeves.

■ 〈Case〉 심장통증

Patient: I have a chest pain.

MTC(Doctor): Do you have difficulty in breathing?

Patient: I am sometimes out of breath when I climb stairs.

MTC: To get an accurate diagnosis of the cause of your chest pain, you need to get some medical tests done.

■ 흉통

Do you have a pain in the chest?

Do you have a pain in the chest when you take a deep breath?

Which part(side) do you have pain in the chest when you have a heart attack?

I feel blocked up in the chest.

I have an alarming pain in my chest.

There is a sudden sharp pain in my chest.

I have a pricking[238] pain in my chest.

■ 〈Case〉 흉통

Patient: I have a fluttering[239] sensation in my chest.

---

236) climb stairs

= walk up stairs.

237) painkiller: 진통제

238) pricking: 따끔하게 찌르는, 따끔따끔한 아픔의

239) fluttering: 두근거리다

MTC(Doctor): When do you feel it?

Patient: Only when I lie down.

My heart beat becomes very strong.

MTC: Have you had any heart diseases in the past?

Patient: No, nothing particular, but I have gained four kilos in the past year and I feel overweight.

MTC: I'd like to take an electrocardiogram.

■ 〈Case〉 흉통

Patient: I have chest a pain[240].

MTC(Doctor): What type of pain do you feel?

Patient: I feel a prickly sensation in my chest[241] and occasionally there is a choking feeling.

MTC: When do you have this pain?

Patient: When I go upstairs.

MTC: Where do you feel the pain?

Patient: Mostly in the left chest.

■ 〈Case〉 흉통

Patient: I sometimes feel short of breath[242] when I walk up stairs.

MTC(Doctor): Do you have a chest pain?

Patient: No, I don't, but I do have a feeling of tightness in my chest.

I have a fluttering sensation in the chest. : 심장이 경련을 일으키는 듯하다.

= I have a twitching sensation in the chest.

I have a burning sensation in the chest.: 가슴이 쓰린 느낌이 든다.

240) I have a chest pain = I have a pain in the chest.

I have a back pain: 등이 아프다 = I have a pain on the back.

I have a knee pain: 무릎이 아프다 = I have a pin in the knee.

241) prickly: 따끔따끔한

I feel a prickly sensation in my chest

= I feel prickly chest pain.

242) feel short of breath: 숨이 차다

■ 〈Case〉흉통

Patient: How did my X-ray turn out?

MTC(Doctor): I can't see any remarkable troubles in your X-ray.

Patient: How did my blood test turn out?

MTC: Your blood test is positive to hepatitis[243].

Patient: Can it be cured?

MTC: It won't take long to recover.

But you need to be hospitalized.

Patient: Am I alright?

MTC: It's in the early stages.

Patient: Really?

MTC: Your blood and urine tests are normal and your heart test is good, also.

Patient: Thank you.

■ 〈Case〉흉통

Patient: I have a severe chest pain.

I think I have a problem in the heart.

MTC(Doctor): When did you feel that problem?

Patient: I had a syncope[244] last night.

I think my heart had a problem.

MTC: Don't you feel any palpitation[245]?

Patient: When I wake up in the morning or when I feel tired, I feel palpitation.

The palpitation comes itself and remain for almost 10 minutes.

■ 〈Case〉흉통

MTC(Doctor): Are you having chest pain? Or feeling pressure around your chest?

Patient: Since a couple of weeks ago, my chest feels very tight.

It's not really a pain.

It gets hard to breathe.

---

243) hepatitis: 간염
244) syncope: 실신
245) palpitation: 심장경련

MTC: Does this happen at any particular time?

Patient: I don't think so.

MTC: I'm going to schedule you for a cardiac catheterization. Hopefully, we can get you scheduled by the end of the week.

Patient: What is cardiac catheterization.[246]

MTC: This is a test that shows us if there's any blockage in the arteries[247] around the heart. What'll happen is that they'll insert a very long, narrow tube into a blood vessel in your thigh area.

Through the thin tube, some dye will be injected. The dye will reach the heart and by using x-rays, they can take pictures of the heart's arteries.

Patient: This sounds like a serious test.

How long will it take?

MTC: The actual test takes about 1.5 to 2 hours. But you'll have to stay about 4 hours after the test to make sure everything is okay.

MTC: It looks like you're healing up really nicely since the thyroidectomy[248]. Have you been feeling better since we adjusted the dosage[249] on the thyroid replacement hormones?

Thyroidectomy is a surgery to remove the thyroid gland.

Patient: I've been feeling much better.

Not feeling as slow and sluggish.

MTC: That's good.

- 〈Case〉 흉통

Patient: I have a severe chest pain.

I think I have angina.[250]

---

246) cardiac catheterization: 심도자법(팔 또는 다리의 큰 정맥을 절개한 후 심도관을 혈관을 통해 심장까지 삽입하는 진단적 검사)

247) arteries: 동맥

248) thyroidectomy: 갑상선 절제술

249) dosage: 투약

adjust the dosage: 투약을 조절하다.

the dosage on the thyroid replacement hormones: 갑상선 대체 호르몬 투약

250) angina: 협심

MTC(Doctor): Since when did you feel that problem?

Patient: I have been having difficulty in breathing for the last two days.

I think my heart has a problem.

MTC: Do you feel pressure, squeezing, burning or tightness in your chest?

Patient: No.

MTC: Do you feel pressure, squeezing, burning or tightness in your arms, shoulders, neck, jaw, throat, or back?

Patient: No.

MTC: Patients have different symptoms.

Do you feel a chest pain when you climb stairs or when you feel tired?

Patient: Yes.

MTC: Do you feel palpitation when you lift something heavy?

Patient: No.

MTC: Do you feel a chest pain when you are having sex?

Patient: No.

MTC: Do you feel shortness of breath, fatigue or weakness?

Patient: I sometimes feel palpitation, but my symptoms often go away soon after I stay still.

MTC: Do you have indigestion[251]?

Patient: No.

MTC: Do you feel dizzy, when you are out in the cold weather?

Patient: No.

MTC: To get an accurate diagnosis of the cause of your chest pain, you need to get some medical tests done.

■ 〈Case〉 흉통

Patient: How are my lungs?

MTC(Doctor): I can hear a wheezing[252] sound.

Have you ever had the symptom before?

---

251) indigestion: 소화불량
252) wheezing: 숨을 쉴 때 기도의 폐색(막힘)에 의하여 생기는 소리

Patient: I had last spring.

■ 〈Case〉 흉통

Patient: I have a pressure in my chest when I walk up stairs.

MTC(Doctor): Let us take an electrocardiography.

(잠시 후)

MTC: The electrocardiogram taken in the resting condition a little while ago doesn't show anything wrong.

It may be because of angina of effort so let us check the electrocardiogram in an exercising condition.

Patient: What is angina?

MTC: It is an obstruction of the coronary arteries[253] and it prevents an adequate amount of blood from reaching the myocardium[254] during exercise.

■ 가슴의 혹

I have a lump[255] in my breast.

I feel a lump at the left breast.

I have a lump at the bottom of my breast.

■ 〈Case〉 가슴의 혹 확인

Patient: I noticed a small lump in my left breast a few days ago.

MTC: Have you had a breast cancer exam?

Patient: Once a year.

MTC: Let us have a look at you.

Please take off your blouse.

■ 겨드랑이의 혹

I felt a lump under the armpit[256].

I have a really bad underarm(armpit) arm odor[257].

---

253) an obstruction of coronary arteries: 관상동맥의 막힘
254) myocardium: 심근
255) lump: 덩어리, 혹
256) odor: 냄새

■ 천식

I have attacks of asthma[258].

I suffer from chronic asthma.

■ 〈Case〉 천식

Patient: I have attacks of asthma[259].

MTC(Doctor): Do you have frequent attacks?

Patient: There is a long period between attacks.

■ 폐렴

I have a pneumonia[260].

I seem to have the symptoms of pneumonia.

You are recommended to have a pneumonia vaccine.

■ 결핵

I have a past history of tuberculosis[261].

I suffered from T.B.[262] in my early 40's.

■ 피부 알레르기

Do you have any allergies?

Are you allergic to any food?

I have allergy to pollen[263].

I have allergy to almond.

I have allergy to peanuts.

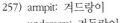

257) armpit: 겨드랑이
    underarm: 겨드랑이 밑의
258) asthma: 천식
    천식: 알레르기염증에 의해 기관지가 반복적으로 좁아지는 만성호흡기 질환이다. 기관지가 좁아
    져서 숨이 차고, 기침이 나며, 가슴에서 색색거리는 소리가 들리며 가슴이 답답해지는 증상이 반
    복적으로 되풀이된다.
259) asthma: 천식
260) pneumonia: 폐렴
261) tuberculosis: 결핵, 폐결핵
262) T.B.=Tuberculosis: 결핵, 폐결핵
263) pollen: 꽃가루

I have allergy to stainless steel.

I have allergy to dust.

I have allergy to dust mites[264].

■ 동상

My ear lobes[265] got frostbitten.

My hands are frostbitten.

I have severe frostbite[266] on my hands.

■ 화상

I have gotten sunburn[267].

I burned my hand.

■ 주름

I want to remove wrinkles on the face.

■ 〈Case〉 주름

Patient: I have lots of freckles and wrinkles so I hear I look older than my age.

MTC(Doctor): Ultraviolet rays are most harmful to freckles so cutting down your UV A and B exposure is most important.

As an anti-aging treatment method, there are chemical peeling treatments as well as laser treatments which accelerate the revival of skin.

And to treat wrinkles, there are methods where you inject botox and collagen.

Patient: Then, what is the treatment that you would recommend for me?

MTC: For freckles, laser treatment would be good.

For wrinkles, I would like to recommend botox.

Patient: Does it hurt?

MTC: During the treatment, it pricks a bit but it doesn't affect daily life.

---

264) dust mite: 집 먼지 진드기
265) ear lobe: 귓불
266) frostbite: 동상
267) sunburn: 햇빛 화상

■ 〈Case〉 피부 트러블

I feel itchy all over my body.

I have a prickly[268] feeling all over.

I have a puffy[269] face.

I want to get rid of blackheads[270] on the face.

I have a growth[271] on my face.

I often have boils[272].

I have got a boil on my face.

I have a boil[273] on my buttocks.

I have rashes[274] all over my body.

I have a skin rash caused by cosmetics.

I've got a prick in my finger[275].

I have red specks[276] on my face.

These pimples[277] are awful.

I can't get rid of the pimples on my face.

This acne[278] is dreadful.

Get rid of the birthmark[279], please.

I want to remove a mole[280].

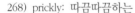

268) prickly: 따끔따끔하는
269) puffy: 부은
270) blackhead: 위가 검은 여드름
271) growth: 부기, 종양
   benign growth: 양성 종양
   malignant growth: 악성 종양
272) boil: 부스럼, 종기
273) boil: 부스럼, 종기
274) rash: 뽀루지
275) 집게손가락: forefinger / first finger / index finger
   엄지손가락: thumb
276) speck: 점
277) pimple: 뽀루지, 여드름
278) acne: 여드름
279) birthmark: 출생모반
   출생모반: 출생할 때 이미 가지고 나오는 혈관성 모반으로 자연적으로 살갗에 나타난 얼룩무늬 또는 점, 사마귀, 주근깨 등을 말한다.
280) mole: 사마귀(Wart)

■ 〈Case〉 피부 여드름

Patient: I have pimples[281].

　　　　 I want an acne treatment.

MTC(Doctor): Since there are many kinds of acne treatment, it's important to choose the one that is right for you.

Patient: What kinds are there?

　MTC: For acne, long-term treatment and maintenance are crucial.

　　　　 Generally, antibiotics such as minomicin are taken.

　　　　 And for ointment you can use antibiotic ointment, vitamin A ointment or benzoyl peroxide ointment.

　　　　 Also, there are surgical treatment, chemical peelings and photochemist treatment available.

Patient: I see.

　MTC: Please decide after consulting with our staffs.

Patient: OK. I understand.

　　　　 Thank you.

■ 〈Case〉 접촉성 피부염

Patient: My skin becomes red and sore.

MTC(Doctor): Let us run a allergy test.

(검사 후)

　MTC: Your test comes out as contact dermatitis[282].

Patient: Then what should I do?

　MTC: Apply the cream sparingly to your face and neck.

　　　　 And take a medicine for a week.

　　　　 After two week please come again.

Patient: How can I take the medicines?

　MTC: Take a pouch of medicine thirty minutes after meals.

　　사마귀: 유두종 바이러스 감염으로 피부 및 점막의 증식이 발생하는 질환이다.

281) pimple: 뾰루지, 여드름

282) dermatitis: 피부염

　　contact dermatitis: 접촉성 피부염

Patient: When do I take the medicine?

MTC: Take this medicine every eight hours.

Patient: Every eight hours?

MTC: Three times a day, thirty minutes after each meal.

Take one does before you go to bed.

Patient: Anything else?

MTC: During taking medicines, you should stay away from irritating[283] foods, alcohol and smoking.

Patient: OK, I will.

■ 피부 가려움

The itching is quite unbearable.

I cannot get over the itching.

My back itches.

My stomach itches all the time.

My legs itch at night.

My feet itch badly.

I feel itchy all over my body.

It's so itchy that I can't help scratching through my shirt.

I have something like a rash all over my back, shoulder, and upper arms.

I have rashes all over the body.

I develop severe hives[284] whenever I eat fish.

I often have boils.

I have rashes all over my body.

I have a prickly feeling all over.

I've got a prick in my finger.

I don't consciously feel a prick.

I'm worried about a node in this area.

---

283) irritating: 자극하는, 귀찮게 하는
284) hive: 두드러기성 구진

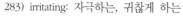
164

- 〈Case〉 피부 가려움

  Patient: My legs have been itchy since this past summer.

  The itching is sometimes quite unbearable.

  MTC(Doctor): When exactly do your legs itch?

  Patient: They get itchy just after taking a bath.

  MTC: What do you usually do when they get itchy?

- 〈Case〉 피부 가려움

  Patient: I can't help scratching the itchy place.

  MTC(Doctor): I'd like to examine your legs.

  Could you take off your panty hose.

- 〈Case〉 피부 가려움

  Patient: In the winter, I feel itchy[285] all over my body.

  MTC(Doctor): Yes, in a dry climate, you may have winter itch.

  Itching can be due the lack of moisture in your skin.

  Itching is sometimes caused by severe allergic reaction, infection, and

  inflammation.

  Patient: I see.

  MTC: How long do you tolerate itching?

  Patient: Over the past couple of weeks.

  MTC: Do you have difficulty in sleeping.

  Patient: The itch skin keeps me awake at night.

  MTC: Let me see.

  The skin looks different in the itching area.

  When you take a bath, What kind of soaps and shampoos do you use?

  Patient: It is just an ordinary soap and shampoo.

  I don't have any allergies to my knowledge.

---

285) itchy: 가려운

■ 〈Case〉 피부 부스럼

Patient: I have got a boil[286] on my face.

MTC(Doctor): Let me see.

What happened to the boil?

Patient: At first the skins turns red and after a few days the color changed into white.

MTC: A boil is a skin infection.

The skin turns red in the area of the infection and a tender lump develops.

After 4 to 7 days, the lump starts turning white as pus collects under the skin.

Patient: What kind of medicine would you recommend?

MTC: Different people can get very different results with the same skin care.

Patient: Please give me a prescription.

MTC: I will give you a prescription to cure the boil.

Let us take a look how the skin care makes a difference.

■ 〈Case〉 피부 두드러기

Patient: I have red rashes[287] on my neck.

MTC(Doctor): It is important to ascertain the cause of the neck rash.

The neck rashes may be caused by detergents, lotions, or soaps.

Do you have anything at home to suspect the cause of red rashes?

Patient: I don't think so.

MTC: Have you exposed yourself to much of the sun's rays?

Patient: No, I haven't.

MTC: If your neck rash is due to a sun burn, then stay out of the sun for a few days.

Do you often work in dirt?

Patient: No, I don't.

MTC: I will give you a prescription.

---

286) boil: 부스럼, 종기
287) rash: 뾰루지, 두드러기

Please clean your neck using an antibacterial cleanser.

This will remove irritants that may be causing your neck rash.

■ 〈Case〉 피부 두드러기

Patient: I have severe hives[288].

I have been to a clinic, but the hives are still here and I decided to see a doctor in Korea.

MTC(Doctor): OK. I will check your condition such as blood test, urine test and kidney function.

After the test, I will give you a prescription to control the hives.

3.6.11 어깨

■ 어깨통증

Do you suffer from shoulder pain?

My shoulders are stiff.

My shoulders are sore.

I have a pain in and around the shoulder blade[289].

My shoulders and arms hurt.

I had a bad fall and put my shoulder out of joint.

Yesterday when I fell down the steps, I seem to have my shoulder dislocated[290].

Because my posture is unnatural[291], my shoulders hurt, too.

My shoulders and arms hurt.

When I fell down the steps, I seem to have dislocated my shoulder.

■ 〈Case〉 어깨통증

MTC(Doctor): Please let me untie your gown so I can examine your lungs.

Patient: Could you push up your shoulders against my resistance.

---

288) hive: 두드러기성 구진
289) shoulder blade: 견갑골, 어깨뼈
290) dislocate: 관절을 삐게 하다
291) unnatural: 부자연스러운

■ 〈Case〉 어깨통증

Patient: My shoulders have been stiff recently.

MTC(Doctor): That is too bad.

When did it start?

Patient: It started about a month ago.

It seems to be getting worse so I am here today.

MTC: Do you think it is related to your job?

Patient: I usually spend a lot of time doing computer work.

I think that is the main cause of my shoulder stiffness.

3.6.12 등

■ 등 질환

My back itches.

I have a rash[292] on my back.

I have a stubborn boil[293] on my back.

My back is hurting me so bad.

■ 등 통증

Do you suffer from back pain when sitting?

I have dull back pain.

I have a severe pain in my back.

My back hurts sometimes.

I have a pulling pain[294] in my back.

When I tried to lift a heavy suitcase, I felt my back snap[295].

I feel pain in the back.

I just started to get terrible soreness in my upper back.

I suffer from back pain.

---

292) rash: 뾰루지
293) boil: 종기
294) pulling pain: 당겨지는 통증이 있다
295) snap: 툭 끊어지다

I have lower back pain.

The lower part of my back hurts so much I can't move.

When I try to straighten my back, the pain hits me.

When I cough, my back hurts down here.

Is the spine or the hip bone fractured?

I have a back pain. When I lie on my back[296], it hurts so much that I can not sleep well.

■ 〈Case〉 등 통증

Patient: I have a dull pain in my lower back and I have been going to the bathroom a lot recently.

MTC(Doctor): Is the color of your urine any different than usual?

Patient: It has been a little red recently.

MTC: You must have pyelonephritis[297].

I'd like to do a urinalysis to see.

■ 〈Case〉 등 통증

Patient: When I tried to lift up a heavy box yesterday, I felt a sharp pain in my back.

MTC(Doctor): Does it still hurt?

Patient: When I try to bend my back, it hurts terribly.

MTC: Compared to the time the pain first started, does it seem less severe?

Patient: It seems to be easing up a little, but I cannot stand it even now.

Anyway, I'd like to take an X-ray. Please get an X-ray on my spine.

3.6.13 허리

■ 〈Case〉 허리통증

Patient: The bottom part of my waist hurts.

MTC(Doctor): Exactly, which part hurts?

---

296) lie on the back: 똑바로 눕다
   lie on the stomach: 엎드려 눕다
   lie on the side: 옆으로 눕다
297) pyelonephritis: 신우신염

Patient: When I try to stretch my waist, it hurts a lot right here.

MTC: Since when did it hurt?

Patient: I think it has been hurting from three months ago.

MTC: First, let's take an X-ray.

Patient: Do I need to have a surgery done(performed)?

MTC: No, first, please lie down on the examination table.

If it hurts, don't hesitate to let me know.

Patient: Yes, Ah. It hurts there.

MTC: I think it is a hernia.

Let's take a closer examination.

Patient: I see. Thank you.

■ 〈Case〉 허리통증

Patient: I can hardly walk because of low back pain.

Yesterday when I tried to stand up from a chair, I felt a crackling.

MTC(Doctor): Do you have numbness on the sole of your feet?

Patient: No particularly.

MTC: When or on what occasions is the pain severe?

Patient: When I stand up or when I sit down.

■ 〈Case〉 허리통증

MTC(Doctor): Which part of your body hurts?

Patient: The bottom part of my waist hurts.

MTC: Exactly, which part hurts?

Patient: When I try to stretch my waist, it hurts a lot right here.

MTC: Since when did it hurt?

Patient: I think it has been hurting from three months ago.

MTC: First, let's take an X-ray.

Patient: Do I need to have a surgery done(performed)?

MTC: No, first, please lie down on the examination table.

If it hurts, don't hesitate to let me know.

Patient: It hurts there.

MTC: I think it is a hernia.

Let's take a closer examination.

Patient: I see. Thank you.

■ 〈Case〉 허리통증

MTC(Doctor): I'm afraid to say that, but your MRI result is not good statement.

The MRI finding shows herniated disc[298] in your back.

Although it probably needs a further evaluation to see what's going on in your body, you seem to have herniated disc in your back.

Patient: Is that serious disease?

MTC: No, if you get segmental surgical resection, you'll be fine.

However, you need to be hospitalized.

Patient: Does the operation hurt?

MTC: No, you're going to be under the anesthesia.

You won't feel any pain at all.

Don't worry about that.

Patient: OK. Sounds like I have no choice.

MTC: If you don't get(have) the surgery done(performed), it could get more complicated.

I'll make a surgery appointment. You'll probably be admitted to the hospital on the day before the day of your surgery.

Patient: All right. How can I get to the admission procedure?

---

298) herniated disc

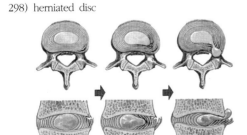

MTC: I will help you with admission procedure.

Let us go down to the registration desk for the foreigners on the first floor.

Fill out the admission form and sign in it.

Patient: All right. Thank you.

■ 〈Case〉 옆구리통증

Patient: I've had a pain in my lower right abdomen for a few weeks.

MTC(Doctor): Does it hurt much?

Patient: It doesn't hurt that much.

It is just uncomfortable.

MTC: How long do you feel the pain?

Patient: It usually last a few hours and then leaves.

For one week I was also a little nauseous[299] but now that is gone.

3.6.14 팔

■ 팔근육 통증

The muscles of my arms and legs ache.

I can't lift my arm over my head.

Because I can't stretch my arms, I have trouble doing house work.

I dislocated my arm joint.

■ 팔꿈치

Do you feel a pain in the elbow?

I dislocated my left elbow joint.

I am suffering from tennis elbow[300].

My tennis elbow began to ache again.

■ 〈Case〉 팔꿈치 통증

Patient: I can't lift my arm over my head.

---

299) nauseous: 구역질하는, 불쾌한
300) tennis elbow: 팔꿈치 과사용 증후군의 일종이다. 팔꿈치 관절과 팔에 무리한 힘이 주어져 팔꿈치 관절에 통증이 생기는 질환이다.

When I start to lift, I feel a little sore.

MTC(Doctor): Since when did you feel the pain?

Patient: A couple of weeks ago.

MTC: It could be tension.

If there was damage to the rotator cuff, this could be a reason for not being able to lift the arm.

Patient: Can I lift my arm after the surgery?

MTC: Even after the rotator cuff is surgically repaired, it often takes about five months to be able to raise the arm over the head.

3.6.15 무릎

I sometimes have a pain in my knees.

I have a severe pain in the knees.

My joints ache.

All my joints are stiff and aching.

My old rheumatism is bothering me again.

■ 〈Case〉 무릎 통증

Patient: Good morning.

MTC(Doctor): Yes, please come in.

Patient: Thank you. My name is Susie Maria.

MTC: What have you come in for today?

Patient: I've been having some pain in my joints, especially the knees.

MTC: How long have you been having the pain?

Patient: I'd say it started three or four months ago. It's been getting worse recently.

MTC: Are you having any other problems like weakness, fatigue or headaches?

Patient: Well I've certainly felt under the weather.

MTC: Right.

How much physical activity do you get?

Do you play any sports?

Patient: Some. I like to play tennis about once a week. I take my dog on a walk every morning.

MTC: OK. Let's have a look.

Can you point to the area where you are having a pain?

3.6.16 생식기 및 항문

■ 음부염증

I have an itchy sensation in the pubic region.

The external genitalia is itchy.

My pubic region has become inflamed[301].

I have a lump[302] in the pubic region.

I have an itchy sensation around the vagina[303].

I have pain while making love.

I'm afraid I might have contracted a veneral disease[304].

I have genital bleeding[305].

The bleeding does not stop.

Although it isn't time for my period, I'm bleeding.

I bleed a lot after delivery.

I bleed a lot after childbirth.

There has been copious bleeding since I had a miscarriage[306].

■ 〈Case〉 음부염증

Patient: My abdomen hurts.

MTC(Doctor): Then, I will take a uterine cancer test, ultrasonic test and internal examination.

Patient: According to the ultrasonic test, I think it is pelvic inflammation[307].

---

301) inflamed: 빨갛게 부은
302) lump: 혹, 덩어리
303) vagina: 질, 음부
304) veneral disease: 성병
305) genital bleeding: 생리
306) miscarriage: 유산

I will give you some medicine for 3 days.

If the pain continues, please come again.

MTC: After paying, get the prescription before you leave.

■ 불감증

I have vaginal discharge[308].

My vaginal discharge has a foul odor[309].

I'm frigid[310].

I don't menstruate[311].

I am having a heavy menstrual flow.

I've missed one period.

My periods haven't started yet this month.

My periods are irregular.

My period is three weeks late.

■ 임신

I think I've become pregnant. But I don't know for sure, so I would like for you to check me.

I want you to see if I'm pregnant.

I'd like to have a pregnancy test done.

When is the baby due?

The contractions[312] last about 20 minutes.

My water broke.

My pelvis[313] is narrow.

We want to have a child, but I can't get pregnant.

I want to have artificial insemination[314].

307) inflammation: 염증
308) vaginal discharge: 질 분비물
309) foul odor: 악취
310) frigid: 냉담한
311) menstruate: 월경하다
312) contraction: 수축
313) pelvis: 골반
314) insemination: 수정

I would like to have some contraceptive[315] medicine.

Once I stop taking the pill, will ovulation[316] be normal?

■ 폐경

When was your last menstrual period?

I have been menopause[317] for 18 months.

■ 생리통증

How may pads do you use in a heavy day?

Are your periods regular?

How many days does your period last?

Do you have abdominal cramps with your periods?

Do you have abdominal pain with your periods?

■ ⟨Case⟩ 생리통증

MTC(Doctor) Have you had any vaginal[318] discharge?

Patient: Yes, I have.

MTC: What is the color of the discharge?

Patient: Yellowish.

MTC: Does it have any bad odor?

Patent: A little bit bad.

MTC: Do you have any vaginal itching?

Patient: No, I don't.

MTC: Are your cycles regular?

■ ⟨Case⟩ 생리통증

MTC(Doctor): I am going to ask you some questions about your obstetric history?

Patient: OK.

---

artificial insemination: 인공수정

315) contraceptive: 피임의

contraceptive medicine: 피임약

316) ovulation: 배란

317) menopause: 폐경

318) vaginal: 질의

MTC: When did have your first menstrual period?

Patient: When I was 17 years old.

MTC: Was it regular?

Patient: Yes, it is.

MTC: How many times have you been pregnant? Any abnormalities or complications? Any mischarges?

Patient: I had mischarge twice.

MTC: How may children do you have?

Patient: Two daughters.

MTC: What are you using for birth control?

■ 〈Case〉 생리통증

MTC(Doctor): Do you have any children?

Patient: Yes, I have two children.

MTC: Have you ever had a miscarriage[319]?

Patient: Yes, I have had one miscarriage.

MTC: When was your first period?

Patient: I was 13 years old.

MTC: Are your periods regular?

Patient: My periods are regular.

It comes about every 38 days.

MTC: How about the amount of blood?

Do you have period pain?

Patient: The amount is normal and I have no pain.

MTC: Have you had a uterine cancer[320] test?

Patient: Yes, I have been tested a year ago.

MTC: What brought you here?

Patient: My abdomen hurts.

---

319) miscarriage: 유산
320) uterine cancer: 자궁암

MTC: Then, I will take a uterine cancer test, ultrasonic test[321] and internal examination[322].

Patient: According to the ultrasonic test, I think it is pelvic inflammation.

I will give you some medicine for 3 days.

If the pain continues, please come again.

MTC: After paying, get the prescription before you leave.

■ 소변통증

Do you have any problems controlling your bladder.

Do you feel pain when you urinate?

Please tell me the number of times you urinated and had a bowel movement yesterday.

When I urinate, it hurts terribly.

It hurts when I begin to urinate.

It's difficult to urinate.

Although I feel I have to urinate, it takes a long time before anything actually comes out.

Absolutely no urine comes out, and my abdomen is extremely painful.

I have pain around my bladder[323].

I seem to urinate very much.

I seem to urinate more often that usual.

After urinating, I don't feel relieved as I used to.

■ 〈Case〉 소변통증

Patient: I have difficulty in urinating.

MTC(Doctor): Do you have to urinate more often than before?

Patient: I don't have to urinate very often during the day, but in the middle of night I sometimes wake up to urinate.

---

321) ultrasonic test: 초음파검사
322) internal examination: 내진
323) bladder: 방광
   gallbladder: 쓸개, 담낭

MTC: I think you prostate gland[324] is enlarged.

I'd like to do a thorough examination and start treatment right away.

■ 〈Case〉 소변통증

Patient: I have difficulty in urinating.

MTC(Doctor): How does the urine come out?

Patient: It dribbles out little by little and it takes a long time.

MTC: You may have a gallstone, so Let us have a echogram.

Try to avoid fatty foods for a while.

■ 〈Case〉 소변통증

Patient: It hurts when I urinate.

MTC(Doctor): Has the frequency of urination been increasing?

Patient: Yes, it seems to be increased as compared to before.

MTC: Do you have cloudy urine?

Patient: Yes, I sometimes notice that it is cloudy.

MTC: You may have a bladder infection.

Let us do a urinalysis.

■ 〈Case〉 소변통증

Patient: I think I go to restroom too much compared to others, even though I drink much water.

MTC(Doctor): For an exact diagnosis, we need several tests.

Patient: What kind of test?

MTC: Please urinate in the bottle and bring it back.

Patient: How much do I need?

MTC: Just a little bit.

One third of the bottle.

Patient: That is it?

MTC: I(The nurse) will attach your name label on the bottle.

---

324) prostate gland: 전립선

The result will come out in a couple of hours.

■ 빈번한 소변 및 요실금

I often have a desire to urinate in the middle of night.

Why do I urine too often?

I am suffering from urinary incontinence[325].

■ 〈Case〉 빈번한 소변

Patient: What seems to be the trouble?

MTC(Doctor): I have been going to the toilet a lot recently.

Patient: How often?

MTC: In the day time I don't have to go often, but I sometimes get up in the middle of the night to go to the toilet.

Patient: Do you have anything to drink before you go to bed?

■ 치질

Do you have hemorrhoids[326]?

I have piles[327].

I'm suffering from piles.

I seem to have hemorrhoids.

Something like pus[328] comes out.

---

325) urinary incontinence: 요실금
326) hemorrhoid: 치질
327) have piles: 치질이 생기다
    치질(치핵): 항문 및 직장에 존재하는 치핵조직이 항문 밖으로 빠져나오는 내치핵과 항문 밖의 치핵조직이 부풀어 올라 덩어리처럼 만져지는 외치핵이 있다.

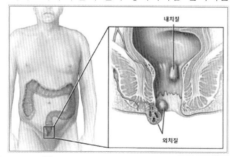

328) pus: 고름

■ 혈변

I bleed quite a bit when I have a bowel movement.

I have bloody stools.

Have you noticed any blood in the stool?

Blood is mixed with my stool.

■ 〈Case〉 혈변

Patient: I found blood in my stool.

MTC(Doctor): When did you notice it?

Patient: Yesterday morning.

I am afraid it might be cancer.

MTC: A bloody stool does not always mean cancer.

Do you have abdominal pain?

Patient: I have a little pain around the stomach.

MTC: Did you have breakfast today?

Patient: No, I didn't.

MTC: OK. let us do a stomach X-ray examination and make a reservation for
endoscopic examination of the large intestine.

You should have an examination for occult blood in the feces.

Patient: I see.

MTC: Please put a fecal specimen in this container and bring it at your next visit.

■ 〈Case〉 혈변

MTC(Doctor): Have you seen blood in the stool?

Patient: No. The color of stool is black.

MTC: Have you had other prominent symptoms besides that?

Patient: No.

■ 〈Case〉 혈변

MTC(Doctor): Have you seen any blood in your urine?

Patient: Yes, I have.

MTC: How many time have you seen blood in your urine?

Patient: I used to see blood in my urine, but it has gone.

MTC: Even though it has gone, I need to check your bladder[329] or kidney[330] infections[331].

■ 항문 가려움

Do you feel itchy around your anus[332]?

My anus is very itchy all the time.

The area around my anus is so itchy. I can't stand it.

I seem to have rash around my anus and it's very itchy.

■ 변비

Do you have constipation[333]?

It's difficult to pass a stool[334].

When my bowels move, it hurts terribly.

I had no bowel movements for two days.[335]

I have loose bowels.

My constipation is bad.

My bowels have stopped.

I have a hard stool.

I've been constipated[336] for the last few days.

I suffer from chronic constipation.

I have a soft stool.

I need to move my bowels. Where is the rest room?

---

329) bladder: 방광
330) kidney: 콩팥, 신장
331) infection: 감염
332) anus: 항문
333) constipation: 변비
      chronic constipation: 만성변비
334) stool: 대변
335) I had no bowel movements for two days.: 이틀 동안 화장실에 가지 못했다.
336) constipate: 변비에 걸리다

■ 〈Case〉 변비

MTC(Doctor): The X-ray shows that you are constipated.

Patient: What should I do?

MTC: To help prevent constipation, be sure to drink lots of water every day and try to eat fiber-rich diet.

■ 〈Case〉 변비

MTC(Doctor): What seems to be the trouble?

Patient: I have been constipated for about 5 days.

MTC: Have there been any changes in your life recently?

Patient: No, nothing in particular.

MTC: How about eating?

Do you eat regularly?

Do you eat a lot of fruit and vegetables?

Patient: I try to, but I sometimes skip breakfast and I tend to eat fastfood.

■ 〈Case〉 변비

Patient: I am suffering from constipation.

MTC(Doctor): Constipation usually results from the slow bowel movements.

It is usually because the bowel contains less water than normal.

Patient: What should I do to release constipation?

MTC: Drink plenty of water.

Your body needs the water in order to process the food you are digesting.

Water also helps weight loss.

Patient: That is what I do every day.

MTC: You had better get some exercise.

Exercising gets things moving, so to speak, so it is good cure for constipation.

■ 〈Case〉 변비

Patient: I have constipation.

MTC(Doctor): Do you drink a lot of water?

Patient: Yes.

MTC: Do you take in fibrous food such as fruits and vegetables?

Patient: Yes.

MTC: You might need to have an enema.[337]

■ 설사

Do you have diarrhea?

How many times per day did you have diarrhea? Was it watery or bloody?

I have a watery stool.

I have diarrhea[338].

I have a touch of diarrhea.

I have terrible diarrhea.

I have diarrhea several times a day.

When I drink milk I get diarrhea.

For two or three days now, I have had terrible diarrhea.

A binding medicine stopped my diarrhea.

■ 〈Case〉 설사

Patient: I have had some diarrhea for the past few days.

MTC(Doctor): Have you been abroad recently?

Patient: Yes, I was in Peking on business for three days last week.

MTC: Did you eat or drink anything unusual?

Patient: No, I don't think so.

MTC: Do you have a fever or stomachache?

Patient: I don't have a fever, but I have a slight pain in the abdomen.

MTC: I will examine your abdomen.

Please lie down on the bed.

■ 〈Case〉 설사

MTC(Doctor): Did you eat any food funny?

Patient: No.

---

337) enema: 관장
338) diarrhea: 설사

MTC: I think you have a food poisoning.

Let us run a test.

■ 〈Case〉 설사

Patient: I have diarrhea.

MTC(Doctor): What did you eat?

Patient: I went to a restaurant this afternoon.

MTC: Don't worry.

Diarrhea is a natural way to flushing toxins from your body.

Patient: I see.

MTC: Diarrhea is a reaction to food allergies, medications, parasites, or bacteria in food or water.

■ 〈Case〉 설사

Patient: I have diarrhea.

MTC(Doctor): Did you eat something that did not agree with you?

Patient: I have no idea.

MTC: I will give you a prescription to stop the diarrhea.

Patient: Thank you.

■ 〈Case〉 통풍[339]

Patient: I think I eat quite a lot of meat and oily food.

I drink almost two bottles of beer every day.

MTC(Doctor): I am afraid you may have gout[340].

Let us measure your uric[341] acid level.

---

339) 통풍: 우리 몸 안에 요산이라고 하는 물질이 몸 밖으로 빠져 나가지 못하고 과도하게 축적되어 발생하는 질병
340) gout: 통풍
341) uric: 오줌의
    uric acid: 요산

3.6.17 손

■ 손의 감각

My fingertips are numb[342].

I feel a tingling[343] in my finger.

■ 손 및 손가락 부상

I have blisters[344] on my palm.

My hands are painful, numb and itchy.

I cut my fingers with a knife.

I scorched[345] my fingers while cooking.

My fingers are hurting.

■ 손가락 통증

I got a splinter[346] in my finger.

I've torn off a fingernail.

I have a pricking sensation in my fingers.

■ 〈Case〉 손가락 부상

MTC(Doctor): How are you today?

Patient: Hello, doctor.

My left hand and fingers are in pain and numb.

MTC: How long have you had this pain and numbness?

Patient: About four months.

But it started to get worse a few weeks ago.

MTC: How is the pain in your left hand?

Is it sharp, dull, crampy, squeezing, or tingling pain?

Patient: My left hand cannot be bent too much.

---

342) numb: 무감각한
343) tingling: 따끔따끔한 느낌
344) blister: 물집
345) scorch: 그을리다
346) splinter: 파편

It hurts and my hand is numb especially at the fingertips[347].

It tingles also.

MTC: What do you do for your living?

Patient: I do sewing for a living.

Lately I cannot hold needle and thread properly.

MTC: How long have you been doing this job?

Patient: About 5 years.

MTC: Do you take any medication[348] for pain?

■ 손목통증

My limbs often get numb[349].

My limbs feel numb.

My limbs are going numb.

My limbs[350] feel numb and paralyzed[351].

My limbs are tingling[352].

3.6.18 다리

■ 다리통증

I feel pain in the legs.

My legs cramp[353] all the time.

My legs are swollen.

My legs are so sore and they hurt tremendously.

■ 〈Case〉 다리통증

MTC(Doctor): Please lay on your left side.

I need to lift your leg and pull it back.

---

347) fingertip: 손가락 끝
348) medications: 복용약
349) numb: 무감각해진
350) limb: 손목
351) paralyze: 마비시키다
352) tingle: 따끔거리다
353) cramp: 경련이 일다

Do you feel any pain?

I am going to move your leg to the side while I press on the side of your knee.

Do you feel any pain?

■ 〈Case〉 다리통증

Patient: My leg feels numb.

MTC(Doctor): Is the leg swollen?

Patient: No, it isn't.

　MTC: Is the calf muscle[354] hard and painful to touch?

Patient: No, it is not.

　MTC: Does it hurt if you pull your foot up towards the ceiling?

Patient: Yes, it does.

　MTC: I need a prescription for anti-inflammatories[355] for a couple of days.

■ 다리부상

My right leg is broken.

I broke my leg.

■ 발목부상

I feel a pain in my ankle. I don't know what is causing it as it just happens.

I sprained[356] my ankle.

I feel pain in the ankles.

■ 발통증

I have unexplainable pain in the left foot for no apparent reason.

I have a very strange pain on the top side of my right foot.

I have a sore foot.

My feet are swollen.

I have a swollen foot.

---

354) calf muscle: 장딴지 근육
355) anti-inflammatories: 항염증 요소
356) sprain: 삐다

My legs feel numb[357] so I can't walk.

■ 〈Case〉 발가락 질환

Patient: The joint of my big toe is swollen and hurt.

MTC(Doctor): Did you hit it against something?

3.6.19 근육

My whole body aches.

Lots of parts of my body crack[358].

I can not stop cracking any part of my body.

■ 〈Case〉 근육통

Patient: Every evening a couple of hours before I usually go to
bed, the joints in my legs seem to stiffen up.

MTC(Doctor): Do you spend a lot of time on the computer?

Patient: Yes, I do.

Is it a possibility that I have arthritis?

MTC: You need to undergo a medical check-up.

Patient: What medical investigation should I undergo?

3.6.20 발열 · 오한

■ 발열

Do you have a fever? Let me check your body temperature.

Do you have a cold?

I have a slight fever.

I feel feverish[359].

I have a high fever.

My fever stayed high for more than two days.

---

357) numb: 감각이 없는
358) crack: 갈라지다, 금이 가다
359) feverish: 미열이 있는

I suddenly developed a high fever.

I haven't taken my temperature, but I feel hot.

I thought I just had a cold but my fever won't go away.

■ 〈Case〉 발열

Patient: I have a high fever and a splitting headache. I lost my appetite, too.

MTC(Doctor): Did you take your temperature?

Patient: Yes, it's 39°C. I took three aspirins, but they didn't work.

MTC: Let me examine you.

Open your mouth.

All right.

Cough, please.

(기침한다)

MTC: You have the flu. You need to stay in bed for three days.

I'll write out a prescription for you.

There you go.

Take this to the drugstore.

■ 〈Case〉 발열

Patient: Good morning.

MTC(Doctor): Good morning, what happened?

Patient: I am feeling fever. My whole body is aching.

MTC: Let me check your fever.

(체온 검사 후)

It's 102 degree Fahrenheit.(38.89 degree Celsius). Show me your throat.

Patient: I also have cough.

MTC: Your throat is also sore.

Did you feel shivering during the night?

Patient: Frequently; I couldn't sleep well.

MTC: What did you eat at night?

Patient: I had simple home-made food. But I have not taken any breakfast.

I am not feeling hungry. And there is a feeling of vomiting.

MTC: Don't worry, I am giving you medicine.

Also get your blood tested today.

Patient: From where shall I get my blood tested?

MTC: The nurse will direct you to the laboratory.

It is on the right-hand side.

Patient: How many doses have you given me?

MTC: Three doses. As soon as you reach your home eat something light and take the first dose.

It contains three tablets and one capsule.

Repeat the same after five hours.

The third one can be taken before going to bed at night.

Patient: Any precautions?

MTC: Don't go to office today.

Take complete rest.

Avoid cold drinks or oily meals.

Patient: Thank you!

■ 〈Case〉 발열

Patient: I seem to have a fever.

MTC(Doctor): When did the fever start?

Patient: Since a couple of days, I have had fever.

MTC: Let me take your temperature with this electric thermometer.

You have a slight fever.

■ 〈Case〉 발열

Patient: Good morning, Doctor!

MTC(Doctor): Good morning! What's wrong with you?

Patient: I have been suffering from fever since yesterday.

MTC: Have you any other problem?

Patient: I also feel headache and shivering.

MTC: Let me feel your pulse and check your fever.

At this time the fever is 100 degree Fahrenheit(37.78 degree Celsius).

Don't worry, there is nothing serious.

I am giving you the medicine, and you will be all right in a few days.

Patient: Thank you, doctor.

MTC: But get your blood tested for malaria.

Patient: OK, doctor.

MTC: I shall recommend at least two days rest for you.

Patient :Would you prepare a medical certificate[360] for me to submit it in(to) my office?

MTC: Sure. This is your medical certificate.

Patient :Thank you very much. Please tell me how shall I take this medicine?

MTC: This medicine is for one day only.

Take this dose as soon as you reach your home and the second at 3 pm and the third at night before sleeping.

Patient: What should I eat doctor?

MTC: You should eat only light food. You can take milk and fresh fruit also.

Patient: Thank you doctor. I shall see you tomorrow.

■ 〈Case〉 발열

Patient: I have had a slight fever for the last few days.

MTC(Doctor): Have you taken your temperature?

Patient: It was over 37 degree Celsius.(98.6 degree Fahrenheit)

MTC: Let me take your temperature.

Can you put this thermometer under your right arm pit?

Patient: OK.

MTC: According to this thermometer, your have a temperature of thirty seven point five degrees celsius.

Do you have any other symptoms?

---

360) medical certificate: 진단서

■ 오한

Do you feel chilly?

Do you feel chills in your spine?

I feel chills all the time.

I have a chill.

After the high fever went away, I began to have chills.

I have a lot of cold sweats[361] and I feel shaky.

I don't have a temperature, but I feel tired.

I feel chilly and suddenly I have a sharp pain in my right side that won't go away.

My feet are cold.

My feet get cold.

My hands feel cold.

My feet arc freezing.

■ 〈Case〉 오한

Patient: My lower back and legs have been feeling cold.

MTC(Doctor): When did it start?

Patient: It started this summer.

MTC: Are your periods regular?

Patient: No, not recently.

MTC: A lack of exercise may be one of the reasons.

Please try to get more exercise.

■ 〈Case〉 오한

Patient: My feet are cold even in the middle of summer.

MTC(Doctor): There are many reasons feet can feel cold no matter how warm it is outside.

Patient: Poor circulation in your legs and arms restrict[362] flow to your feet and hands. It can make them feel cold.

---

361) cold sweats: 식은 땀
362) restrict: 제한하다

But persistently[363] cold feet can be the sign of a serious medical condition.

3.6.21 비만과 몸무게 감소

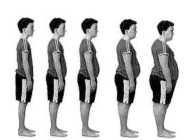

Do you think you are overweighted?

I don't want to gain more weight.

I am getting fatter and fatter.

I am getting fat day by day.

I am putting on weight.

I'm obese[364].

I am overweight.

I look fat but I am not overweight.

I've suddenly started to gain weight.

■ 〈Case〉 몸무게 증가

Patient: I have gained a lot of weight lately.

MTC(Doctor): How many kilos have you gained?

Patient: I used to weigh 70 kilos, but I have put on more than 4 kilos.[365]

MTC: Why do you think that is?

Patient: I have been eating at late in the evening because I have been busy.

MTC: That is too bad.

Do you drink a lot?

Patient: Unfortunately, yes, because I have to do a lot of company entertaining.

MTC: You need to have dietary[366] therapy and should change your life-style.

■ 몸무게 감소

I am losing weight everywhere but my stomach is still bloated.

I've lost a lot of weight and became as thin as a rail.

---

363) persistently: 지속적으로

364) obese: 비만의

365) I used to weigh 70 kilos, but I have put on more than 4 kilos.

= I used to weigh 154 pounds, but I have put on more than 8.8 pounds.

366) dietary: 음식의

I have suddenly lost weight.

I am slim-figured.

I keep losing weight.

My weight suddenly keeps going down.

I am losing weight, even though I am eating well.

■ 〈Case〉 몸무게 감소

Patient: My weight keeps going down gradually.

I've been losing my appetite a lot.

Every time I get on the scale, it is getting

lower and lower.

I used to be 180 pounds then I dropped

to about 143 pounds.[367]

Is that normal?

MTC(Doctor): Do you exercise?

Patient: Yes, I do.

MTC: Let me check your height and weight.

This is within the normal weight range for your weight.

Patient: I have been trying to lose weight for the last two months.

I am a diet and I've struggled with my weight.

My weight keeps going up and down.

MTC: Do you exercise?

Patient:Yes,Iexercisedailyandeatright.

I have been following a healthy eating plan.

MTC: I will examine your blood for several factors.

■ 〈Case〉 몸무게 감소

MTC(Doctor): Did you gain or loss weight recently?

---

367) I used to be 180 pounds then I dropped to about 143 pounds.

= I used to be 81.65kg then I dropped to about 65kg.

1kg = 약 2.2 pounds

1 pound = 약 0.45kg

Patient: I lost 3 kilos recently[368].

MTC: How about your daily meals?

Patient: I live apart from my family because of my business, so I eat at irregular times.

MTC: Let us have a blood sugar test done just in case.

3.6.22 부작용 문의

Is there any danger?

Is a recurrence[369] likely?

Isn't there any adverse reaction?

What kind of adverse reaction can I expect?

What kind of adverse reaction can happen ton me?

What kind of adverse effects can this have?

What kind of adverse effects can occur?

What kind of adverse effects can be expected?

■ 〈Case〉 부작용 문의

Patient: Is there a risk of losing my eyesight during a double eyelid operation?

MTC(Doctor): You may lose eyesight due to complications[370].

However, in most cases, Patients will recover from it through treatments in the hospital.

3.6.23 동반 증상

Do you have any other associated problems like nausea, fever, headache, neck stiffness?

Do you have any other medical conditions like high blood pressure, diabetes, high cholesterol?

---

368) I lost 3 kilos recently.

= I lost 6.6 pounds recently.

369) recurrence: 재발

370) complication: 합병증

Do you have any accompanying symptoms like numbness or weakness in your arms?

It is important to find out if there are any accompanying symptoms.

3.6.24 과거 병력

Have you ever had similar problem before?

Have you ever been hospitalized?

Did you have any surgeries in the past?

Have you ever suffered from insomnia[371]?

Have you ever had a surgery?

Have you ever had a surgical operation?

3.6.25 가족력

Does anybody in your family have the same problem?

Are there any medical conditions that run in your family like diabetes, high blood pressure, cancer?

Did your father suffer from heart disease?

Did your mother have diabetes[372]?

Have you a family history of mental or nervous disorders to the best of your knowledge?

■ 〈Case〉 가족력

MTC(Doctor): Is there anybody in your family who has had cancer or heart disease?

Patient: Yes, my father has had angina[373].

---

371) insomnia: 불면증
372) diabetes: 당뇨병
373) angina: 협심증

■ 〈Case〉 가족력

MTC(Doctor): Is there anyone else in your family who has high blood pressure or heart disease?

Patient: My father died of heart attack the year before the last.

MTC: Do you exercise regularly?

Patient: I rarely exercise.

MTC: Please tell me about your eating habits.

Patient: I try to avoid salty food and alcohol.

3.6.26 주의해야 할 음식

What foods should I avoid?

What can I eat?

What about my diet?

What kind of foods should I avoid to lose weight?

What kind of foods should I avoid to help my colon heal better?

What kind of foods shuld I avoid to heal heartburn?

■ 〈Case〉 주의해야 할 음식 ₩

Patient: What kind of foods should I avoid not to gain weight?

MTC(Doctor): You should eliminate coke from your diet. You had better eat plenty of fruit.

Chapter 4

건강검진 및 검사 표현

건강검진 진행과정 및 주의사항

Checkup procedure	Information
Telephone reservation or online reservation	
Confirming reservation by texting or e-mail	You may receive the message right after the reservation has been confirmed.
One day before the checkup calling service	We confirm the reservation schedule again and introduce about things you should prepare at forenoon[1] the day before checkup.
	If you take the vasopressin, cardiac disease pills, phenytoin, bartiturate pills, please take those pills with minimal amount of water before 6:00 am.
	Please don't take insulin or diabetic pills if you are diabetes.
	Please don't take any accessories or valuables.
Arrival at ABC Hospital	You are required to arrive at ABC Hospital at the time you have appointed.
Pay the cost on the day of the checkup.	
Taking checkup	It takes about 2 to 6 hours.
Making reservation for result counseling	7 to 10 days after the checkup
Result counseling	You may visit or have telephone counseling after receiving certified mail.

---

1) forenoon: 오전

4.1 건강검진 안내 및 주의사항

4.1.1 건강검진 전날 주의사항

■ 〈Case〉 건강검진 전날 주의사항

MTC(Nurse): Tomorrow you will get the medical checkup.

From now on, I would like to tell you about very important precautions[2] you should take before the medical checkup.

Do not worry too much about the checkup in advance and go about your activities as usual.

The blood test and urinalysis[3] requires fasting[4] so you must finish all meals by 7:00 pm.

Do not drink water.

Absolutely no food is allowed after 7:00 pm

Do not smoke.

Generally speaking, taking medicine is not allowed, but you can take medicine for hypertension[5], heart diseases[6], or diabetes[7] after consulting and confirming about the medicine with the doctor.

■ 〈Case〉 건강검진 전 주의사항 문의

Patient: Am I allowed to at least drink water before my examination?

MTC(Nurse): No food and nor drink will be permitted before the examination

Even a cup of water is not allowed within 12 hours before the examination.

The ingestion of food further activates metabolism and thus lowers the test accuracy especially in sonogram.

---

2) precaution: 예방조치, 주의
3) urinalysis: 소변검사 = urine test
4) fasting: 금식
5) hypertension: 고혈압
   hypotension: 저혈압
6) heart disease: 심장병
7) diabetes: 당뇨병

Also, any foreign substances inside the body disable endoscopy and gastric endoscopy[8].

So, there should not have food or liquids of any kind including water, candy, gum before the examination.

4.1.2 알레르기

Are you allergic to anything, food or medicine?

Are you allergic to any medicine?

What drugs are you allergic to?

Are you allergic to anything?

■ 〈Case〉 알레르기

MTC(Nurse): Are you allergic to any medicine?

Patient: I am allergic to aspirin.

4.1.3 건강검진 당일 주의사항

■ 〈Case〉 건강검진 당일 주의사항

MTC(Nurse): Would you please change into a gown in the dressing room?

Please take off your clothes except for underwear.

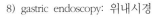

8) gastric endoscopy: 위내시경

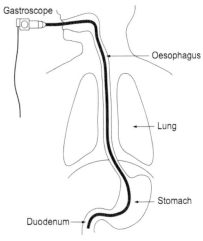

Remove watch, earing and dentures[9], if you are wearing them.[10]

Patient: Can I exercise before the examination.

MTC: You can do light exercise and brush your teeth. You are allowed to wear eyeglasses or contact lenses, but please avoid wearing any other accessories including the watch and neckless.

■ 〈Case〉 건강검진 당일 주의사항

MTC(Nurse): You are schedule to get the medical check-up 10 o'clock tomorrow morning.

Patient: 10 o'clock.

MTC: Let me explain about the instructions regarding the medical check-up.

Patient: Am I scheduled to a colonoscopy[11].

MTC: Yes, I will give you a medicine one day before the colonoscopy as well as on the day of the colonoscopy to keep your colon[12] clean.

Patient: I see.

MTC: You need to fast[13] from 8:00 pm the night before the test.

---

9) denture: 틀니
10) If you are wearing jewelry, watch, earing and dentures, please remove them.
   If you are wearing glasses or contact lenses, please don't bring them with you.
11) colonoscopy: 대장내시경
12) colon: 대장(맹장·결장·직장)의 일부인데, 상행결장, 횡행결장, 하행결장, S상결장의 4부분으로 이루어져 있고, 이 4부분은 각각 길이와 형태가 다르다. 전체는 4부분으로 되어 있다.

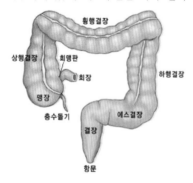

13) fast: 금식하다.

If you are on medication[14], you are required to stop taking them one day before the test.

Patient: I understand.

MTC: For the colonoscopy, you need to fast for at least 9 hours before the test. Do not drink water. Do not smoke. Do not chew gums.

Patient: OK.

MTC: Here is the instructions for the medical check-up.

(다음 날)

MTC: Did you have a good sleep last night?

Patient: Yes, I did.

MTC(Nurse): Sit down and wait until I call your name.

Patient: OK

MTC: Maria Hans.

Patient: Yes

MTC: Please come in.

4.2 탈의

4.2.1 전체 탈의

- 〈Case〉 전체 탈의

MTC(Nurse): Now, you have to wear the Patient gown of the hospital.

In the dressing room[15], there are rockers.

The right hand side dressing room is for ladies.

The left hand side dressing room is for gentlemen.

Patient: OK.

---

14) be on medication: 약을 복용하다.
= take medicine
be on a diet: 다이어트 중이다.

15) dressing room = changing room

MTC: Please come this way.

MTC: OK, here we are.

Please wait until I have left the room for you to begin changing.

Remove your shoes and socks as well, but keep on your undergarments[16].

As you see, there are two compartments[17] in the rocker. After you take off the shoes, put them in the lower compartment in the rocker.

Please wear the slipper in the rocker room, after you take off the shoes.

Patient: OK

MTC: From now on, I will explain to you how to wear the gown.

(뒤가 터진 가운 제공)

MTC: Place your hands through arm holes. Make sure the gown opening is in the back before you tie the gown. A gown has two sets of ties.

One is at the top and the second is in the middle of the gown. Tie each pair of tries together as you would tie a shoe lace.

Patient: Like this?

MTC: Yes, that is right.

MTC: If you bring with you any accessories including the watch, ring, or neckless, please put them in the rocker.

Do you have any precious things with you? I will keep them in custody[18] until you finish examination.

Patient: Here you are.

MTC: OK. I will keep them in the safety box.

Now I will leave the room.

Do you have any question?

Patient: Do I have to remove my bra?

MTC: Yes, you do. Please remove the bra as well.

---

16) undergarment = underwear
17) compartment: 서랍
18) keep something in custody: 부관하다

4.2.2 상의 탈의

Please strip to the waist.

Please loosen your belt and show your abdomen.

Please pull up your undershirt and show your chest.

Please put on your clothes.

- ■ 〈Case〉 상의 탈의

MTC(Nurse): Please pull up your undershirt and show your chest.

The doctor will listen to your heart beat with the stethoscope[19].

Patient: OK.

MTC: The doctor wants to find out whether you have a heart murmur[20] that is likely caused by a heart valve problem.

The doctor wants you to breathe in and breathe out.

The doctor wants to check for fluid buildup[21].

〈Case〉 상의 탈의

MTC(Nurse): Now, it is time to wear the Patient gown of the hospital.

In the dressing room[22], there are rockers.

OK, let us move.

Please come this way.

Patient: Thank you.

MTC: OK, here we are.

This is the gown.

---

19) stethoscope: 청진기
20) heart murmur: 심장음(심장 내에서 난기류가 발생하면서 생기는 비정상적인 소리)
21) fluid buildup: 체액 누적
   Signs and symptoms of heart failure: Swelling in feet, legs, and abdomen caused by the buildup of fluid in your body from weight gain.(심부전의 징조와 증상: 체중 증가로 몸속에 체액이 쌓여 발, 다리, 배에 생기는 부종)
22) = in the changing room

Please wear the gown like a jacket with the button in the front.

As you see, there are buttons in the front of the gown.

Please button up all the buttons of the gown.

Patient: OK

MTC: Remove your shoes and socks as well, but keep on your undergarments[23].

As you see, there are two compartments[24] in the rocker. After you take off the shoes, put them in the lower compartment in the rocker.

Please wear the slipper in the rocker room, after you take off the shoes.

Patient: OK

4.3 건강검진 및 예진

I am going to ask you about lifestyle?

I am going to ask you about your family's health?

Thanks for answering all these questions. Now, I will need to do your physical exam.

Is there anything else you'd like to tell me?

■ 예진방법

> Before the physical exam, I am going ask you some question.
> I am going to ask you about your A.
>
> **질문과 답변**
> Now, I am going to ask you about your B.
>
> **질문과 답변**
> Is there anything else you'd like to tell me?
> Thanks for answering all these questions. Now, I will need to do your physical exam.

---

23) undergarment = underwear : 속옷
24) compartment: 서랍

- ⟨Case⟩ 예진(흡연)

  MTC(Doctor): Do you smoke?

  Patient: Yes, I do.

  MTC: How many packs a day do you smoke?

  Patient: About 5 to 8 cigarettes a day.

  MTC: For how many years?

  Patient: For about 10 years.

- ⟨Case⟩ 예진(약복용)

  MTC(Doctor): Are you currently taking any prescription drugs?

  Patient: No, I am not.

- ⟨Case⟩ 예진(약복용)

  MTC(Doctor): Are you currently taking any prescription drugs?

  Patient: Yes, I am.

  MTC: What kind of medications are you taking?

  Patient: I am taking medicine for hypertension[25] regularly for the last three years.

- ⟨Case⟩ 예진(음주)

  MTC(Doctor): Do you drink alcohol?

  Patient: I sometimes drink for business.

  MTC: What do you drink, Soju or beer?

  Patient: Soju.

- ⟨Case⟩ 예진(식욕)

  MTC(Doctor): How is your appetite?

  Patient: I have a good appetite.

  MTC: Any recent weight changes?

  Patient: No. My weight has remained exactly the same.

---

25) hypertension: 고혈압

　　I am taking medicine for hypertension.

　　= I am taking medicine for high blood pressure.

■ 〈Case〉 예진(직업)

MTC(Doctor): What kind of work do you do?

Patient: I work in the office.

MTC: How often do you exercise on weekends?

Patient: I hardly exercise on weekends.

■ 〈Case〉 예진(운동)

MTC(Doctor): How often do you exercise?

Patient: I hardly exercise.

MTC: How often do you check your weight?

■ 〈Case〉 예진(여성)

MTC(Doctor): Do you have any children?

Patient: Yes, I have two children.

MTC: Then, have you had a miscarriage?

Patient: Yes, I have had one miscarriage.

■ 〈Case〉 예진(여성)

MTC(Doctor): When was your first period?

Patient: I was 13 years old.

MTC: Are your periods regular?

Patient: My periods are regular.

It comes about every 38 days.

■ 〈Case〉 예진(여성)

MTC(Doctor): How about the amount of blood?

Do you have period pain?

Patient: The amount is normal and I have no pain.

MTC: Have you had a uterine cancer test?

Patient: Yes, I have been tested a year ago.

■ 〈Case〉 예진(건강검진)

MTC(Nurse): When did you last come in for a physical examination?

Patient: I had my last physical two years ago.

MTC: Have you had any other exams recently?

A blood test, an EKG (Electrocardiography[26])) or an ultrasound[27])?

Patient: Well, I had a few X-rays at a clinic.

MTC: How have you been feeling in general?

Patient: Pretty well.

MTC: Do you exercise regularly?

Patient: No, not really.

If I run up stairs[28]), it takes me a while to get my breath back.

MTC: How about your diet?

Patient: I think I eat a pretty balanced diet[29]).

You know, I'll have a hamburger from time to time, but generally I have well-balanced meals.

■ 〈Case〉 예진(건강검진)

MTC(Nurse): Welcome to our hospital's health check up center.

Patient: Hi, How can I receive a health check up?

MTC: First of all, please register and go through the formalities[30]) here.

Patient: Could you explain the check up process?

MTC: Please change into your gown over there before you get a check up.

Patient: I changed into my gown.

What should I do next?

MTC: Please fill in this simple questionnaire.

Have you had any chronic[31]) disease such as tuberculosis[32]), hepatitis[33]),

---

26) Electrocardiography: 심전도
27) ultrasound: 초음파
28) run up stairs: 계단을 뛰어오르다
    walk up stairs: 계단을 오르다
29) = a well-balanced diet
30) go through the formalities
    = undergo the procedure : 절차를 밟다
31) chronic: 만성의
    acute: 급성의
32) tuberculosis: 결핵

hypertension[34], diabetes[35] or have you ever had a surgery?

Patient: Yes, I am taking medication for hypertension.

MTC: Do you smoke?

If you do, how much do you smoke per day?

Patient: I do smoke.

I smoke about 10 cigarettes a day.

MTC: How many times do you drink alcohol per week and when you do, how much do you drink?

Patient: I drink about twice a week and I drink about 3 glasses of beer in one sitting.

MTC: Is there anybody in your family who had cancer or heart disease?

Patient: Yes, my father had angina[36].

MTC: Thank you for filling out the form.

Patient: What kind of test do I get now?

MTC: First, you should take a physical examination and blood test and then, take a radiation test such as X-ray and endoscopy[37].

Patient: Where should I go first?

MTC: Please come this way.

Patient: Okay. Thank you.

4.4 건강검진 및 검사 종류

4.4.1 건강검진 문의 및 순서 안내

You need to make a thorough examination. Please go to the room A.

You need to take some urinary and blood tests, please go to the room B.

---

33) hepatitis: 간염
34) hypertension: 고혈압
    hypotension: 저혈압
35) diabetes: 당뇨병
36) angina: 협심증
37) endoscopy: 내시경검사

You need to take an X-ray. Let us go to the room C.

You need to take an electrocardiogram. Let us go to the room D.

■ 〈Case〉 건강검진 문의

Patient: I've come for a consultation about my health
in general.

I want to know what's wrong with me.

MTC(Doctor): Have you ever had any trouble with
your health?

Patient: I've never had any trouble with my health.

I want to have a complete medical checkup.

■ 〈Case〉 건강검진 문의

Patient: When can I receive the results of the medical checkup?

MTC(Doctor): I understand that you are very anxious to see the result as soon as
possible.

Approximately 80% of the results can be provided on the day of the
examination.

Final results will be available in a week.

■ 〈Case〉 건강검진 종류

Patient: What can I expect at the medical checkup?

MTC(Doctor): The medical checkup basically includes an ophthalmic[38] examination,
hearing examination, blood test, urine/feces[39] test, gastric[40] endoscopy,
abdominal sonogram, pulmonary[41] function test, chest X-ray, electrocardiogram[42],
gynecologic[43] test, anus examination, and dental examination.

---

38) ophthalmic: 안과의
39) feces: 대변
40) gastric: 위의
    gastric endoscopy: 위내시경
41) pulmonary: 심폐의
42) electrocardiogram: 심전도
43) gynecologic: 부인과의

■ 〈Case〉 건강검진 소요시간

Patient: How long does the examination take?

MTC(Nurse): It takes approximately 1 hour starting at 8:30 in the morning. Please note that conscious sedation endoscopy[44] requires an additional 30 minutes to 50 minutes for the time to administer the sedation.

■ 〈Case〉 건강검진 소요시간

Patient: How long does it take to finish the medical checkup?

MTC(Nurse): It will take approximately 1 hour and a half, however, it depends on the number of Patients. I am proud to tell you that most Patients are satisfied with the medical checkup.

Patient: Is the endoscopy[45] painful?

MTC: Most Patients experience only a slight pain[46] when the local anesthesia

---

44) conscious sedation endoscopy: 수면내시경
45) endoscopy: 내시경검사
46) splitting pain: 쪼개질 듯한
   tearing or ripping pain: 찢어지는 듯한 통증
   terrible pain: 끔찍한 통증
   colic pain: 위, 장에 나타나는 극심한 통증
   stabbing pain: 칼로 찌르는 듯한 통증
   sharp pain: 날카롭게 찌르는 듯한 통증
   twinge pain : 예리한 급성 통증 = smart pain
   shooting pain: 쏘는 듯한 통증
   lancinating pain: 찌르는 꿰뚫는 통증 = piercing pain
   gnawing pain: 위통, 쪼는 듯한 통증(위궤양)
   burning pain: 작열감
   burning sensation: 작열감
   soreness: 쑤시거나 따끔거림(피부, 근육)
   raw sensation: 쓰라린
   tenderness: 누르거나 건드리면 느끼는 통증
   pressing pain: 압통
   squeezing pain: 조이는 듯한 통증
   constricting pain: 꽉 조여오는 듯한 통증
   prickling pain: 찌르는 듯한 통증
   pinching pain: 꼬집는 듯한 통증
   stinging sensation: 따끔거리는 느낌
   dull pain: 둔통

is used. A pain-free surgery is also available. If you choose the pain-free[47] operation, you will experience almost no pain.

■ 〈Case〉 건강검진 문의

MTC(Nurse): Welcome to our hospital's health check up center.

Patient: How can I receive a health check up?

MTC: First, please register and go through the formalities here.

Patient: Could you explain the check up process?

MTC: First, please change into your gown over there before you get a check up.

Patient: I changed into my gown.

What should I do next?

MTC: Please fill in these simple questions. Have you had any chronic[48] disease such as tuberculosis[49], hepatitis[50], hypertension[51], diabetes[52] or have you ever had any surgery?

Patient: Yes, I am taking medication for hypertension.

MTC: Do you smoke?

If you do, how much do you smoke per day?

Patient: I do smoke.

I smoke about 10 cigarettes a day.

MTC: How many times do you drink alcohol per week and when you do, how much do you drink?

Patient: I drink about twice a week and I drink about 3 glasses of beer in one sitting.

---

tingle/tingling sensation: 저릿저릿한 감각
pins and needles: 저리는 느낌
pounding: 지끈거리는
pounding headache: 지끈거리는 두통
throbbing: 욱신거리는 통증
47) pain-free: 무통의
48) chronic: 만성의
　　acute: 급성의
49) tuberculosis: 결핵
50) hepatitis: 간염
51) hypertension: 고혈압
52) diabetes: 당뇨병

MTC: Is there anybody in your family who has had cancer or heart disease?

Patient: Yes, my father has had angina[53].

MTC: Thank you for filling out the form.

Patient: What kind of test do I get now?

MTC: First, you should take a physical exam and blood test and then, take a radiation test such as X-ray and endoscopy.

Patient: Where should I go first?

MTC: Please come this way.

Patient: Okay. Thank you.

■ 〈Case〉 X-Ray

MTC(Nurse): The doctor will detect cancer by an X-ray capture image of your breasts.

Patient: I understand.

■ 〈Case〉 치과검진 종류 설명

Patient: What do you check in the dentistry?

MTC(Nurse): The doctor will check if you have a decayed[54] tooth or a tartar[55] on the teeth.

(건강검진 프로세스)

(예): 병원 도착 ⇒ 문진표 작성 ⇒ 접수 ⇒ 탈의 ⇒ 신체 계측 ⇒ 치과 ⇒ 청력검사 ⇒ 흉부 방사선 ⇒ 혈압측정 ⇒ 시력측정 ⇒ 채혈 ⇒ 채뇨 ⇒ 진찰 ⇒ 접수반 납 ⇒ 탈의 ⇒ 귀가

미국 등 장거리 여행을 한 의료관광객은 건강검진을 위한 금식 기간이 길어질 수 있으므로 공복 시에 필요한 검사를 먼저 한 후에 간단한 간식을 준다.

■ 〈Case〉 건강검진 순서 설명

MTC(Nurse): This is the order of the medical tests you will take.

It is useful for you to understand the medical procedures.

---

53) angina: 협심증
54) decayed: 썩은
55) tartar: 치석

Patient: Thank you.

MTC: You are scheduled to follow the procedures that the hospital set up.

In the pre-examination, your past disease history and general questionnaire will be asked.

Please answer their questions honestly.

And then, you will check height and weight.

After the height and weight measurement, there will be eye vision test.

건강검진 및 진단을 위한 조사에는 어떤 것들이 있을까?

건강검진 또는 진료를 목적으로 한국을 찾은 영어권 의료관광객을 응대할 때, 의료관광코디네이터로서 어떤 표현들을 사용하게 될까?

4.4.2 신장과 몸무게 측정

〈Case〉 신장과 몸무게 측정

MTC(Nurse): Please stand on the height and weight measuring instrument.

Lean against the ruler with your back straight up.

The ruler will examine your amount of fat[56] based on height and weight.

■ 〈Case〉 신장과 몸무게 측정

MTC(Nurse): The instrument will measure automatically your height and weight.

Please step on the scale.

The bar will come down from the top to measure your height.

Your height is 168 cm.[57]

Your weight is 82 kg.[58]

Now you can step down.

Patient: Am I overweight?

---

56) fat: 지방

57) Your height is 168cm.
   = Your height is about 5.5 feet.

58) Your weight is 82kg.
   = Your weight is about 180.78pounds.

MTC: I am afraid that you are overweight[59].

■ 〈Case〉 신장과 몸무게 측정

MTC(Nurse): Come right this way.

We are going to need to get your height and weight first.

Will you stand here?

Patient: I think I've grown a bit since I was here last.

MTC: You've grown by an inch[60] and a half since we last saw you.

Now for your weight.

Stand on this scale, please.

Patient: Should I take off my shoes?

MTC: Yes, go ahead and take them off.

Please put your shoes in this basket.

Take anything out of your pockets.

We want to get an accurate[61] figure.

---

59) obese: 비만
   overweight: 과체중
   underweight: 저체중
   normal: 정상

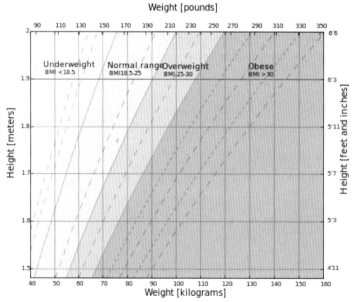

60) 1 inch = 2.54cm

Patient: I guess I've gained some weight since last time, too.

MTC: Not too much, just a couple of pounds[62].

That's healthy for a man at your age.

■ 〈Case〉 신장과 몸무게 측정

MTC(Nurse): I am going to measure your height and weight first.

Will you stand on the scale?

Patient: Should I take off my shoes?

MTC: Yes, take them off.

Take anything out of your pockets.

We want to get an accurate measurement.

4.4.3 비만도 측정

■ 〈Case〉 비만도 측정

MTC(Nurse): The instrument will check your body fat by ultrasound[63].

It will take a few minutes.

Step on the shape of the feet.

Hold these handles lightly.

Stretch your arms downward.

Hold them away from your body.

Maintain the posture for about two minutes.

(측정 후)

Now it is done.

Your body fat is a little above the normal range.[64]

---

61) accurate: 정확한

　　accurate diagnosis: 정확한 진단

　　The early and accurate diagnosis is important.

62) pound = 약 0.45kg

　　80kg = 176.37 pound

63) ultrasound: 초음파

64) Your visceral fat is a bit above the normal range.

　　visceral fat: 내장지방

4.4.4 피하지방검사

■ 〈Case〉 피하지방검사

MTC(Nurse): This is to measure your body fat composition[65].

Taking skinfold measurement is a common method for determining body fat composition.

I will pinch the right side of your body.

All skinfold measurements will be taken on the right side of the body.

Please stand upright and relaxed.

I will gently grasp the skin with the caliper.

Please wait until the nurse read the level.

Body fat percentage

	Excellent	Good	Average	Below Average	Poor
Male	60-80	81-90	91-110	111-150	150+
Female	70-90	91-100	101-120	121-150	150+

4.4.5 시력검사

■ 〈Case〉 시력검사

MTC(Nurse): Sit on the chair, please.

You are advised to wear glasses before the test.

Please keep both eyes open, gently place the eye test blind in front of the eye that is not being evaluated.

I will start with the big letters and proceed to the smaller ones.

All you have to do is to identify every letter and communicate it to me.

If you are not sure of the letter, you may guess.

---

65) composition: 구성

This test will be done on each eye, one at a time.

Change the eye test blind to the other eye after the first eye is checked.

And the procedure is the same.

After both eyes have been evaluated, remove the eye test blind.

■ 〈Case〉 시력검사

MTC(Nurse): I will start your visual acuity test.

Please read the line I am pointing.

Patient: A, B, C, D

MTC: OK.

Do you wear reading glasses[66])?

Patient: Not yet.

■ 〈Case〉 시력검사

MTC(Nurse): I will start your visual acuity[67]) test.

Please read the line I am pointing.

Now, please cover the other eye.

Please place your forehead here and open both eyes.

If you wear glasses or contact lenses, I will check both the naked[68]) vision and corrected[69]) vision.

You need to tell me where the opening is right or left.

The test is now finished.

Patient: Thank you.

---

[66]) reading glasses: 돋보기

[67]) 예민함

visual acuity: 시력

[68]) naked vision: 나안시력

[69]) corrected vision: 교정시력

4.4.6 색맹검사

■ 〈Case〉색맹검사

You passed the color vision test.

The color vision test will be accomplished before the eye vision test.

MTC(Nurse): Your color vision will be examined.

　　　　　Can you tell me the number on the page.

Patient: 12, 29

　MTC: Thank you.

4.4.7 안압검사

■ 〈Case〉안압검사

MTC(Doctor): Please remove your glasses.

　　　　　Have a seat here.

　　　　　From now on, I will check your intraocular[70] pressure by puffing air.

　　　　　The test will take about five minutes.

　　　　　Place your chin on the bar and put your forehead in front.

　　　　　Don't be startled when a puff of air is shot at your eyes.

　　　　　I will measure the intraocular pressure three times on each eye.

　　　　　From this test, I will find out if you have glaucoma[71].

---

70) intraocular: 안구 내의
　　intraocular pressure: 안압

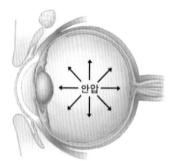

71) glaucoma: 녹내장
　　cataract: 백내장

Do you see the green dot on the screen?

Please keep watching the green dot.

Thank you for your cooperation. The test is finished.

Patient: Thank you.

4.4.8 혈압측정

I will measure your blood pressure.

Your blood pressure is within the normal range.

Your blood pressure is 145 over 90.

Your blood pressure is a little bit above the normal range.

Your blood pressure indicates that you have prehypertension[72].

Stage	Systolic (First number)	Diastolic (Second number)
Normal	Less than 120	Less than 80
Prehypertension	120~139	80~89
High blood pressure stage 1	140~159	90-99
High blood pressure stage 2	160 or higher	100 or over

■ 〈Case〉 혈압측정

MTC(Nurse): I will take your blood pressure.[73]

Please roll up your sleeves.

Do not talk nor move, please.

Patient: OK.

(혈압측정 후)

MTC: Your blood pressure is a little above 130 over 80, but your risk of cardiovascular[74] disease is low, you can lower your blood pressure by making some changes to your lifestyle.

---

72) prehypertension: 고혈압이 될 수 있는
73) = I will measure your blood pressure.
74) cardiovascular: 심장혈관의

■ 〈Case〉 혈압측정

MTC(Nurse): Will you sit over here.

I will get your blood pressure.

Now roll up your sleeves.

Please do not move until the nurse() read

your blood pressure.

(혈압측정 후)

Patient: is my blood pressure within the normal range?

■ 〈Case〉 혈압측정

MTC(Nurse): A typical normal blood pressure is 120 over 80.

The first number represents the pressure when the heart contracts and

the second number represents the pressure when the heart relaxes.

Patient: I see.

MTC: Let me check your blood pressure.

Please roll up your sleeves.

■ 〈Case〉 혈압측정

MTC(Nurse): This is the automatic blood pressure monitor.

Please put your arm through the hole.

You're going to feel a little squeeze.

Do not talk nor move, please.

Patient: I see.

(혈압측정 후)

MTC: Your blood pressure is 120 over 80.

Your blood pressure is within normal limits.

■ 〈Case〉 혈압측정

MTC(Nurse): Could you roll up your left sleeve?

I'd like to take your blood pressure.

Patient: Certainly.

MTC: Your blood pressure is 130 over 80.

Your blood pressure is within the normal range.

You don't seem to be overweight.

Patient: I am glad to hear that.

■ 〈Case〉 혈압측정

MTC(Doctor); Will you sit over here so we can get your blood pressure?

Patient: Should I put my arm through here?

MTC: Yes, Now roll up your sleeves.

You're going to feel a little squeeze.

■ 〈Case〉 혈압측정

MTC(Nurse): You will sit on the chair.

Please sit with your feet flat on the floor.

Rest your arm on the table so that the cuff[75] is at the same level as your heart.

You have to remain still and please do not talk during the measurement.

Patient: OK.

■ 〈Case〉 혈압측정

MTC(Nurse): Please sit on the chair with your feet flat on the floor.

Put in your arm though the apparatus and unfold[76] your hands and match your hands exactly to the position of the image of the hands.

Please do not move.

You have to remain still and please do not talk during the measurement.

Patient: OK.

MTC: Your blood pressure is 120 over 80.

Your blood pressure is within the normal range.

---

75) cuff: 손목
76) unfold: 펴다

■ 〈Case〉 혈압측정

MTC(Nurse): The pulse checks will be performed automatically by the medical apparatus.

I will check your pulse rate.

The pulse rate will be measured by the heart beats directly.

The normal pulse rate for a healthy adult is between 60 beats and 80 beats per minute.

Patient: OK.

4.4.9 혈액채취

■ 〈Case〉 혈액채취

MTC(Nurse): I will draw a sample of your blood.

Please roll up your sleeve.

do not move.

You will feel a sting.

Patient: I see.

■ 〈Case〉 혈액채취

MTC(Nurse): Please roll up your left arm sleeve and make your fist tight.

While I draw your blood, please do not move.

Patient: OK.

■ 〈Case〉 혈액채취

MTC(Nurse): I will draw your blood.

It won't hurt you much, because I am well-trained and professional.

The doctor will let you know the results.

Patient: Thank you.

- ⟨Case⟩ 혈액채취

MTC(Nurse): I am going to wrap this elastic[77] band around the upper arm to apply pressure to make the vein[78] swell with blood.

I am going to insert a needle into the vein.

While the blood collects into a tube, please do not move.

I am going to remove the elastic band from your arm.

I am going to cover the area with the bandage.

Please gently press the bandage to stop any bleeding.

Patient: OK.

4.4.10 청력검사

- ⟨Case⟩ 청력검사

MTC(Nurse): Your hearing will be examined.

Before you take the hearing check, you will wear a headset in order to confirm your hearing sensitivity.

If you can hear any beep sound at the left ear, please raise your left hand.

Patient: I understand.

- ⟨Case⟩ 청력검사

MTC(Nurse): A hearing test is an evaluation of your sensitivity of hearing.

It will take about three minutes.

Please wear the headset.

If you hear the beep sound in the right hand

side, please raise your right hand.

Patient: OK.

- ⟨Case⟩ 청력검사

MTC(Nurse): Please press the button every time you hear a beep sound.

Patient: What if I press the button when there is no beep sound.

---

77) elastic: 고무줄의
78) vein: 정맥

MTC: There is no need to worry if you give an incorrect response, because I will check multiple times at a particular volume to make sure accurate results.

4.4.11 소변검사

■ 〈Case〉 소변검사

MTC(Nurse): This is for the urine test.

Urine is a waste product of the kidneys so that the doctor will use this information to identify a bladder[79] or kidney infection[80], diabetes[81], and other conditions. Please fill one third of the cup with your mid-stream[82] urine and bring it back.

Patient: I see.

■ 〈Case〉 소변검사

MTC(Nurse): Please urinate in this container and bring it back here.

Patient: How much do I need?

MTC Just one third of the container.

Patient: I see.

■ 〈Case〉 소변검사

MTC: Please dip the test paper with your mid-stream urine.[83]

Show the paper to the nurse(to me).

OK.

Dispose the paper into the garbage.

Patient: I see.

---

79) bladder: 방광
80) infection: 감염
81) diabetes: 당뇨병
82) mid-stream: 흐름의 중간쯤
83) Please wet the test paper with your mid-stream urine.

■ ⟨Case⟩ 소변검사

MTC(Nurse): We need to take some urinary tests.

I give you a cup and you should fill it half or one third of the cup with your urine.

After you get the urine, please wash your hands with the soap in the rest room.

The pre-examination of adrenal[84] or urogenital[85] disorders and a urine glucose[86] test for diabetes[87] are also performed.

Patient: I see.

■ ⟨Case⟩ 소변검사

MTC(Nurse): I am going to give you a cleansing towelette to clean your perineum[88].

Please put the specimen container in the stream.

■ ⟨Case⟩ 소변검사

Patient: Why do you want to do another test?

What kind of test is it?

MTC(Doctor): Okay. Let me explain.

Since there was quite a bit of sugar in your urine sample, I am going to order a glucose tolerance test.

Patient: I see.

4.4.12 대변검사

■ ⟨Case⟩ 대변검사

MTC(Nurse): The container[89] is for your stool specimen.

There is a bathroom at the end of the hall.

---

84) adrenal: 부신의
85) urogenital: 비뇨 생식기의
86) glucose: 포도당
87) diabetes: 당뇨병
88) perineum: 회음, 남성과 여성의 성기
89) container: 용기

If it is difficult now, you can bring your stool specimen until tomorrow morning.

Patient: OK.

■ 〈Case〉 대변검사

MTC(Doctor): Feces[90] examination will be performed to see whether several kinds of parasites[91] and liver fluke[92] occur in the digestive system.

The day before the medical checkup a container will be distributed.

A sufficient quantity of the morning specimen[93]

must be collected in a dry container and given to the nurse.

Patient: OK.

Abnormal consistency	Expected reasons
pale[94], bulky[95], frothy[96]	poor fat digestion
hard	constipation[97]
flattened[98] and ribbon like	obstruction in the lumen of the bowel
semisolid	digestive upset, mid diarrhea[99]
watery	bacterial infection[100]
rice water stools	cholera

90) feces: 대변, 대소변
91) parasite: 기생충
92) liver fluke: 간디스토마, 간흡충
93) specimen: 표본
94) pale: 색깔이 흐릿한
95) bulky: 부피가 큰
96) frothy: 거품이 떠있는
97) constipation: 변비
98) flattened: 납작한
99) diarrhea: 설사
100) infection: 감염

228

4.4.13 폐기능검사

- 〈Case〉 호흡

MTC(Nurse): I am going to check your respirations.

I am going to evaluate your bed to 50 degrees.

Please place your arms across your abdomen.

I am going to place my index and middle

fingers on your writs to check your pulse rate.

Please stay relaxed and do not move.

I am going to count your respirations.

Patient: OK.

- 〈Case〉 호흡

MTC(Doctor): Now, I'm going to listen to your heart.

Please breathe in and hold your breath.

Please pull up your shirt

(상의탈의 후)

MTC: Breathe deeply.

Everything sounds good.

Let's take a look at your throat. Please open wide and say 'Ah'.

Patient: 'Ah'

MTC: I'm going to order blood test and X-Ray test to be done.

Patient: I see.

MTC(Nurse): Please take this slip to the front desk.

After you pay the bill.

They'll arrange an appointment for the blood test.

Patient: Thank you.

- 〈Case〉 폐기능검사

MTC(Nurse): This test is for the lung function.

It will take about five minutes.

You will breathe through the mouthpiece.

The mouthpiece is clean.

Patient: OK.

MTC: Please hold the hose and put the mouthpiece about a half into your mouth. I will block your nose with a nose clip for you to breathe only with your mouth. Please breathe normally twice.

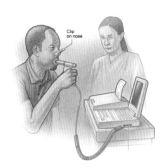

When the doctor says "breathe", please breathe in as deeply as you can until the doctor says "Hooh".

You need to breathe in strongly and continuously.

When the doctor says "Hooh", please breathe out until the doctor says "Breathe".

You need to breathe out strongly and continuously.

You need to do it once more. This time, please blow much harder.

Breathe.

More.

Hooh.

Thank you for your cooperation.

Please take off the mouthpiece.

You have done well.

Patient: Thank you.

4.4.14 심전도검사

■ 〈Case〉 심전도검사

MTC(Nurse): This test is for electrocardiography[101].

The electrocardiography detects[102] and records the heart's electrical activity.

---

101) electrocardiography: 심전도검사
   electrocardiogram: 심전도
102) detect: 발견하다

The electrocardiography can detect an irregular heart beat and signs of a previous heart attack. It also can show whether your heart chambers are enlarged.

The test will take about three minutes.

The electrocardiography checks the current cardiac functions.

The doctor will check the heart rate as well as to detect for the arrhythmia[103] or myocardial infarction[104].

Please take off your slipper and lie down on the bed.

Could you open your gown please?

Please relax and stay still.

Please do not move. Abrupt movements will give inaccurate results.

The test is finished.

Patient: Thank you.

■ 〈Case〉 심전도검사

MTC(Nurse): Please lie on the bed facing the ceiling.

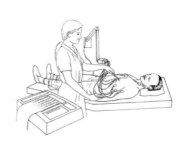

The electrocardiogram checks your heart.

It will give doctors information about the rhythm of the heartbeat[105] of blood going to the heart muscle.

The small plastic stickers are electrodes.

I will attach electrodes on the chest, arms and legs.

Please do not move.

Relax.

Do not talk during the test.

The electrocardiography is done.

The stickers will be taken off.

---

103) arrhythmia: 부정맥
104) myocardial infarction: 심근경색증
105) heartbeat: 심장박동

You will feel like taking off a small band-aid[106] when the stickers are taking off.

The doctor will consult with you after the doctor is looking at the graph paper of your heartbeat.

Patient: Thank you.

4.4.15 운동부하 심전도

■ 〈Case〉 운동부하 심전도

MTC(Nurse): This is for the treadmill[107] test.

This test checks the physiological[108] changes and reactions of the heart during the exercise.

This test is for checking potential coronary artery[109] diseases by burdening the heart through the exercise.

It will take about 20 minutes.

Please step on the treadmill.

Hold the bar, please.

You need to walk faster or run on the treadmill during the test.

Do you feel dizziness now?

Patient: No, I don't.

MTC: This test has four stages and each stage takes about three minutes.

As you proceed the test, the speed and the incline will increase.

I will notify you of changes in the stage.

During the test, the nurse will check your blood pressure and heart rhythm.

If you feel fatigued and have a headache, dizziness or chest discomfort, please raise your hand.

Before getting started, the nurse will check your blood pressure and

---

106) band-aid: 반창고
107) treadmill: 러닝머신
108) physiological: 생리적인
109) coronary artery: 관상동맥의

electrocardiography for the basal data.

Now, are you ready?

Now, let us get stared.

When the treadmill starts moving, please walk slowly.

This is stage one.

Now the nurse will raise the stage.

This is stage two.

The test is finished.

Please take a seat here and take a rest.

4.4.16 초음파 심장검사

■ 〈Case〉 초음파 심장검사

MTC(Doctor): This test is for diagnosing heart valve disease.

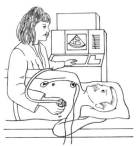

Echocardiography uses waves to create a moving picture of your heart as it beats.

It takes about 10 minutes.

A device called a transducer is placed on the surface of your chest.

The echocardiography shows the size and shape of your heart valves and chambers.

It also shows how well your heart is pumping blood.

The echocardiography also shows whether a heart value is narrow or has backflow[110].

4.4.17 흉부 X-ray 촬영

Put your chin on the board.

Hold your hands on your back.

Push your shoulder forward.

Hold your breath for a second.

---

110) backflow: 역류

Lie on your back.

Lie on your face up.

■ 〈Case〉 흉부 X-ray 촬영

MTC(Radiologist): This test is for X-ray.

It will take about three minutes.

Could you please stand up and face this board.

Please raise your chin a little bit and put your shoulder close to the board.

When I say "Hold your breath," stop breathing and do not move.

Breathe in and hold your breath.

(X-ray 촬영 후)

MTC: You can breathe now.

Thank you for your cooperation.

The test is finished.

Patient: Thank you.

■ 〈Case〉 흉부 X-ray 촬영

MTC(Radiologist): You are going to have a chest X-ray taken[111].

Please take all your clothes off except for your underwear and change into the examination wear in the dressing room over there.

Are you ready?

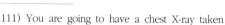

Patient: Yes, I am ready.

MTC: Please stand on closely in front of the X-ray machine.

Move forward a little bit more.

MTC: Take a deep breath and hold it just one minute.

Don't move.

---

111) You are going to have a chest X-ray taken

= The nurse is(I am) going to take your chest X-ray.

■ 〈Case〉 흉부 X-ray 촬영

MTC(Radiologist): You should take off all your clothes except for your underwear, and change into the examination wear in the dressing room.

Patient: I'm ready.

MTC: Good.

Please stand on closely in front of this machine.

Put your chin on here, both hands back and push your shoulder forward.

Now, take a deep breath and hold it just a few seconds to X-ray.

OK.

Good. That's all.

I've got your chest shot.

Patient: Thank you.

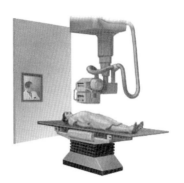

■ 〈Case〉 흉부 X-ray 촬영

MTC(Radiologist): Are you wearing any jewelry?

Patient: Yes, I am wearing earrings.

MTC: Will you please take them off?

You can put them in this tray.

Patient: OK. How should I sit?

MTC: Sit straight up and try not to move.

Please wear this vest.

It's to protect your body from radiation.

Patient: Thank you.

MTC: I am going to step outside and instruct you from there.

Are you ready?

Patient: OK. Yes, I am ready.

MTC: Can you hold your breath for about five seconds, then exhale[112] slowly?

---

112) exhale: 숨을 내쉬다

■ 〈Case〉 흉부 X-ray 촬영

Patient: I am here for an x-ray exam.

MTC(Nurse): Please be seated on the chair. While
　　　　　you are waiting, you may read a magazine.
　　　　　A technician will call you soon.

Patient: Thank you.

(간호사 호출)

　MTC: The nurse calls your name. Please follow
　　　　me.

Patient: Alright.

MTC(Radiologist): This is a dressing room. Remove your top and put on a gown
　　　　　with an opening in the back.

(X-ray 촬영실 안에서)

　MTC: Lie with your back on this table. When I say 'hold your breathing', stop
　　　　breathing and do not move.

Patient: OK.

　MTC: Hold your breath. OK, you can breathe now. I'll take a front of view.
　　　　Turn on your left side. I'll take a left side of view.
　　　　Turn on your right side. I'll take a right side of view. All done. Please
　　　　wait out side until X-ray is developed.
　　　　I'll let you know when you can go.

Patient: Thank you.

4.4.18 유방 X-ray 촬영

Have you ever taken a mammography[113] before?

Do you have any symptoms related with the breast?

Are there any family members who have breast cancer?

---

113) mammography: 유방 X선 촬영

■ 〈Case〉 유방 X-ray 촬영

MTC(Radiologist): This test will take about five minutes.

The plate on this machine will press your breast to make pictures.

Please take off your gown and put it on the hanger.

Please stand in front of this machine.

Relax and don't be nervous.

I will start checking with the right side.

Turn your head to the left and look at the wall.

Pull back your right shoulder.

Pull your left breast with your left hand.

Relax your shoulder and I will put pressure on your breast.

Please let us know if you feel uncomfortable during the test.

Patient: I will

MTC: Turn your head to the right and look at the wall.

Hold on for three seconds.

Thank you for your cooperation.

The test is finished.

Patient: Thank you.

4.4.19 체온측정

I will measure your temperature.

Your temperature is 36.5 celsius.[114]

---

114) Your temperature is 36.5 Celsius.

= Your temperature is 97.7 Fahrenheit.

■ 〈Case〉 체온측정

MTC(Nurse): Please put this thermometer[115] under your arm, so we can measure your temperature.

Patient: OK.

MTC: Are you pregnant?

Patient: No, I am not.

■ 〈Case〉 겨드랑이 체온 측정

MTC(Nurse): I will use the thermometer to check your body temperature.

I will place the thermometer under the armpit[116].

Patient: OK.

MTC: Please raise your arm to check your temperature.

■ 〈Case〉 겨드랑이 체온 측정

MTC(Nurse): I will close the curtain for your privacy.

I am going to check your temperature.

I am going to move your gown away from your shoulder and arm.

Please place your right arm over your head.

I will clean your armpit with tissue.

I am going to place the thermometer into the center of your axilla[117].

Please put your right arm over the thermometer.

Just a second please.

Patient: OK.

■ 〈Case〉 이마 체온 측정

MTC(Nurse): I will place the thermometer on your forehead.

Please do not move.

Patient: OK.

---

115) thermometer: 체온계, 온도계
116) armpit: 겨드랑이
117) axilla: 겨드랑이

MTC(Nurse): I am going to place the thermometer in the center of your forehead.

Please do not move. Just a second please.

Your temperature is 36.5 degree Celsius[118].

Patient: Thank you.

■ 〈Case〉 귀 체온 측정

MTC(Nurse): I will put the thermometer in your ear.

Please do not move.

Patient: OK.

■ 〈Case〉 구강 체온 측정

MTC(Nurse): I will put the thermometer in your mouth.

Open your mouth, please.

(입을 연 후)

Patient: Close your mouth, please.

MTC: Your temperature is 36.5 degree Celsius.

Patient: Thank you.

■ 〈Case〉 구강 체온 측정

MTC(Nurse): Have you had anything to eat or drink in the last 30 minutes?

Patient: No, I haven't.

MTC: Please open your mouth.

I am going to place the thermometer under your tongue.

Please close your lips.

■ 〈Case〉 구강 체온 측정

Patient: I think I might have a fever. It's so cold in here!

MTC(Doctor): Here, let me check your forehead.

Patient: What do you think?

---

118) Your temperature is 36.5 degree Celsius.

= Your temperature is 97.7 degree Fahrenheit.

MTC: Your temperature seems raised.

Patient: How do I raise my bed? I can't find the controls.

MTC: Here you are.

Is that better?

Patient: Could I have another pillow?

MTC: Certainly, Here you are. Is there anything else I can do for you?

Patient: No, thank you.

MTC: OK, I'll be right back with the thermometer.

Patient: Oh, just a moment. Can you bring me another bottle of water, too?

MTC: Certainly, I'll be back in a moment.

■ 〈Case〉 직장 체온 측정

MTC(Nurse): I am going to take a rectal[119] temperature.

For your privacy, I will close the curtain.

Patient: Thank you.

MTC: I need you to roll onto your side.

The right knee forward, please.

That is good.

I am going to expose your anal area.

Patient: Please cover my upper body and legs.

MTC: Sure.

I need you to breath slowly and try to relax.

I am going to insert the thermometer one and a half inches into your anus.

Please do not move.

Your temperature is 99 degree Fahrenheit.[120]

I am going to wipe your anal area with tissue.

---

119) rectal: 직장의

rectal cancer: 직장암

120) Your temperature is 99 degree Fahrenheit.

= Your temperature is 37.2 degree Celsius.

4.4.20 UGI(위장 조영술)

■ 〈Case〉 위장 조영술

Please lie on the bed.

Please turn your back.

Please lie on your back, and face up.

Please lie on your stomach and face down.

■ 〈Case〉 위장 조영술

MTC(Radiologist): You need to make a reservation, if you want to select the gastroscopy[121] or an upper gastrointestinal[122] (UGI) series examination.

Patient: I will take UGI series examination.

MTC: You should not eat or drink for 8 hours before the UGI series examination. Smoking and chewing gums are also prohibited during this time.

Patient: OK.

---

121) gastroscopy: 위내시경
122) upper gastrointestinal: 상부 위장관 조영술
   위내시경은 내시경 끝에 장착된 고성능 카메라를 통해 위 속을 HD급 영상으로 관찰하는 방식이며, 상부 위장관 조영술은 위벽에 코팅된 바륨의 모습을 X선 영상을 통해 간접적으로 보는 검사이다.

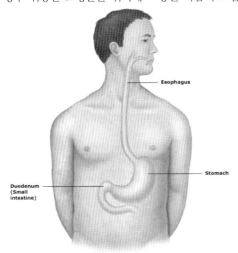

MTC: Do you have any allergies to medications or foods?

Patient: No, I don't think I have.

MTC: Are you pregnant?

Patient: No, I am not.

MTC: I see. If you are pregnant, you must take an alternative examination such as upper gastrointestinal Endoscopy.

(다음 날)

MTC: Let me check if you did not eat anything after 8:00 pm.

Patient: No, I didn't.

MTC: The Upper Gastrointestinal Series Examination consists of a checkup on the esophagus[123], stomach and duodenum[124].

You drink this.

This is barium[125] liquid.

It coats the lining of the upper gastrointestinal tract[126] and makes signs of diseases show up more clearly on X rays.

The doctor will view the barium liquid moving through the esophagus, stomach, and duodenum.

Please lie down on the table.

To fully coat the upper gastrointestinal tract with barium liquid, the radiologist may press on the abdomen or ask you to change the position.

123) esophagus: 식도
124) duodenum: 십이지장

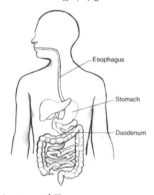

125) barium: 바륨
126) gastrointestinal tract: 위장관

You must hold still in various positions.

The radiologist will take X rays of the upper gastrointestinal tract at different angles.

4.4.21 복부 초음파검사

■ ⟨Case⟩ 복부 초음파검사

MTC(Nurse): Please take off your slippers and lie down on the bed.

Please open your robe to see your abdomen for the examination.

Raise both your hands over the head.

The doctor will apply a clear water-based gel on the abdomen.

The gel is used to make secure contact with the body and eliminate air pockets between the instrument and the skin.

Please take a deep breath and hold it.

Now breathe out.

Turn slightly to your left side.

Turn slightly to your right side.

Please lie on your back.

Please wipe your abdomen with this towel and put your robe on.

Patient: Thank you.

■ ⟨Case⟩ 복부 초음파검사

MTC(Doctor): You should not have anything to eat for about 4 to 6 hours before the abdomen sonography.

Patient: Can I drink water?

MTC: You can drink as much water as you like.

I am going to apply a gel to the skin of your lower abdomen to ensure a better interface between the surface and the ultrasound transducer.

The computer generates several images per second and you can see the images on the monitor.

It is done.

Please wipe the gel with this towel.

Patient: Thank you.

4.4.22 전립선 초음파검사(Transrectal Ultrasonography)

■ 〈Case〉 전립선 초음파검사

MTC(Nurse): This test will see the prostate[127]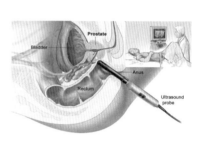
by inserting the equipment into your anus.

It will take about 15 minutes.

Please take off your underwear. Put your clothes in this drawer.

You need to wear these gown with a hole.

The side with the hole goes to the back.

Please lie on your left side facing the wall.

Bend your knees and bring them up to your chest as much as you can.

The ultrasound[128] equipment will go into your anus.

Now, the doctor will start the test.

(검사종료 후)

MTC: The test is finished.

You have done well.

Patient: Thank you.

---

127) prostate: 전립선
128) ultrasound: 초음파

4.4.23 골밀도검사

■ 〈Case〉 골밀도검사

MTC(Radiologist): Please lie down on the table.

This is the bone densitometry[129] test.

This test will check your bone density by scanning your spine, hip and leg bone.

It will take about five to six minutes.

Let us start with the spine first.

Now I will check your leg bone.

Please stretch your legs.

Turn your legs inward.

Relax your legs.

Thank you for your cooperation.

The test is finished.

Patient: Thank you.

■ 〈Case〉 골밀도검사

MTC(Doctor): How old are you?

Patient: I am 40 years old.

MTC: If you have a family history of osteoporosis[130], the bone densitometry test is a must.

MTC(Radiologist): You need a bone densitometry test.

Are you pregnant?

Patient: No, I am not.

---

129) bone densitometry test: 골밀도검사

인체 특정부위의 뼈의 양을 측정하기 위한 검사이다. 골다공증, 골연화증과 같은 대부분의 대사성 골질환 환자에서는 뼈의 양이 감소하게 되는데, 뼈의 양을 골밀도라고 하는 지표로 측정하고 이를 정상인의 골밀도와 비교하여 얼마나 뼈의 양이 감소되었는지를 평가하고자 하는 것이 검사목적이다.

130) osteoporosis: 골다공증

MTC: This bone densitometry test will use the least amount of X ray to produce images of the spine, hip, and the whole body.

Patient: I am glad to hear that.

MTC: It takes about 5 to 6 minutes.

Please lie still and breathe normally on the table.

Stretch your legs, please.

Turn your legs inward.

Relax your legs.

Thank you for your cooperation.

Patient: You are welcome.

4.4.24 위내시경검사

Have you ever taken an endoscopy before?

Have you ever had a surgery on your stomach or intestine[131]?

Are you taking any blood thinner such as aspirin?

■ 〈Case〉 위내시경검사 전

MTC(Doctor): This test is for endoscopy.

It will take about five minutes.

Before the endoscopy test, I will give you some medicine.

This liquid medicine is for removing the bubbles in your stomach and decreasing the bowl movement.

Drink the medicine, please.

Patient: OK.

■ 〈Case〉 위내시경검사

MTC(Nurse): The tube has a camera, so the doctor can visualize the lining of the esophagus and stomach.

I will take samples and photos.

Patient: I understand.

---

131) intestine: 장

MTC: Please drink this medicine.

Patient: What is this for?

MTC: This medicine will remove the bubbles in the stomach as well as decrease the bowl movement.

Patient: I see.

MTC: Just wait a second until the medicine permeates into the esophagus and stomach.

4.4.25 수면내시경검사

▪ 〈Case〉 수면내시경검사

Patient: I cannot imagine having a long tube stuck down my throat.

Is it painful?

I am afraid I would have a panic attack right on the table.

MTC(Nurse): Then, do you want sleep endoscopy?

Patient: What is sleep endoscopy?

MTC: The endoscopy will be preformed, while you are sleeping.

If you want the sleep endoscopy, you should make an appointment in advance.

Patient: I see

MTC: After the sleep endoscopy, you will remain in the recovery room until you regain conscious awareness.

▪ 〈Case〉 수면내시경검사

MTC(Nurse): You will have sleeping sedatives through the intravenous line.

Place your right arm on the table.

May I roll up your sleeve?

Would you clench[132] your fist firmly?

---

132) clench: 꽉 쥐다

It might sting a little bit when the needle gets in.

Now let us move to the endoscopy room.

The preparation for the endoscopy is done.

Relax.

(수면내시경 후)

　MTC: Are you awake?

4.4.26 대장내시경검사

■ 〈Case〉 대장내시경검사

MTC(Nurse): This test is for colonoscopy[133].

Could you pull your knees toward your chest more tightly?

I will put the side rail down, so do not lean back.

The doctor will examine the rectum[134] with the finger.

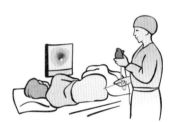

Don't be startled.

The doctor is inserting a rectal rube into your anus.

The doctor is inserting gas so that you might feel like passing gas.

Pass gas, because it is normal.

It might be painful when the tube goes in, because the colon is curved.

Now it is almost done.

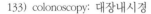

133) colonoscopy: 대장내시경

항문으로 내시경이라는 특수한 카메라를 삽입하여, 대장 내부 및 대장과 인접한 소장의 말단 부위까지를 관찰하는 검사법이다. 최근 사용되는 대부분의 내시경은 유연한 튜브의 끝에 광섬유로 연결된 카메라가 달려 있는 길이 1.3~1.7m의 기구이다.

대장내시경은 특히 대장암과 염증성 장질환의 진단에 매우 중요한 검사이다. 갑작스러운 혈색소(헤모글로빈 hemoglobin)의 감소 등 빈혈의 징후가 있는 경우에는 대변에서 혈색소가 검출되지 않더라도 상부 위장관(위, 식도, 십이지장)내시경과 함께 흔히 대장내시경을 시행한다. 직접 대장의 내부를 보면서 눈으로 진단을 하고, 필요에 따라 지혈을 하거나 조직검사 또는 의심스러운 병변을 제거하는 치료적인 목적도 가지고 있다. 최근에는 다양한 기구와 술기를 이용하여 출혈 부위를 지혈하거나 용종과 점막의 종양을 제거하는 치료 내시경이 확대되고 있다.

134) rectum: 직장

The doctor is pulling out the tube.

Relax.

Let us move to the recovery room.

Patient: Thank you.

■ 〈Case〉 대장내시경검사

MTC(Doctor): Your bowel must be empty so that I can clearly view the colon.

It take about 30 minutes.

Please drink this fluid to relax you during the procedure.

Patient: OK.

(마신 후)

MTC: Please lie on your lift side and bring your knees toward your chest.

Patient: Like this?

MTC: OK. Are you comfortable?

Patient: Yes, I am.

I am going to insert the colonoscope into the rectum as well as to the large intestine.

You will feel a little pressure.

I am going to fill your colon with a small quantity of air through the endoscope.

This discomfort will be gone away when the air is withdrawn.

You might feel bloated.

I am going to take a small amount of tissue.

It is almost done.

I am going to remove the tube from your anus.

Patient: OK.

4.4.27 자궁경부암검사

■ 〈Case〉 자궁경부암검사

MTC(Nurse): This is pap test[135] to examine you're your vagina[136] and the cervix[137].

During the Pap test, the doctor will use a plastic or metal instrument to widen your vagina.

This helps the doctor examine the vagina and the cervix, and collect a few cells and mucus[138] from the cervix and the area around it. The cells are then placed on a slide or in a bottle of liquid and sent to a laboratory.

The laboratory[139] will check to be sure that the cells are normal.

Patient: OK.

4.4.28 알레르기 테스트

■ 〈Case〉 알레르기 테스트

Patient: I feel itchy all over my body.

MTC(Doctor): What did you eat?

Patient: Nothing particular.

I just had an ordinary meal just like any other day.

MTC: Where you live and where you work?

Patient: I live in downtown.

I work in the office.

---

135) pap test: 자궁경부암검사 = cervical cancer screening test
자궁암검사는 자궁경부 세포진 검사로 자궁경부나 질에서 떨어져 나온 세포를 현미경으로 관찰하여 비정상 세포유무를 관찰하는 것이다. 골반 내진을 하여 작은 솔로 자궁경부의 세포를 묻혀 유리 슬라이드에 펴 바른 뒤 현미경으로 관찰한다.
136) vagina: 음부
137) cervix: 자궁
138) mucus: 진액
139) laboratory: 실험실

MTC: OK.

These allergy skin tests will find out which substances cause you to have an allergic reaction.

■ 〈Case〉 알레르기 테스트

MTC(Nurse): You need an allergy test.

This is a test slip. Please register this at the front desk and make an appointment for you. When I receive the results, I'll notify you.

Patient: Thank you.

■ 〈Case〉 알레르기 테스트

MTC(Nurse): This test will take about 15 minutes.

The skin is scratched or pricked[140] with a tiny bit of liquid extract of an allergen[141] such as pollen or food.

If the area swells up and becomes red like a mosquito bite, the result of the allergy test is positive. It means that you are allergic to that substance.

4.4.29 CT검사

■ 〈Case〉 CT검사

MTC(Radiologist): The doctor found something abnormal and the doctor needs further examination.

Patient: Is it serious?

MTC: You must change into a special gown.
Before you wear the gown, you must remove any jewelry or metallic objects. Such objects will interfere with the X-ray signals.

---

140) prick: 찌르다
141) allergen: 알레르기 유발 항원

Patient: Do I have to remove hearing aids[142] and dentures[143] as well?

MTC: Yes, you do.

Please lie down on a table.

The table will slide into the circular machine.

■ 〈Case〉 CT검사

MTC(Radiologist): The CT scanning combines special X-ray equipment with sophisticated computers to produce multiple images of the inside of the body.

The cross-sectional images of the area will be examined on a computer monitor.

I will inject iodine-containing[144] fluid into the vein in order to highlight certain areas in the chest for clear images.

Patient: OK.

4.4.30 MRI검사

만약 임신을 했거나 간 기능에 문제가 있으면, MRI를 위한 조영제를 사용할 수 없다. 밀실공포증이 있으면 진정제를 투여받는다.

■ 〈Case〉 MRI 검사

MTC(Radiologist): This is MRI.

As you can see, it is a large cylinder-shaped tube surrounded by a circular magnet.

You will lie on the table. The table is moveable.

The technician will slide the table into the center of the magnet.

MTC: Now please remove jewelry, watches, credit cards, hearing aids, hairpins, eyeglasses, pens, and body piercings.

142) hearing aid: 보청기
143) denture: 틀니, 의치
144) idodine-containing: 요오드가 담긴

The similar metallic[145] items can distort MRI images.

Please tell us if you have medical or electronic devices in your body, because they may interfere with the examination.

Patient: I see.

　MTC: Now, wear this gown.

(가운으로 갈아입은 후)

　MTC: You are required to receive an injection of contrast material into the bloodstream.

Patient: I see.

　MTC: Do you have allergies of any kind such as allergy to drugs or food?

■ 〈Case〉 MRI검사

MTC(Radiologist): You are required to sign at the consent form for the operation.

　　　　Please read the consent form and sign it.

Patient: Here you are.

　MTC: Have you ever performed a MRI?

Patient: Yes, I have.

　　　　I have allergy to contrast materials.

　MTC: I see. Instead of Iodine, we will use gadolinium.[146]

　　　　Gadolinium does not contain iodine.

　　　　It can be used safely in patients with contrast allergies.

■ 〈Case〉 MRI검사

MTC(Radiologist): Have you recently had any surgery?

Patient: No, I haven't.

　MTC: Do you have problems with the kidney?

Patient: No, I don't.

　MTC: Are you pregnant?

Patient: No, I am not.

---

145) metallic: 금속의
146) iodine: 요오드
　　　Gadolinium: 가돌리늄(MRI 조영제)

MTC: Do you have claustrophobia[147])?

Patient: Yes, I have.

MTC: Then, the doctor will give you mild sedative[148]) before the examination.

4.4.31 PET-CT검사

신장에 문제가 있는 환자의 경우, PET-CT검사로 인해서 신장이 상할 수 있다.

■ 〈Case〉 PET-CT검사

MTC(Radiologist): You will lie down on a table.

You are required rest quitely, avoid movement and talking.

A radioactive[149]) material called radiotracer will be injected into your bloodstream[150]). You may feel a slight pin prick when the needle is inserted into your vein for the intravenous line.

When the radioactive material is injected into your arm, you may feel a cold sensation moving up your arm.

The radioactive material accumulates in the organ or area of your body. It will take approximately 60 minutes for the radiotracer to travel through your body and to be absorbed by the organ.

The radioactive material gives off a small amount of energy in the form of gamma rays, the PET scanner detects this energy.

Patient: I understand.

■ 〈Case〉 PET-CT검사

MTC(Radiologist): You should be fast.

You must not drink beverages except for water at least 4 to 6 hours before the test.

---

147) claustrophobia: 밀실 공포증
148) sedative: 진정제
149) radioactive: 방사성의
150) bloodstream: 혈류

It takes about two to three hours to complete the test.

(4~6시간 금식 후)

MTC: I will take a small blood sugar sample and place an intravenous line for a simple injection of the radioactive tracer.

When the nurse places the intravenous line, it will be slightly painful.

After the radioactive injection, you will drink two bottles of contrast agent.

Patient: Do you use anesthesia?

MTC: No, anesthesia will not be used.

Do you feel anxiety in small, enclosed spaces?

Patient: Yes

MTC: I see, then I will give you a light sedative to help calm your anxiety and help you relax.

After the injection, you will be asked to sit quietly for 45 to 60 minutes. This allows the drug to distribute in your body.

(약 45~60분 후)

MTC: Please lie down on the table.

You will receive another injection of enhancing agent.

You may notice warmth and flushing when the tracer is injected. This is normal.

■ 〈Case〉 PET-CT 검사

MTC(Radiologist): Do you have any allergy?

Patient: I am allergic to nuts.

MTC: I see, then you must have an allergic reaction test[151] done before PET-CT.

(검사 후)

MTC: The test turns out that you are allergic to radioactive tracers so I will treat you with antihistamines or steroid medications.

Now the PET-CT scanner will take images of your body for approximately 30 to 40 minutes.

---

151) allergic reaction test: 알레르기 반응 테스트

The table will move slowly through a doughnut-shaped ring.

You need to lie still while the images are being taken.

(종료 후)

MTC: OK, it is finished.

You are encouraged to drink water to clear the radioactivity from your body.

■ 〈Case〉 PET-CT 검사

MTC(Radiologist): Please swallow the contrast material.

It has no taste.

Lie on the table.

You will be moved into the PET-CT scanner and the imaging will begin.

You need to remain still during imaging.

The CT exam will be done first, then PET scan will be done later.

In the second CT scan, I will inject intravenous contrast for the PET scan.

It will take 20 to 30 minutes.

If you are claustrophobic[152], you may feel some anxiety while you are being scanned.

It is finished.

Patient: It is too noisy inside the circle.

MTC: Yes, it is.

Please drink plenty of water to help flush[153] the radioactive material out of your body.

Patient: OK.

---

152) claustrophobia: 밀실 공포증
153) flush: 씻어내다

4.4.32 수면검사

■ 〈Case〉 수면검사

MTC(Nurse): Please take no nap during the day.

No coffee or tea.

You can take shower before you come for sleep study.

Please do not use hair spray or skin lotion.

You can take dinner before you come for sleep study.

Patient: Can I bring my own pajamas?

MTC: You can bring your comfortable pajamas or any comfortable uniform.

You can bring your own pillow or slipper, shaving utensil[154].

When you arrive sleep study room, doctor will attach sleep study devices on your body such as sensor, belt and etc.

Specialists will check your condition while you are awake.

Doctors will monitor your snoring, breathing, heart palpitation, movement of your eyes, muscle stress degree, oxygen in your blood.

4.4.33 치아 X-ray

■ 〈Case〉 치아 X-ray

MTC: Please, come here[155].

Let me take an X-ray.

Open your mouth, please.

Tap your back teeth together.

Open your mouth, please.

Close your mouth slightly.

Press the film with your finger.

Use your thumb to hold it.

Put your head back.

154) utensil: 도구
155) = Please follow me.

Close your eyes.

Don't move.

Patient: OK.

■ 〈Case〉 치아 X-ray

MTC: The radiologist(I) will take an X-ray.

Take off your glasses, please.

Keep your teeth together.

Open your mouth, please.

Close your mouth slightly.

Grab the film with your finger.

Use your thumb to hold it.

Put your head back.

Close your eyes and don't move.

It is finished.

Now you can open your eyes.

Patient: Thank you.

4.5 조사결과

■ 결과설명

Your test results have come out.

I'm afraid the prognosis[156] isn't good.

You have a long road to recovery.

We have several options to discuss.

The blood test turned out negative.

We'll know more in a few days.

Your blood test turned out almost ideal levels of cholesterol.

---

156) prognosis: 예후, 질병치료 뒤의 경과 예상

I am afraid that you are diagnosed[157] with a cancer.

I am afraid that you have been diagnosed with a cancer.

■ 자세한 설명 요구

What do you think your diagnosis[158] is?

Could you explain my diagnosis in more detail?

Will you explain more concretely?

Could you tell me more specific about my diagnosis?

■ 추가증상 질문

Do you have any other symptoms?

Are you having any other symptoms such as palpitation, shortness of breath, jaundice[159], thirst, or a sensitivity of cold or heat?

■ 〈Case〉 추가증상 질문

MTC(Doctor): Have you had any other symptoms with your headache?

Patient: I had a fever.

■ 〈Case〉 추가증상 질문

MTC(Doctor): Did you have other symptoms with your stomachache?

Patient: I had nausea[160] and vomiting.

■ 〈Case〉 추가증상 질문

MTC(Doctor): Do you feel any other symptoms with your chest pain?

Patient: I feel nauseated[161].

■ 조사 결과

The test turns out you are suffering from a disease.

---

157) diagnose: 진단하다
    be diagnosed with: 어떤 병으로 진단받다
    I have been diagnosed with pancreatic cancer.: 췌장암으로 진단받았다.
158) diagnosis: 진단
159) jaundice: 황달
160) nausea: 욕지기, 구역질
161) nauseate: 구역질나게 하다

I hope the tests turn out that you don't have glaucoma[162].

The X ray shows that you have tuberculosis[163].

The X ray tells me that you have a malignant[164] cancer.

The urine test shows that you suffer from osteoporosis[165].

■ 〈Case〉 X-Ray 결과

Patient: How did my X-ray turn out?

MTC(Doctor): I can't see any remarkable troubles in your X-ray.

Patient: How did my blood test come out?

MTC: The result of your blood test is normal.

■ 〈Case〉 X-Ray 결과

MTC(Doctor): The chest X-ray shows your lungs are healthy.

Patient: Thank you.

■ 〈Case〉 혈액 및 소변검사 결과

MTC(Doctor): Your blood and urine tests are normal.

Patient: I am glad to hear that.

How about the result of the heart test?

MTC: It is normal.

■ 〈Case〉 혈액검사 결과

MTC(Doctor): Your blood test is positive to hepatitis[166].

Patient: Is it serious?

MTC: You need to be hospitalized.

It won't take long to recover because it is in the early stages.

---

162) glaucoma: 녹내장
163) tuberculosis: 결핵
164) malignant: 악성의
165) osteoporosis: 골다공증
166) hepatitis: 간염
    hepatitis A: A형 간염
    hepatitis B: B형 간염

■ 〈Case〉 내시경검사 결과

MTC(Doctor): According to the endoscopy[167], there is a slight inflammation[168] of the stomach.

However, it can be cured with some medication.

The colonoscopy[169] result turn out that your colon is clean.

No polyps[170] were found.

Patient: I am glad to hear that.

■ 〈Case〉 비만도검사 결과

MTC(Doctor): You are overweight.

You need exercise and change your eating habit. Exercise is very beneficial in lowing high blood pressure.

I will make a copy of the check-up before you leave the hospital.

Patient: Thank you.

■ 〈Case〉 건강검진 결과

Patient: I will stay only for 5 to 6 days in Korea. Can I get the result of medical checkup before I leave Korea?

MTC(Nurse): I takes more than 8 to 10 days to get the result of medical checkup.

You may have telephone counseling after receiving certified mail.

■ 〈Case〉 건강검진 결과

MTC(Doctor): Here are the results of your medical check-up.

I found some potential problems in your circulatory[171] system.

Patient: I see.

MTC: The test shows that your cholesterol level is high and your blood pressure is also high.

---

167) endoscopy: 내시경
168) inflammation: 염증
169) colonoscopy: 대장 내시경
170) polyp: 폴립, 용종
171) circulatory: 순환의
    circulatory system: 순환계

■ 〈Case〉 건강검진 결과

MTC(Doctor): I will explain about the result of your medical tests.

Patient: OK.

MTC: Your overall condition is healthy except for the weight problem.

Your body mass index[172] is high.

You need to exercise and eat a healthier diet.

Patient: I see.

MTC: Obesity[173] can lead to many medical problems such as heart attack, diabetes, problems with the liver[174].

You need to have a well-balanced diet[175].

You should avoid fast food and cut down on fats.

Patient: I see.

■ 〈Case〉 건강검진 결과

Patient: When can I get the result of the medical up?

MTC(Nurse): The details of the medical check up will be sent by e-mail.

---

172) Body mass index

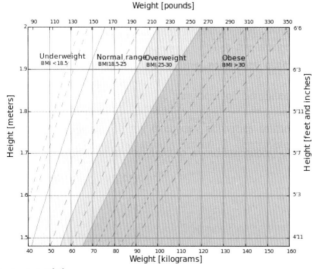

173) obesity: 비만

174) liver: 간

175) = a pretty balanced diet

Chapter 5

수술 및 진료

5.1 수술 결정

■ 〈Case〉 수술결정

MTC(Doctor): You need a surgery.

Patient: Do I need a surgery?

What if I don't get the surgery done(performed)?

MTC: If you don't get the surgery, it could get more complicated.

I'll make a surgery appointment.

You'll probably be admitted to the hospital on the day before the day of your surgery.

Patient: All right. How can I get to the admission procedure?

MTC: I will help you with admission procedure.

Patient: Thanks a lot.

MTC: Please fill out the admission form and sign in it.

Patient: All right.

■ 〈Case〉 수술일정

MTC(Nurse): I'm here to schedule your appointment to have a surgery done(performed) by Dr. Kim.

Can you come in on April twenty-sixth or April twenty-ninth?

Which day do you prefer?

Patient: How about Monday?

MTC: Okay, so that is Monday the twenty-ninth.

Now I have to ask you some allergy questions.

Do you have any allergy to medications?

■ 〈Case〉 예진표 작성

MTC(Nurse): Please fill out the medical questionnaire including a list of your medications.

Patient: OK.

MTC: I need to confirm the time of the appointment with the operating room, so I'll give you a call once I've confirmed the time.

Patient: OK.

MTC: As soon as you arrive at the hospital, you need to do some paperwork before the surgery.

■ 〈Case〉 수술시간 안내

MTC(Nurse): Your surgery will be scheduled to begin at either 10:00 am or 10:20 am tomorrow.

Patient: I feel nervous.

MTC: Please do not feel so nervous.

There is a waiting room in front of the operating room on the second floor of the hospital.

I will wait for you in front of the operation room until the operation(surgery) is over.

Patient: Thank you.

MTC: Your surgery will be performed by the most experienced doctors.

I believe that they will do their best to prepare for the successful surgery(operation).

They are very concerned about your health.

■ ⟨Case⟩ 수술시기 문의

Patient: Is it true that it is not good to have operations performed in the summer?

MTC(Nurse): As long as you do not wash your face on the day of the operation then getting an operation in the summer does not affect the result of the surgery and/or recovery.

With the advanced medical techniques used these days, Patients can wait until the day following the operation to wash the face.

In other words, it is perfectly fine to have operations performed in the summer.

■ ⟨Case⟩ 수술시간 연기

MTC(Nurse): The operation has been postponed because of the unexpected emergency in the hospital.

There is a serious Patient who needs surgery right now.

Patient: I see. Then, when can I have the surgery done(performed)?

MTC: I will check right away.

Please wait here.

Patient: Okay.

MTC: The doctors say that they are very sorry about this kind of delay and your operation will begin in about one hour(30 minutes).

Patient: I see.

MTC: Would you like to read some magazines?

■ ⟨Case⟩ 수술 소요시간

Patient: How long does the operation take?

MTC(Nurse): It depends on the type of operation.

In general, hair transplants in the front of the head take approximately 4 to 5 hours.

5.2 수술 전 주의사항

■ 〈Case〉 수술 전 확인

MTC(Nurse): Good morning.

Your surgery is schedule to begin(take place/start) tomorrow morning.

Patient: I am nervous.

MTC: Don't worry.

Now I have to ask you some allergy questions.

Please take this form and complete the questions, including a list of your medications[1].

■ 〈Case〉 수술 전 주의사항

MTC(Nurse): Well, good communication between you and your physician is very important.

The surgeon will ask what you'd like your nose to look like.

Patient: I want my nose to look much better after the surgery.

MTC: That is what I want, too.

The doctor will recommend you the most appropriate ideas after the doctor check your physical conditions and expectations.[2]

Patient: Okay, I am listening.

MTC: The doctor will also explain about the possibilities of complications[3] as well as the factors that can influence the results.

---

1) medications: 복용약

2) The doctor will recommend you the most appropriate ideas after the doctor check your physical conditions and expectations.

= The doctor will recommend you the most appropriate ideas after the doctor check the shape of your face, the thickness of your skin, your age, and your expectations.

3) complications: 합병증

Patient: I will pay attention to the doctor's advise.

MTC: Yes, it is important.

Your surgeon will also explain the techniques and anesthesia[4] he or she will use, the type of facility where the surgery will be performed as well as the risks involved.

Patient: Okay

MTC: Be sure to tell your surgeon if you've had any previous nose surgery or an injury to your nose, even if it was many years ago.

You should also inform your surgeon if you have any allergies or breathing difficulties; if you're taking any medications, vitamins, or recreational drugs; and if you smoke.

Patient: I see.

MTC: Do not hesitate to ask your doctor any questions you may have, especially those regarding your expectations and concerns about the results.

Patient: Okay

MTC: I hope that you will be very much satisfied with the surgery.

■ 〈Case〉 수술 전 주의사항

MTC(Nurse): Your surgeon will give you specific instructions on how to prepare for the surgery, including guidelines on eating and drinking, smoking, taking or avoiding certain vitamins and medications.

Please follow these instructions carefully so that your surgery will go more smoothly.

Patient: I know.

MTC: A special bus has been arranged for you, so that we will drive you to the hotel after your surgery and help you out for a few days.

Patient: Thank you.

---

4) anesthesia: 마취

MTC: The plastic surgery usually takes an hour or two.

■ 〈Case〉 수술 전 주의사항

MTC(Nurse): You are required not to eat or drink anything after 11:00 pm the day before your surgery.

The hospital says that smoking increase the likelihood of breathing problems during and after anesthesia[5].

Patient: I do not smoke.

MTC: I am glad to hear that.

You need to prepare for your surgery(operation) by bathing or showering, removing all make-up, nail polish and jewelry.

Patient: Okay, I will do.

MTC: You have to wear loose-fitting[6] casual clothing and comfortable shoes.

Please leave all your valuables[7] at the room in the hotel.

Patient: Thank you for your advise.

MTC: You are welcome.

5.3 수술과 진료

5.3.1 수술비용

■ 〈Case〉 수술비용

Patient: How much does the surgery cost?

MTC(Staff): The cost of surgery ranges from about USD 500 to USD 800.

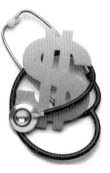

■ 〈Case〉 수술비용

Patient: How much does the surgery cost?

5) anesthesia: 마취
6) loose-fitting: 낙낙한, 헐렁한
7) valuables: 귀중품

MTC(Staff): Surgery costs vary based on many factors including the surgeon's fees, the type of surgery, operating room fees, the type of anesthesia used, what tests are performed before and after surgery, and the length of time required in the hospital after surgery.

■ 〈Case〉 수술비용

Patient: Is the surgery expensive?

MTC(Staff): The cost of the hair transplant[8] surgery is determined according to the state of hair loss and the number of hairs that are needed to be transplanted.

■ 〈Case〉 수술비용

Patient: Which forms of payment do you accept?

MTC(Staff): Cash or credit cards are acceptable.

Patient: Are there additional charges such as anesthesia[9] fee or bank fees besides the surgery cost?

■ 〈Case〉 수술비용 할인

Patient: I read on the webpage that ABC Clinic is having a promotional sale going on for the prices.

I am wondering if I get multiples procedures, would I still be able to receive a 10% percent discount on the already reduced prices?

MTC(Staff): I am afraid that there is no double discount.

But we can reduce a little more.

■ 〈Case〉 수술예약비 납부

Patient: Is it possible to have check up on June 1st and have a surgery done (performed) on June 2nd and go back home on June 3rd?

MTC(Staff): I can promise that I can meet your schedule.

You can consult with the doctor and get an operation on each day you want.

---

8) transplant: 이식
9) anesthesia: 마취제

If you want to make a reservation, you must send deposit a 10% of operation fee.

The operation fee is USD 3,000.

Patient: Then USD 300 must be paid in advance for reservation.

MTC: Please send an e-mail to us after paying to the account of ABC Hospital. Moreover, we need to know about your date and time when you arrive in korea flight name, your name and contact information.

5.3.2 수술횟수 및 종류

■ 〈Case〉 수술횟수

Patient: How many times should I receive the surgery?

MTC(Doctor): Most patients are satisfied after only a single surgery.

However, if greater results are necessary, then a second surgery may be administered and is conducted at least 10 months after the first surgery.[10]

■ 〈Case〉 수술일정

Patient: I am wondering when is the soonest date I can have chin and zygoma[11] reduction surgery?

MTC(Nurse): Let me check the schedule.

You can operate 2:00 pm on the 21st of July.

---

10) However, if greater results are anticipated by having another surgery, then a second surgery may be administered and is conducted at least 10 months after the first surgery.

= However, if you want to have another surgery to obtain much better results, then a second surgery may be performed at least 10 months after the first surgery.

11) zygoma: 광대뼈

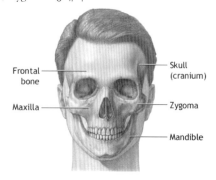

Frontal bone —
Maxilla —
Skull (cranium)
Zygoma
Mandible

A 10% deposit will be required for reservation.

Patient: Please let me know the account information by e-mail.

■ ⟨Case⟩ 수술일정

Patient: When is the best season for surgeries?

What season is better to get recovery faster?

MTC(Doctor): There is no best season.

It depends on the doctor's skill. the season doesn't matter.

■ ⟨Case⟩ 수술샘플

Patient: Can I bring a picture of who I want to look like?

MTC(Doctor): Yos, you can.

Patient: If I did facial contouring at the clinic and eye surgery at another clinic, which one should I show you first?

MTC: You had better show me all the pictures.

■ ⟨Case⟩ 수술종류

Patient: Do you perform neck lift in your clinic?

MTC(Nurse): We do not perform neck lift.

Instead of neck lift, S-lift is available.

5.3.3 수술 후 회복

■ ⟨Case⟩ 수술오류

Patient: Can you tell if by any chance nerve get damage during surgery?

Can the damaged nerve be recovered? What will happen afterwards?

MTC(Doctor): Even if nerve is cut, I can repair the nerve.

The recovery rate depends on individual characteristics.

■ ⟨Case⟩ 수술 후 회복

Patient: I am interested in Mandible angle reduction as well as liposuction under chin.

How many days should I stay in Korea?

Can I have my consultation and surgery on the same day?

MTC(Nurse): You can consult and operation on the same day.

        After 3 days since surgery the doctor will remove the bandages, and on the 5th day tapes will be removed, so after one week you can come back to your normal life.

        I recommend you to stay more than 6 days in Korea.

■ 〈Case〉 수술 후 회복

Patient: Is sleep anaesthesia used for S lift?

        Would I have to stay overnight in clinic after surgery?

MTC(Nurse): S-lift is operated under the intravenous local anesthesia[12).

        You will be discharged after surgery.

5.3.4 마취

■ 〈Case〉 마취

Patient: What kind of anesthesia[13) is used for rhinoplasty[14)?

MTC(Doctor): For pain-free anesthesia, a hemostatic[15) agent[16) or local anesthetic is injected after inducing[17) sleep.

Through this process, the Patient will experience no pain during the surgical procedure.

The period of inducing sleep is adjusted according to the recovery time required after surgery and the individual's overall health.

If the surgery is conducted under a conscious sedation[18), the Patient must return home after sufficiently recovering from the anesthesia.

---

12) intravenous local anesthesia: 정맥 국부마취
13) anesthesia: 마취제
14) rhinoplasty: 코 성형술
15) hemostatic: 지혈의, 지혈제
16) agent: 약품
    hemostatic agent: 지혈제
17) induce: 유도하다
    induce sleeping: 수면을 유도하다
18) sedation: 진정제

5.3.5 치과

■ 〈Case〉 치과 의사능력 문의

MTC(Nurse): Hello. This is the global healthcare center.

This is Kim speaking.

Patient: I am interested in the dental care in ABC Hospital.

MTC: Thank you for choosing ABC Hospital.

Patient: How qualified are the physicians at your hospital?

MTC: Most of the doctors have either studied, practiced or become licensed in the U.S.

Their qualifications are usually available for your review at the homepage.

Patient: How soon must I make the payment?

MTC: You will be required to make a deposit prior to going for your procedure.

The balance of the payment is due either before or upon treatment.

Patient: What does my doctor need to know?

MTC: It is wise to let your primary care physician know your plans to receive medical treatment overseas.

■ 〈Case〉 스케일링

Patient: Is scaling not good as it grinds off part of the tooth?

MTC(Doctor): Scaling is a treatment used to remove plaque[19] and calculus[20] stuck to teeth, and it does not cause any damage to your teeth.

When the calculus is removed, inflammation[21] of the gums[22] caused by the calculus, which shrinks the gums and exposes the roots of teeth.

This may cause teeth to hurt when drinking cold water, but you should recover from this effect within several days.

---

19) plaque: 치석
20) calculus: 결석, 치석
21) inflammation: 염증
22) gums: 잇몸

■ 〈Case〉 임플란트

Patient: Is an implant painful?

MTC(Doctor): In general, an implant is administered[23] under local anesthesia.

As it is carried out under anesthesia, Patients will experience absolutely no pain.

Pain may be experienced after coming out of the anesthetic, but this can be easily remedied[24] by taking an ordinary pain killer.

The pain is less than the pain experienced when pulling out a wisdom tooth[25].

■ 〈Case〉 임플란트 존속기간

Patient: How long does an implant last?

MTC(Doctor): Implanted teeth can last for as long as 10~30 years, or even longer, but the lifespan[26] of implanted teeth vary according to various conditions, such as the individual's overall health, and state of oral hygiene[27].

5.3.6 안과

■ 〈Case〉 라식수술

Patient: I am interested in Lasik surgery.

Ever since I was young, I've had bad eyesight, so I've always had to wear glasses.

I would like to have a consultation about sight adjustment surgery.

---

23) an implant is administered
    = an implant is places
24) remedy: 고치다, 치료하다
25) wisdom tooth: 사랑니
26) lifespan: 수명
27) hygiene: 위생
    public hygiene: 공중위생
    mental hygiene: 정신위생

MTC(Doctor): Is there any surgery that you are interested in?

Patient: I am interested in Lasik surgery.

MTC: Lasik is the most generalized laser sight adjustment surgery.

The recovery is fast and it is easy to get back to your daily life right after the surgery.

Patient: Doctor, then what about Lasek surgery?

MTC: It is suitable when the cornea is thin or your eyes are small.

It takes about 2~3 weeks to regain your full eyesight.

Patient: Are there any other treatments?

MTC: There is something called ICL where contact lenses are injected inside the eyes.

Patient: I see. In my case, what kind of operation would be best?

MTC: After a test, I will explain a suitable operation.

Patient: Thank you.

It was a pleasure to meet you.

■ 〈Case〉 라식수술

Patient: I have bad eyesight, but I do not want to wear glasses any more.

I would like to have a consultation about sight adjustment surgery.

MTC(Doctor): OK.

There are two options. Lasik and lasek.

Patient: Can you tell me the difference between Lasik and lasek?

MTC: Sure.

In case of Lasik, the laser cuts eye's surface and then lift the surface.

The laser reshapes the eye and the flap is replaced as a type of natural bandage for quicker healing.

Lasik is used when your corneas are too thin or too steep for Lasik.

In many ways, Lasik vision recovery is slower than Lasik recovery.

Patient: Can I go back to daily lives within a couple of days?

MTC: Yes.

Your eye may feel irritated during the first day or two afterward.

Lasik compared with Lasik, it often takes longer to recover good vision up to four to seven days.

You also may experience more pain with Lasik compared with Lasik.

■ 〈Case〉 라섹수술

Patient: Ever since I was young, I've had bad eyesight, so I've always had to wear glasses.

I would like to have a consultation about sight adjustment surgery.

MTC(Doctor): Ah, I see.

Is there any surgery that you are interested in?

Patient: I am interested in Lasik surgery.

MTC: Lasik is the most generalized laser sight adjustment surgery.

The recovery is fast and it is easy to get back to your daily life right after the surgery.

Patient: Doctor, then what about Lasek surgery?

MTC: It is suitable when the cornea[28] is thin or your eyes are small.

It takes about two or three weeks to regain your full eyesight.

Patient: Are there any other treatments?

MTC: There is something called ICL where contact lenses are injected inside the eyes.

Patient: I see. In my case, what kind of operation would be best?

MTC: After a test, I will explain a suitable operation.

Patient: Thank you.

It was a pleasure to meet you.

5.3.7 피부과

■ 〈Case〉 피부관리

Patient: I am interested in skin care program.

MTC(Nurse): ABC Hospital offers anti-aging[29] skin care program.

---

28) cornea: 각막
29) anti-aging: 노화방지

You can have the latest[30] laser skin care program.

The doctor will prescribe a laser program after he(she) assess[31] your skin condition.

Patient: Does it help improve the skin tone and texture[32]?

　MTC: Yes, it does.

■ 〈Case〉 머리카락 이식

Patient: When are hair transplants possible?

MTC(Doctor): Hair transplants are applicable to general baldness, deficiency of eyebrows and eyelashes[33], female atrichia[34], and scars.

■ 〈Case〉 머리이식 안정 정도

Patient: What is the hair settlement rate?

MTC(Doctor): The average rate of settlement is more than 90%.

However, the actual settlement rate may vary largely according to the surgical method used and the competency[35] of the surgeon.

So it is very important to receive the surgery from an experienced specialist.

■ 〈Case〉 여드름

Patient(Nurse): I came here because of my pimples[36].

So, I came for an acne[37] treatment.

　MTC: Since there are many kinds of acne treatment, it's important to choose the most suitable treatment for you.

---

30) latest: 최근의
31) assess: 평가하다
32) texture: 감촉
33) eyelash: 속눈썹
34) atrichia: 무모증
35) competency: 소관
　　competency of the surgeon: 의사의 능력
　　= skills of the surgeon
36) pimple: 여드름, 뾰루지
37) acne: 여드름

Patient: What kinds are there?

MTC: For acne, long-term treatment and maintenance are important and necessary.

Generally, you are to take antibiotics[38].

And for ointment[39] you can use antibiotic ointment and vitamin A ointment.

Also, there are surgical treatment and chemical peelings.

Patient: I see.

MTC: Please decide after consulting with the doctor.

Patient: OK. I understand.

Thank you.

■ 〈Case〉 여드름 치료

Patient: What is the general method to treat a pimple[40]?

MTC(Doctor): The most basic treatment is to take medication and to apply an ointment[41].

■ 〈Case〉 여드름 치료

Patient: What is the best pimple treatment?

MTC(Doctor): It takes a long time until the skin clears up when only taking medication while you are using an ointment.

However, chemical peeling produces quick results.

■ 〈Case〉 피부관리 후 일상생활 복귀

Patient: Can I return to my everyday activities immediately after the plastic surgery?

MTC(Doctor): You are advised to avoid strenuous[42] exercise or going to saunas even after the surgery.

---

38) antibiotics: 항생제
39) ointment: 연고
40) pimple: 여드름
41) ointment: 연고
42) strenuous: 격렬한
    make strenuous efforts: 분투하다, 힘껏 노력하다

■ 〈Case〉 머리이식 후 일상생활 복귀

Patient: Can I get back to my daily life after the hair transplant?

MTC(Doctor): The hair transplant procedure will not impact your ordinary daily activities, such as going to work or school.

■ 〈Case〉 보톡스 후 일상생활 복귀

Patient: Can I wash my face and wear makeup immediately after a botox injection?

MTC(Doctor): It is advised not to press down on the injection area for 3 to 4 hours after the botox injection.

Also, you are advised not to lie down for 3 to 4 hours.

You may continue your daily life activities, and you can even wash your face or wear makeup[43] 4 hours after the injection.

5.3.8 성형외과

■ 〈Case〉 가슴성형 가격

Patient: I am not satisfied with the size of my breast.

MTC(Doctor): Do you want to increase the size of your breast.

An implant will be placed under the breast tissue[44] or under the chest muscle beneath the breast.

Patient: What is silicon made of?

MTC: The silicon shell is filled with gel or salt water.

Patient: How much is breast enlargement surgery in ABC Clinic.

Is it possible to have breast surgery together with facial bone surgery at once?

MTC: You can get breast enlargement surgery and facial bone surgery together.

If you get two surgeries at once, we can give you discount up to 20%.

The cost of breast enlargement surgery is 6,500,000 Korean Won, equal to USD 5900.

---

43) makeup: 화장
   wear makeup: 화장하다
44) tissue: 조직

■ 〈Case〉 성형수술자국 제거

Patient: I had blepharoplasty[45] a year ago and I have scars on my upper eyelids.

Is it possible to do something about that?

MTC(Doctor): I can remove the scar, but I must inspect the size and depth of scar first.

■ 〈Case〉 보톡스

MTC(Nurse): Hello. This is the global healthcare center.

This is nurse Kim speaking.

Patient: I am interested in the plastic surgery.

MTC: Have you visited the homepage of ABC Hospital?

Patient: Yes, I have.

MTC: Then, you must know the general information about the hospital.

What do you want to know more specific about the hospital?

Patient: I want to know how much it cost to remove the wrinkles from my face.

MTC: The price range to remove lines is from USD 1,000 to USD 3,000.

It depends on how deep and how long the wrinkles are.

There are two options, botox or filler.

Patient: What is the difference between botox and filler?

MTC: Botox injections reduce[46] wrinkles by relaxing the facial muscles.

On average the effects of botox last for three months.

Botox is best to remove frown lines[47], crows' feet and forehead wrinkles.

---

45) blepharoplasty: 안검성형수술(눈꺼풀 처짐 수술)

Excess skin removed

— Stitches

46) reduce: 줄이다, 감소시키다, 축소하다, 낮추다

Dermal fillers are also treatment for crow's feet, smile lines as well as for fullness of the lips and cheeks.

Patient: Does it hurt much?

MTC: Botox injections do not cause much pain.

Patient: How long does it take?

MTC: It only takes approximately 30 minutes.

Including consultation with the doctor it will take up to 45 minutes to 60 minutes.

Patient: Are there any adverse effect[48]?

MTC: In case of botox, you may feel slight hardness to the treated area.

This will be reduced after approximately one week.

In case of filler treatment, there may be a little swelling[49], immediately after your dermal filler treatment

This is normal and you should not panic[50].

After a few days, the swelling will go down and you will see the final result.

Patient: What else?

MTC: Botox injection and dermal filler are something that involves skill so that it should be performed by well-trained practitioners.

---

47) frown lines = glabella frown lines

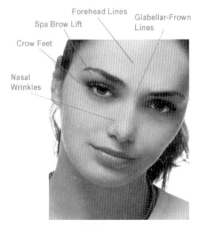

Forehead Lines
Spa Brow Lift
Glabellar-Frown Lines
Crow Feet
Nasal Wrinkles

48) adverse effect: 부작용 = adverse reaction
49) swelling: 부기
50) panic: 공황에 빠지다

Patient: I see, however, what if there is adverse effect[51]?

MTC: ABC Clinic has proper insurance cover.

The insurance cover will protect you in the case something does not go correctly.

Patient: I see. Thanks for your information.

What is the price?

MTC: Before I tell you the exact price, I need the front view and the side view of your face.

Please send your pictures to my e-mail address, then I will be able to tell you the price more precisely.

Patient: OK. Thank you.

What is your e-mail address.

MTC: Can you visit the homepage of the global healthcare Center of ABC Hospital.

At the bottom of the web site, you can find the e-mail address.

Patient: Please tell me by phone, I will write it down right now.

MTC: OK.

I will tell you each alphabet of my e-mail address.

Are you ready?

Patient: OK

MTC: fatherofsusie@hanmail.net[52]

Patient: F is for Fox?

MTC: Yes, it is.

■ 〈Case〉 눈 확대수술

Patient: I want my eyes to look bigger.

MTC(Doctor): Big eye operations include ptosis[53] surgery, medial epicanthoplasty[54],

---

51) adverse effect: 부작용
52) F for Fox, A for Alpha, T for Tango, H for Hotel, E for Echo, R for Romeo, O for Oscar, F for Fox, S for Sierra, U for Uniform, S for Sierra S, I for India, E for Echo at (@) hotmail.com
53) ptosis: 눈꺼풀 처짐
54) medial epicanthoplasty: 앞트임

lateral canthoplasty[55]).

Ptosis surgery can make your eyes look much bigger.

- 〈Case〉 쌍꺼풀수술

Patient: I came to have double eyelid[56] surgery.

  MTC(Doctor): Please close your eyes a bit.

           Now, open your eyes slowly.

           What about this much?

Patient: I think it is a little bit thin.

  MTC: Then, close your eyes again.

       Open your eyes again.

       What about this much?

Patient: I think this looks much natural.

  MTC: You seem to want your eyelid to look natural and not too thick, right?

Patient: Yes, when is it possible to have the surgery done(performed)?

  MTC: It will cost 2,000,000 Korean Won, equal to about USD 1820.

Patient: How long does the swelling[57] stay?

  MTC: In a week, the swelling goes down, so that you can go back to your daily life.

       But it takes about 6 months for the double eyelid to become natural.

Patient: How many times do I have to come to the hospital?

  MTC: On the day after the surgery, and then three days after that.

Patient: I see. Thank you for your consultation.

  MTC: You are welcome.

- 〈Case〉 주름제거

Frontal Wrinkle : 이마에 수평으로 생기는 주름(Worry Line)

Crow's Feet : 눈가에 부채살처럼 생기는 주름(Periorbital Lines)

Glabellar Wrinkle : 미간에 내 천자 주름

Perioral Wrinkle : 입술주변에 방사상으로 생기는 주름

---

55) latearl canthoplasty: 뒤트임
56) double-eyelid: 쌍꺼풀
57) swelling: 부기

Neck Wrinkle : 목주름

Patient: Hello.

MTC(Doctor): This is global healthcare center.

This is nurse Kim speaking.

How may I help you?

Patient: I would like to remove wrinkles from my face.

MTC: There are two options in order to remove your wrinkles from your face.

They are botox and filler.

In case of botox, it will cost USD 1,500.

In case of filler, it will cost USD 1,600.

Patient: Does the price include the airfare and the pickup service between the hospital and the airport.

MTC: No, it does not.

Patient: The price is reasonable.

I will undertake the botox treatment.

MTC: When can you visit Korea?

Patient: I think this coming Friday would be OK.

MTC: I will fit the schedule for you.

Patient: Thanks.

■ ⟨Case⟩ 주름제거

Patient: I have crow's feet[58]. I want to remove them.

MTC(Doctor): To get rid of the wrinkles around the eyes, botox is usually used.

---

58)

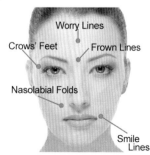

Patient: How long does the effect last?

MTC(Doctor): It may last for about six months.

Patient: Does it hurt?

MTC: You will have localized pain when you receive the injection.

Within a couple of days, you can go back to your daily life.

■ 〈Case〉 주름제거

MTC(Nurse): This is global healthcare center.

This is nurse Lee speaking.

How may I help you?

Patient: This is an international call from USA.

I'd like to make an appointment to see a skilled specialist in the plastic surgery.

A couple of days ago, I talked with you about the plastic surgery.

MTC: May I have your name, please?

Patient: Maria Hans.

MTC: Maria Hans.

I remember that you are interested in removing the wrinkles from the face.

I talked about your case with the plastic surgeon and the doctor recommended the filler surgery.

The doctor said that it takes only a couple of hours to remove the wrinkles from your face.

Patient: It is wonderful.

How much is the total cost for the cosmetic surgery?

■ 〈Case〉 주름제거

Patient: I have lots of freckles[59] and wrinkles so I hear I look much older than my real age.

---

59) freckle: 주근깨

MTC: Ultraviolet rays[60] are most harmful to freckles so cutting down your untraviolet A and B exposure is most important.

As an anti-aging treatment method, there are chemical peeling treatments as well as laser treatments.

Those anti-aging treatments accelerate the revival[61] of skin.

And to treat wrinkles, there are botox and collagen.

Patient: Then, what treatment would you recommend for me?

MTC: For freckles, laser treatment would be good.

For wrinkles, I would like to recommend botox.

Patient: Does it hurt?

MTC: During the treatment, it pricks a bit but it doesn't affect daily life.

Patient: How much does it cost?

■ 〈Case〉 이마수술

Patient: I have some questions about fat graft[62] to forehead[63].

What percentage of the fat is expected to survive? Will I need a second fat graft later?

MTC(Doctor): The percentage of fat to survive is 50 to 70%. It depends on your body.

Patient: Where is the scar on the face? Will there be swelling? How long is the recovery period?

Patient: The scar is on the scalp.

A 70 to 80% of swelling will be gone within 2 weeks.

The minimum recovery period is 1 week[64].

---

60) ultraviolet ray: 자외선
61) revival: 재생
62) fat grafts: 지방이식
   chin augmentation by fat graft: 턱 지방이식
   fat graft on eyelid: 눈꺼풀 지방이식
63) fat grafts to forehead: 이마 지방이식
64) = You need at least one week to recover.

■ 〈Case〉 눈썹수술

Patient: Is there a way to augment the brow bone[65], so that it protrudes[66] about 1 cm above the eye socket?[67]

Can this be done with fat injections?

MTC(Doctor): The methods of brow[68] augmentation are the fat graft[69] and the implant.

The brow can be augmented more by the implant.

I can do fat graft for augmentation of the brow about 0.5cm

■ 〈Case〉 웃을 때 보이는 잇몸 제거수술

Patient: Is two jaw surgery a solution for fixing gummy smile[70]?

My upper jaw showing gums and I feel very uncomfortable to smile. Is it possible to help with surgery?

Is it possible to make my smile smaller and no gum showing?

MTC(Doctor): Two jaw surgery or laser gum contouring[71] is a solution for gummy smile.

After two jaw surgery, you lips will be smaller and gums will be little shown.

Patient: Also my jaws are protruding. How much can you push it back?

I can push the chin more than 1.5 cms.

If your mouth is protruded[72], I can push the mouth in up to 7 to 8 mms.

---

65) brow bone: 눈썹 아래의 뼈
66) protrude: 튀어 나오다
67) eye socket: 눈구멍, 안와
68) brow: 눈썹
69) graft: 이식
    fat graft: 지방이식
70) gummy smile: 잇몸이 들어나는 미소

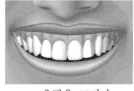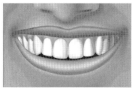

71) contour: 윤곽을 그리다
72) protrude: 돌출하다, 튀어나오다

■ 〈Case〉 광대뼈수술

Patient: I have wisdom teeth growing on both sides of my mouth on the bottom rows.

I am wondering if I can get zygoma[73] and mandible reduction with muscle reduction surgery?

I know mandible reduction and muscle reduction are done with an intraoral[74] incision[75].

MTC(Doctor): Wisdom tooth doesn't matter to get zygoma and mandible reduction surgery.

The location is different.

■ 〈Case〉 광대뼈수술

Patient: I wonder if the scars after zygoma reduction are very visible?

MTC(Doctor): The scar is barely[76] visible.

---

73) zygoma: 광대뼈

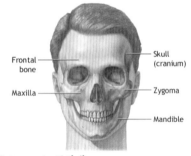

Frontal bone
Maxilla
Skull (cranium)
Zygoma
Mandible

74) intraoral: 구강내
75) incision: 절개
   intraoral incision: 구강내 절개

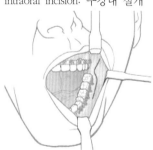

76) barely: 거의 -- 않다
   I barely heard any noise in the car.: 차안에서 거의 소리가 나지 않았다.

Although slight redness remains, but scars will be invisible.

Patient: I want to do zygoma reduction, but after 2 weeks I want to come back to work.

Will my scars be very visible after 2 weeks?

MTC: On 2 weeks after zygoma reduction, you can go back to work.

At that time, the scar is small and barely visible.

■ 〈Case〉 양악수술

Patient: How much can face become shorter after 2 jaw surgery?

What is the maximum of reduction? 2 or 4 cms?

My face is very long and I have protruding[77] mouth. Can two jaw surgery help?

MTC(Doctor): After two jaw surgery, face will be shorter.

But it depends on your face.

The maximum reduction maybe from 1 to 2 cms.

Protruding mouth[78] can be corrected with two jaw surgery.

---

77) protrude: 튀어 나오다
78) protruding mouth: 돌출 입

- 〈Case〉 턱수술

  Patient: Does mandible[79] reduction have to be done under general anesthesia[80]?

  What kind of pain medication do you give afterwards?

  MTC(Doctor): Mandible reduction surgery is done under general anesthesia.

  The pain killer[81] is usually used to reduce pains.

- 〈Case〉 턱성형

  Patient: I have a strong jaw with muscle[82].

  What is the procedure for this surgery?

  Does mandible reduction includes masseter[83] muscle reduction?

  MTC(Doctor): The purpose of mandible reduction surgery is to reduce the angle of mandible bone.

  Masseter muscle reduction surgery is not included within mandible reduction surgery.

---

79) mandible: 하악골, 턱뼈
   mandible reduction: 턱 축소

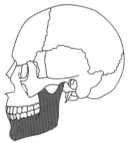

80) general anesthesia: 전신마취
   local anesthesia: 국소마취
81) pain killer: 진통제
82) muscle: 근육
83) masseter: 교근

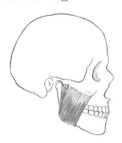

The cost of mandible reduction surgery is 5,000,000 Korean Won and masseter muscle reduction is 1,500,000 Korean Won.

■ 〈Case〉 턱성형

Patient: How much can you shorten the long face?

What is the surgery for reducing face length?

MTC(Doctor): For long face, two jaw surgery and chin reduction surgery are helpful.

I can reduce 2 cms or more, but it depends on your facial bone structure.

■ 〈Case〉 짧은 턱성형

Patient: I have a short chin.

What is the maximum mm two jaw surgery can increase the length of chin?

How many mm can I lengthen my chin if I use the bones cut from mandible?

MTC(Doctor): If you want to lengthen your chin more than 12 mms, you need two jaw surgery.

The maximum length depends on your facial bone.

Patient: May I know the cost of two jaw surgery?

How much is the surgery for mandible bone for chin?

MTC: If you get two jaw surgery, there is no extra charge for the surgery to lengthen the chin.

Patient: What is the suture[84] material for fixation?

MTC: I use a titanium plate and screw for two jaw surgery.

■ 〈Case〉 턱성형

Patient: I have a small and short chin and I want a V-line shape, but I think I don't need V-line surgery, but I just need chin augmentation.

Does the chin implant have the V shape or I can choose the shape I want?

MTC(Doctor): There are many kinds of chin implants.

---

84) suture: 봉합

> If you want v-shape chin and augmentation, we can make your chin look longer.

■ 〈Case〉 코성형

Patient: I came to consult with you about my nose.

MTC(Doctor): What part of your nose don't you like?

Patient: My nose bridge is extremely flat.

I would like to heighten[85] my nose.

MTC: Pleaser turn your face to the left side.

Your nose is a little bit low.

Patient: Also, I think it is a little bit wide.

MTC: If you heightened your nose, it would make your nose a bit narrower.

■ 〈Case〉 코성형

Patient: I think that my nose is a bit bent?

MTC(Doctor): Does your nose become clogged[86] easily?

Patient: No, it doesn't get clogged too easily.

MTC: Let me take a look inside your nose.

There can be a little unpleasant feeling.

The middle part of your nose is not bent. Have you had an accident where you injured it?

Patient: No, I haven't.

MTC: Your nose could bend as you grow older.

In your case, the degree of bending is insignificant so I think it would be good to have a surgery that would heighten the nasal bridge and nasal tip.

Patient: How much would that cost?

---

85) heighten: 높게 하다
86) clog: 막히다

5.3.9 외과

- 〈Case〉 담석 제거수술

MTC(Doctor): The gallstones[87] can be broken up with the ultrasonic shock wave. About 3,000 to 4,000 shock waves are fired in 30 minutes.

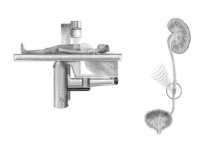

The ultrasonic shock wave will break gallstones into small pieces. You are then able to pass these stones through urine.

Patient: I am glad to hear that.

MTC: Please lie face up on the table.

The ultrasound device will be placed directly over your gallbladder.

- 〈Case〉 목디스크 수술

Patient: I am experiencing neck pain that has lasted for longer than a week.

I would like to make an appointment with a doctor.

MTC(Nurse): May I have your name?

Patient: My name is Susie Hans.

Is it possible to see the doctor tomorrow afternoon?

MTC: 2:30 pm is available.

Would that be OK with you?

Patient: Yes, 2:30 is OK with me.

(다음 날 오후)

MTC: Good afternoon. How may I help you?

Patient: I made a reservation at 2:30 pm.

MTC: What has brought here?

Patient: I feel pain in the neck.

MTC: Just a second, please.

---

87) gallstone: 담석

(잠시 후)

MTC: Please come in.

Please be seated.

(앉은 후)

MTC(Doctor): What is your problem today?

Patient: I have a severe pain in the neck.

MTC: Do you feel pain in the arm or numbness[88] in the fingertips[89].

Patient: Yes, I do.

MTC: You need neck X-ray.

(X-ray 촬영 후)

MTC: You have a herniated disc in the neck.

■ 〈Case〉 척추수술

MTC(Doctor): Do you have a persistent[90] leg pain?

Patient: Yes, I do.

You need to take a MRI scan.

(MRI Scan 검사 후)

MTC: I am afraid that you have a herniated disk.

The herniated disc presses on a nerve root.

The surgery will be performed under general anesthesia[91].

Patient: How long will it take to finish the surgery?

MTC: It will take about one hour, depending on the extent of the herniated disc

In order to remove the fragment of herniated disc, I will make an incision[92]

over the center of your back.

The incision is usually about 3 centimeters in length.

---

88) numbness: 무감각, 마비
89) fingertip: 손가락 끝
90) persistent: 지속하는
91) general anesthesia: 전신마취
   local anesthesia: 부분마취
92) incision: 절개

5.3.10 한의학

■ 〈Case〉 침

Patient: I came because my waist hurts.

MTC: Your waist hurts.

Then come inside the consultation room.

MTC: Since when did your waist start to hurt?

Patient: It started a month ago.

I think I sprained my waist when I was lifting a heavy flower pot.

MTC: Which part hurts the most?

Patient: Under the waist, especially my right side.

MTC: In what position does it hurt especially?

Patient: It hurts the most when I stand up from a chair.

MTC: Then I suggest acupuncture.

It takes about an hour.

After the acupuncture, don't do any hard work or heavy lifting for about half a day.

Taking a shower is okay but refrain from taking a bath.

I will guide you to the acupuncture room.

Please change into this gown.

(병원 가운으로 갈아입은 후)

Patient: How many times do I have to receive acupuncture?

MTC: It is good to get the acupuncture treatment at least 3 times a week.

Since the effect of acupuncture differs according to each person, we decide the treatment period after 2 to 3 shots through individual consulting. Also, taking an herbal medicine along with the treatment accelerates the effect.

Patient: I see. What do I do about the herbal medicine?

MTC: First, we diagnose the physical condition and make the herbal medicine[93] that suits your symptoms.

---

93) herbal medicine: 한약

Patient: I fully understand.

Thank you.

■ 〈Case〉 침

MTC: Since when did your waist start to hurt?

Patient: It started a month ago.

MTC: Did you hurt your waist?

Patient: I think I sprained my waist when I was lifting a heavy flower pot.

MTC: Which part hurts the most?

Patient: Under the waist, especially my right side.

MTC: In what position does it hurt especially?

Patient: It hurts the most when I stand up from a chair.

MTC: Then I suggest acupuncture[94].

It takes about an hour.

After the acupuncture, don't do any hard work or heavy lifting for about half a day.

Taking a shower is okay but refrain from taking a bath.

I will guide you to the acupuncture room.

Please change into this gown.

Patient: How many times do I have to receive acupuncture?

MTC: It is good to get the acupuncture treatment at least 3 times a week.

Since the effect of acupuncture differs according to each person, we decide the treatment period after 2~3 shots through individual consulting.

Also, taking an herbal medicine along with the treatment accelerates the effect.

Patient: I see. What do I do about the herbal medicine?

MTC: First, we diagnose the physical condition and make the herbal medicine that suits your symptoms.

94) acupuncture: 침

Patient: I fully understand.

Thank you.

■ 〈Case〉 한약복용

Patient: Maybe you should try some traditional Chinese medicine(Oriental medicine).

MTC(Doctor): Actually, it might not make a difference with this cold, but it can make your whole body stronger so you won't catch so many colds.

Patient: What's so special about traditional Chinese medicine?

MTC: One special point is that it's all natural.

Chinese medicine is made from plants, not chemicals, which means there are few side-effects.

Patient: That's a big advantage.

Some people can't stand the thought of taking medicine because of all the chemicals.

MTC: Another advantage is that Chinese medicine works slowly, so it keeps your body healthy in the long run.

Patient: That sounds like just what I need!

But, how does traditional Chinese medicine work?

MTC: Basically, it helps balance two opposing forces in your body.

In Chinese, we call these forces "Yin", which is cold, dark and quiet, and "Yang", which is hot, bright and active.

If you have either too much "Yin" or too much "Yang", your body is out of balance, and you are more likely to get sick.

The purpose of traditional Chinese medicine is to put "Yin" and "Yang" back in balance.

Patient: I see. So how can I get my hands on some Chinese medicine.

MTC: First, you should be examined by a traditional doctor.

Patient: I'm a bit afraid.

Will he give me any shots or anything like that?

MTC: Don't be afraid.

I will just feel your pulse and check the color of your tongue.

It's very simple and painless!

Patient: I came because my waist hurts.

MTC(Doctor): Your waist hurts.

Then come inside the consultation room.

■ 〈Case〉 한약복용

Patient: Is Oriental medicine fattening?

MTC(Doctor): Fattening is a result of individual diet and exercise habits, not because of Oriental medicine.

Oriental medicine strengthens stomach functions, enhances the appetite and improves digestion, which leads to weight gain.

However, it is not true that all Oriental medicines make people gain weight. On the contrary, since Oriental medicine is often effective in treating pathological[95] obesity[96].

5.4 진단 및 처방

5.4.1 의사의 조언

Please eat balanced meals.

Please don't push yourself too hard.

Please avoid hard exercise.

Please stay in bed and rest at home.

Please don't take a bath or shower for three days.

Please come back for a check-up a week from now.

---

95) pathological: 병치료의
96) obesity: 비만

You'll get the results of the examination four days from now.

Please go to the pharmacy and receive your medicine before you go home.

I need to renew my prescription[97].

■ 〈Case〉 검사결과

MTC(Doctor): I'll check your temperature through your ear.

(체온검사 후)

　　MTC: Your temperature is 99.6 degrees Fahrenheit(37.5 degree Celsius).

　　　　　I am going to check your purse and blood pressure.

Patient: Thank you.

(맥박검사 후)

　　MTC: Your purse rate is 88 beats per minute.

　　　　　And your blood pressure is 140 over 90.

　　　　　You have the symptoms of high blood pressure.

Patient: Really?

　　　　　What shall I do?

■ 〈Case〉 검사결과

Patient: I couldn't bear the pain so I had to meet you immediately,

MTC(Doctor): Tell me how you feel. Where does it hurt?

Patient: Doctor, I have this terrible pain on my left side and my back.

　　　　　My mouth is dry and I fed nauseous[98], I throw up whatever I eat.

MTC(Doctor): Let me check your temperature.

(환자 체온 검사)

MTC(Doctor): Your temperature is normal. Have you been drinking?

Patient: Yes doctor. A little more than usual.

MTC(Doctor): Let me check your heartbeat.

(환자의 심장 검사)

Please lie down and I am going to checks your stomach.

---

97) prescription: 처방
98) nauseous: 구역질 나는, 속이 메스꺼운

(환자의 복부 검사)

MTC(Doctor): Your liver is slightly enlarged[99].

Let me see your eyes.

(환자의 눈 검사)

MTC(Doctor): Yes, your eyes too are discolored and slightly yellow.

You are heading for a liver disease problem.

It could be infectious hepatitis[100], through a virus or a starting process of damage through excessive and destructive food habits.

We willgo in for all the required tests and start treatment. But as for now, the nurse in the next room will give you an injection to reduce your pain and I will prescribe some medicine for relief.

(처방전 작성)

MTC(Doctor): Keep off spicy food and drinking for now. Avoid oil. You have to go slow on these if you need to be fit. Meet me again after two days. I advise full rest till then.

Patient: Thank you, Doctor.

■ 〈Case〉 검사결과

MTC(Doctor): Your medical examination turned out that you have a high blood pressure.

Is there anyone else in your family who has high blood pressure or heart diseases?

Patient: My grandfather died of heart attack the year before last.

MTC: Do you exercise regularly?

5.4.2 질병에 대한 질문

What is my diagnosis?

What caused my condition?

Can my condition be treated?

---

99) enlarge: 확대하다
100) hepatitis: 감염

How will this condition affect my vision now and in the future?

Should I watch for any particular symptoms and notify you if they occur?

Should I make any lifestyle changes?

5.4.3 필요한 조사에 대한 문의

What is the treatment for my condition?

When will the treatment start, and how long will it last?

What are the benefits of this treatment, and how successful is it?

What are the risks and side effects associated with this treatment?

Are there foods, drugs, or activities I should avoid while I'm on this treatment?

If my treatment includes taking a medication, what should I do if I miss a dose?

Are other treatments available?

What kind of tests will I have?

What do you expect to find out from these tests?

When will I know the results?

Do I have to do anything special to prepare for any of the tests?

Do these tests have any side effects or risks?

Will I need more tests later?

■ 〈Case〉 검사결과

MTC(Doctor): Please roll up your left arm sleeve and make your fist tight[101].

It will hurt little, but it will be done in one second.

Patient: I see.

MTC: Go to the third floor to get an urine test.

After the urine test you can go home.

You'll find out the results back in a week.

Patient: Thank you.

---

101) make your fist tight

= make a tight fist: 주먹을 꽉 쥐다

■ 〈Case〉 처방

MTC(Doctor): Apply the cream sparingly to your face and neck.

　　　　　　And take a medicine for a week.

　　　　　　After one week please come again.

Patient: How can I take the medicines?

　MTC: Take a pouch of medicine thirty minutes after meals.

Patient: When do I take the medicine?

　MTC: Take this medicine every eight hours.

Patient: Every eight hours?

　MTC: Three times a day, thirty minutes after each meal.

　　　　Take one does before you go to bed.

Patient: Anything else?

　MTC: During taking medicines, you should stay away from irritating foods, alcohol and smoking.

Patient: OK, I will.

■ 〈Case〉 전원

MTC(Doctor): You need to be transformed to a tertiary medical care center.

　　　　　　I will get the referral slip.

　　　　　　The nurse will get a copy of the results of the tests you have undergone.

5.4.4 약 복용

■ 약 형태의 종류

가루약 : Powder medicine

고약(연고) : Ointment

알약 : Pill

물약 : Liquid medicine

좌약 : Suppository

한약 : Chinese Medicine

■ 약 효과의 종류

항생제 : Antibiotic

해독제 : Antidote

진통제 : Analgesics, Painkiller

지혈제 : Styptic, Hemostatic

진정제 : Tranquilizer, Sedative

제산제 : Antacid

발한제 : Sudorific, Diaphoretic

마취제 : Anesthetic

Are you taking any medicine regularly?

Are you taking any medications?

Are you taking any other medication?

I am taking a medicine for thyroid[102].

I am taking aspirin.

■ 복용량

These are medicines for seven days.

There are two kinds of capsules and tablets to take.

If you feel pain, please take one of these red tablets.

If you feel itchy, please take two of these tablets.

If you feel pressure in the chest, please take one of these tablets.

If it is hard to sleep, please take one of these tablets.

If your temperature is over 38 degree celsius(100.4 degree Fahrenheit), please take one of these tablets.

This is enough medicine for one month.

■ 약 보관

Please keep the medicine in a refrigerator.

Please store the medicine in a refrigerator.

Do not store the medicine in the freezer.

---

102) thyroid: 갑상선

Please store in a cool place, away from moisture.

Keep the medicine at room temperature.

These medicine should be taken within one month.

You must keep our of reach of children.

■ 복용방법

Please dissolve the medicine with hot water and drink.

Take the medicine with a glass of water.

Put the medicine in the mouth to dissolve[103] slowly, and do not chew.

Put the medicine under the tongue to dissolve slowly, and do not chew.

Dissolve the medicine in water before use.

Shake the bottle well before use.

This is an undiluted[104] solution[105]. Please mix the medicine with water before you take it.

This is suppository[106]. Please insert it anally. The color of your stools will change but don't worry.

■ 복용시기

Please take three times a day after meals.

Please take three times a day before meals.

Please take two tablets after every dinner.

Please take three tablets after breakfast and after dinner.

Take the medicine in the morning and in the evening.

Please take two tablets before you go to bed.

Please take two tablets every 8 hours.

Take the medicine after each meal.

Take the medicine between each meal.

---

103) dissolve: 용해하다
104) undiluted: 물을 타지 않은, 희석하지 않은
105) solution: 용액
106) suppository: 좌약

■ 연고

Apply this ointment where you feel pain.

Apply this ointment when it feels itchy.

Apply this ointment to your knee.

Apply the ointment to the wound.

Apply the salve[107] to the wound.

Apply the ointment and put a bandage around it.

■ 주의사항

Please read the directions well.

As it might affect your stomach, please take a stomach medicine.

After you take the medicine, the color of your urine will change but don't worry.

Please avoid driving and dangerous work because this medicine will make you sleepy.

Please do not drive nor operate machinery because these medicines may cause drowsiness[108].

Please avoid drinking because the medicine may have strong effects when taken with alcohol.

Please continue to use this medicine until all prescribed doses completed, even if the symptoms disappear.

Please do not breast-feed while you are taking this medicine because the medicines are discharged[109] in breast milk.

You must consult your doctor or pharmacist immediately when there is a possibility of pregnancy.

Stop taking these medicines and consult your doctor or pharmacist if you have the following symptoms, or if you feel something is wrong while taking them.

• Stomachache

• anemia[110]

• inability to make muscle movement

---

107) salve: 연고
108) drowsiness: 기면 상태, 졸음
109) discharge: 나오게 하다, 빼다
110) anemia: 빈혈

- Urticaria[111]

- Headache

- Nausea[112]

- Abdominal pain

- Rash

- Hot flush[113]

- Dizziness

■ 약 효과

The medicine will ease pain.

The medicine will calm disconcertedness[114] and excitement.

The medicine will reduce inflammation[115].

The medicine will stop itching.

The medicine dilates blood vessels[116] and make blood flow more smoothly.

The medicine will lower blood pressure.

The medicine will stop diarrhea[117].

The medicine will promote digestion.

The medicine will stop coughing

The medicine will reduce phlegm[118].

The medicine will bring fever down.

The medicine will promote bowel movements[119].

The medicine will alleviate nausea[120].

This is stomach medicine.

This medicine for colds.

---

111) urticaria: 두드러기
112) nausea: 구역질, 뱃멀미, 욕지기
113) hot flush: 안면 홍조증
114) disconcertedness: 불안
115) inflammation: 염증
116) blood vessel: 혈관
117) diarrhea: 설사
118) phlegm: 가래
119) bowel movement: 배변
120) nausea: 구역질, 뱃멀미

This is an antibiotic.

This is an antirheumatic[121].

This medicine is for hermorrhoids[122].

This medicine is for athlete's foot[123].

This medicine is for asthma[124].

This medicine is for gout[125].

This medicine is for diabetes[126].

■ 〈Case〉 약 복용방법

Patient: Hi, I am here to pick up a prescription.

MTC(Pharmacist): What is your last name?

Patient: Susie.

Pharmacist: One moments.

　　　　Here it is.

　　　　Do you know how to use it?

Patient: I do not know.

Pharmacist: Take two pills, three pills a day.

　　　　Take the medicine after meals and wash it down with water.

Patient: When should I begin?

Pharmacist: You should start as soon as get home.

　　　　Make sure you don't drive while taking this and don't mix it with alcohol.

■ 〈Case〉 약 복용방법

MTC(Doctor): I don't think it's anything serious.

　　　　I'm going to give you a prescription for some antibiotics[127].

Patient: Thanks, doctor.

---

121) antirheumatic: 항류마티즘약
122) hermorrhoid: 치질, 치핵
123) athlete's foot: 무좀
124) asthma: 천식
125) gout: 통풍
126) diabetes: 당뇨병
127) antibiotic: 항생제

MTC: They're not very expensive, but you need to make sure that you take them all and follow the instructions carefully.

Even if you start to feel better, you have to finish the whole bottle.

Patient: I understand.

Where can I pick it up?

MTC: If there's pharmacy, that's convenient for you.

I'll have the nurse call it in.

Patient: There's a drug store near my house that I usually use.

MTC: You're also going to need a booster shot[128].

We can give that to you right down the hall.

It should help reduce the swelling.

Patient: I hate needles.

Is it a big one.

MTC: Don't worry.

■ 〈Case〉 약 수령 소요시간

Patient: How long does it take to fill the prescription?

MTC(Pharmacist): About 10 minutes.

Patient: I am running late. Is there any way you can speed it up?

MTC: There are four orders ahead of yours.

Patient: I understand.

■ 〈Case〉 약국 위치 및 처방전 제출방법 설명

MTC(Doctor): We will issue you a prescription for a pharmacy out of the hospital.

Please go to the pharmacy and receive your medicine before you go home.

Patient: I see.

MTC: Please submit this prescription to the pharmacy.

---

128) booster shot: 효능 촉진제, 경기 부양책

■ 〈Case〉약 효과

Patient: Good morning. Do you have a medicine for indigestion[129]?

MTC(Pharmacist): Yes, I recommend these tablets. But if it gets any worse, you should see your doctor.

Patient: Thanks a lot.

■ 〈Case〉주사처방 및 처방전 발급

MTC(Doctor): The treatment is finished.

Patient: Thank you.

MTC: Come to the injection room[130].

It is a shot on the hip

(주사 후)

Up your hip, please.

It is done.

Patient: Thank you.

MTC: Please take the prescription[131] with you.

Patient: Thank you.

MTC: Please come back in three days.

Go to the pharmacy on the first floor and present this prescription to the pharmacist.

Patient: Could you please fill[132] this prescription?

MTC(Pharmacist): Sure, I'll be right back.

Take two of these white pills within 30 minutes after each meal.

Patient: Will this medicine make me sleepy[133]?

MTC: Yes, please do not drive a car after you take these medicines.

---

129) indigestion: 소화불량
130) injection room: 주사실
131) prescription: 처방전
132) fill a prescription: 처방약을 받다
   How long does it take to fill the prescription: 처방전의 약을 받으려면 얼마나 걸릴까요?
133) Will this medicine make me sleepy?
   = Will this medicine make me drowsy?
   drowsy: 졸리는

■ ⟨Case⟩ 약 추가

Patient: I am out of pills.

MTC(Nurse): What do you take the pills for?

Patient: I take them for high blood pressure.

MTC: Who is your primary doctor?

Patient: Doctor Lee.

■ ⟨Case⟩ 약 부작용

Patient: I took the pills that the doctor prescribed for me and I feel sick.

MTC(Doctor): What do you mean by sick?

Could you give me your symptoms in detail?

Patient: I feel dizzy, weak and tired all the time.

MTC: These are all side effects of the medication that you are taking.

Chapter **6**

의료기관에서 빈번하게
사용되는 의료용어 약어

6.1 의료용어 약어

의료관광코디네이터는 의료인과 환자 사이에서 커뮤니케이션
다리 역할을 한다. 따라서 의료기관에서 사용하는 약어를 이해할
필요가 있다.

hospital

a.c: Before meals(식전)

p.c: After meals(식후)

Tx: Treatment(치료)

Sx: Symptom(증상)

MD: Mid day(정오)

MN: Mid night(자정)

bid: Twice a day(하루에 두 번)

tid: Three times a day(하루에 세 번)

qid: Four times a day(하루에 네 번)

q.d: Every day(매일)

q.h: Every hour(매 시간)

Bin: Twice a night(하룻밤에 두 번)

Prn: 필요할 때마다(Whenever Necessary)

SOW: 물을 조금씩 마심(Sips of Water)

P/E: 신체검진(Physical Examination)

Stat: Immediately(즉시)

h.s: at bed time(취침시간시)

p.o: By mouth(경구로)

c: with(함께)

Med: Medication(투약)

Inj: Injection(주사)

Cx: Complication(합병증)

Cc: Chief Complaint(주호소)

Admi: Admission(입원)

D/C: Discharge(퇴원)

I&O: Intake and Output(섭취량과 배설량)

Lab: Laboratory(실험실)

OP: Operation(수술)

Fx: Fracture(골절)

Relaxation: 이완

Tepid Message: 온수마사지

N/V: Nausea/Vomiting(오심, 구토)

ABR: Absolute Bed Rest(절대안정)

NPO: Nothing by Mouth, Nothing Pre Oral, Nulla Per Os, Nil Per Os(금식)

D.O.A: Dead on Arrival(도착시 사망)

LUQ: Left Upper Quadrant(좌측상부 1/4)

LLQ: Left Lower Quadrant(좌측하부 1/4)

RUQ: Left Upper Quadrant(우측상부 1/4)

RLQ: Left Lower Quadrant(좌측하부 1/4)

s.s enema: Soap Solution Enema (비눗물 관장)

BE enema: Barium Enema(바륨관장)

CPR: Cardio Pulmonary Resuscitation (심폐소생술)

ROM: Range of Motion(운동범위)

Foley Catheterization: 인공배뇨

Grav: Gravida(임신)

Pora: Parere(출산)

Metastasis: 전이

Needle: 바늘

Syringe: 주사기

Ointment: 연고

Pt: Patient(환자)

I&D: Incision and Drainage(절개와 배액)

Dx: Diagnosis(진단)

Transfer: 전실, 전원

Stool: 변

Urine: 소변

Castor Oil: 윤활제

Irrigation: 세척

Soft Diet: 죽

Regular Diet: 일반식이

Specimen: 검사물

Sputum: 객담

Steam Inhalation: 증기흡입

Deep Breathing: 심호흡

Secretion: 분비물

Defecation: 배변

Dehydration: 탈수

Decubitus: 욕창

Asepsis: 무균

bleeding: 출혈

Edema: 부종

Tourniquet: 지혈대

Vein: 정맥

Faint: 기절

Vision Disturbance: 시각장애

Abortion: 유산

Nausea: 오심(메스꺼움)

Infection: 감염

Suction: 흡인

Aspiration: 흡입

Contamination: 오염

Injury: 손상

Isolation: 격리

Pillow: 베개

Enema: 관장

Immunity: 면역

Conscious: 의식

Remove: 제거하다

Connect: 연결하다

Dressing: 소독

O.P.O: 외래진료

BR: 안정(Bed Rest)

ABR: 절대안정(Absolute Bed Rest)

Suture: 봉합

Sprint: 부목

Dextrose in Water: 포도당

Hepatitis B Virus: B형 바이러스

Hypertension: 고혈압

Hypotension: 저혈압

RBC: 적혈구(Red Blood Cell)

6.2 진료 및 인체 설명용어

6.2.1 수술의 종류

미용성형외과 : Cosmetic Surgery

지방흡입술 : Abdominal etching

복부성형술 : Abdominoplasty, Tummy Tuck

쌍꺼풀수술 : Asian Blepharoplasty, eyelid surgery

가슴성형술 : Mammoplasty

유방축소술 : Breast Reduction

유방하수교정술 : Breast Lift

화학적 박피술 : Chemical Peel

레이저 박피술 : Laser Skin Resurfacing

코수술 : Phinoplasty, Nose Job

안면거상술 : Phytidectomy, Face Lift

지방흡입술 : Suction-Assisted Lipectomy, Liposuction

턱 축소, 턱 확대수술 : Chin Reduction, Chin Augmentation

광대뼈 축소, 확대수술 : Cheek Reduction, Cheek Augmentation

콜라겐이나 보톡스 등의 필러 주사 : Filler Injection

6.2.2 신체 이름

■ 호흡기계

nasal cavity : 비강   epiglottis : 후두개

soft pharynx : 연구개   glottis : 성문

base of tongue : 혀의 기저부   trachea : 기관

hyoid : 설골   esophagus : 식도

■ 눈 EYE

pupil : 동공   lens : 수정체

iris : 홍채   conjunctive : 결막

cornea : 각막

■ 중추신경계

cerebrum : 대뇌   skull : 두개골

cerebellum : 소뇌   frontal : 전두부

medulla : 연수   parietal : 두정부

spinal cold : 척수   temporal : 측두부

두부 및 경부 head and neck   occipital : 후두부

■ 흉부 및 배부 CHEST AND BACK

lung : 폐   pericardium : 심막

heart : 심장   trachea : 기관

pleura : 늑막   bronchus : 기관지

rib : 늑골

■ 복부 및 배부 ABDOMINAL AND BACK

esophagus : 식도   stomach : 위

small intestine : 소장

duodenum : 십이지장

jejunum : 소장

ileum : 직장

large intestine : 대장

cecum : 맹장

appendix : 충수돌기

colon : 대장

rectum : 직장

liver : 간

spleen : 비장

pancreas : 췌장

gall bladder 담낭(쓸개)

kidney : 신장

■ 척추 SPINE

cervical spine : 경추

thoracic spine : 흉추

lumbar spine : 요추

sacrum : 천골

■ 골 BONE

clavicle : 쇄골,

humerus : 상완골, 상박골

radius : 요골

ulnar : 척골

femur : 대퇴골

tibia : 경골

fibular : 비골

6.2.3 질병 이름

tonsillitis : 편도선염

carditis : 신염

pancreatitis : 췌장염

brain abscess : 뇌농양

lung abscess : 폐농양

liver abscess : 간농양

benign tumor : 양성종양

malignant tumor = cancer : 악성종양

stomach cancer : 위암

lung cancer: 폐암

colon cancer : 대장암

hepatic cancer : 간암

gastric ulcer : 위궤양

duodenal ulcer : 십이장 궤양

Chapter 7

퇴원

7.1 퇴원

의료관광객이 퇴원하기 위해서 의사가 발급한 퇴원 확인서가 필요하다.

■ 〈Case〉 퇴원

If you have a normal delivery[1], you will be able to be discharged from the hospital the very next day.

You can leave the hospital shortly after the surgery.

You will be able to leave the hospital the next day as long as your pain is under control and you are able to eat.

You will be discharged from the clinic with prescription[2] for postoperative[3] recovery medications such as antibiotics[4] and pain medicine.

You will be discharged from the clinic the morning after the operation.

■ 〈Case〉 퇴원 시기

MTC(Doctor): It looks like you are ready to go home.

Patient: I am happy to hear that.

1) delivery: 분만
2) prescription: 처방전
3) postoperative: 수술 후의
4) antibiotic: 항생제

MTC(Doctor): I think you will be able to be discharged from the hospital on Monday.

The nurse will call you one or three days after your discharge to see how you are feeling.

■ 퇴원 연기

I'd like to keep you here over night.

You have to stay at the hospital another 24 hours.

You will be able to leave the hospital after a few days.

■ 〈Case〉 퇴원

MTC(Nurse): You've been much better than when you were first in the hospital.

Patient: Really?

I appreciate.

MTC: You can be discharged from the hospital tomorrow.

Patient: How do I get to the discharging procedure?

MTC: Go down to the registration desk for foreigners on the first floor.

Patient: What should I do first?

MTC: To be discharged from the hospital, you pay for your medical charge.

Fill out the discharging form and sign in it.

That's all you need to do.

Patient: Is that all?

MTC: Don't forget to take your medicines in time after leaving the hospital.

You should come back to the clinic every Wednesday to see how you are feeling for one month.

Patient: Thanks.

■ 〈Case〉 퇴원

MTC(Doctor): Tomorrow you will be discharged[5].

The check out time is two o'clock in the afternoon.

---

5) discharge: 퇴원하다.

I will tell the staff to prepare the receipt of the bill.

(퇴원절차 종료 후)

MTC: Now, it is time to leave the hospital.

In front of the hospital, a mini-bus is waiting for you.

The bus will start to the airport.

The flight schedule is five o'clock.

Patient: I see.

MTC: Here is the receipt of the bill.

Patient: Thank you.

■ 〈Case〉 퇴원

MTC(Doctor): You've been much better than when you were first in the hospital.

Patient: Really?

I appreciate.

MTC: You can be discharged from the hospital tomorrow.

Patient: What should I do first?

MTC: To be discharged from the hospital, you pay for your medical charge.

Fill out the discharging form and sign in it.

That's all you need to do.

Patient: Is that all?

MTC: Don't forget to take your medicines on time after you leave the hospital.

You should come back to the clinic next Wednesday to see how you are feeling for a week.

Patient: Thanks.

7.2 설문서 배포

의료관광객이 외국인환자 유치의료기관에 입원해서 의료서비스를 받은 경우는 병원을 떠나기 전에, 의료서비스를 받고 관광을 나중에 한 경우는 호텔을 체크아웃하기 전에, 무작위로 선택된 의료관광객에게 한국 의료관광에서 느낌과 불편했던 점에 관한 설문서를 배포하고 수거한다.

수거된 설문서는 Excel, SPSS, Minitab을 이용해서 빈도분석, 교차분석, 독립된 두 집단의 t검정, 분산분석, 회귀분석을 실시해서 의료관광객의 서비스 만족도를 과학적으로 분석할 수 있다.

구체적인 분석 방법은 백산출판사에서 발간한 Excel활용 마케팅통계조사분석(보건·의료관광·관광경영 사례 중심) 또는 SPSS활용 통계조사분석(보건·의료관광·관광경영 사례 중심)을 참고한다.

Please fill out this questionnaire.

Please fill out this customer satisfaction survey.

Please complete and return the survey before you leave the room.

■ 〈Case〉 설문서 배포

MTC(Staff): Would you please fill out the questionnaire concerning the evaluation[6] of the medical tour in Korea.

Patient: That's O.K.

MTC: When you write it, please make the sentences simple and persuasive[7].

Patient: Simple and persuasive.

MTC: That's right.

Patient: I'll do my best.(utmost)

MTC: Please submit the questionnaire to us until tomorrow afternoon.

(작성 후)

Patient: Here is the questionnaire you wanted me to write yesterday in the morning.

MTC: Thank you very much.

Patient: You are welcome.

---

6) evaluation: 평가
7) persuasive: 설득력이 있는

- 〈Case〉 설문서 배포

MTC(Staff): I would like to ask you to fill out this customer satisfaction survey. (설문서를 주면서)

Patient: OK.

MTC: We need your suggestions and feedback to improve the customer service.

7.3 기념사진 촬영

- 〈Case〉 기념사진 촬영

MTC(Staff): Do you mind if we take a picture for memory's sake?

Patient: No. It is my pleasure.

- 〈Case〉 기념사진 촬영

MTC(Staff): Will you take a picture with us for memory's sake?

Patient: It is great.

Can I have one copy of the pictures before I leave Korea?

MTC: Sure.

- 〈Case〉 기념사진 촬영

MTC(Staff): All the members are going to take a picture in front of the hospital in a few minutes.[8]

Let us go down stairs.

Patient: Okay, I'd better wear my jacket.

만약 의료관광객이 휠체어를 타고 있다면 휠체어 부분을 플래카드 등으로 가려주거나 함께 앉아서 사진을 촬영하는 것이 바람직하다.

---

8) All the members are going to take a picture in front of the hotel in a few minutes.

= We are going to take a picture in front of the hotel in a few minutes.

Chapter 8

영송

8.1 귀국 항공편 재확인

72시간 전에 출국 비행기편을 재확인해야 한다.

■ 〈Case〉 귀국 항공편 재확인

Patient: I'd like to reconfirm your return flight.

MTC(Staff): When do you plan to leave?

Patient: This Friday.

MTC: Then, September 20th.

Please schedule your hotel departure three to four hours before flight departure due to the traffic conditions in Seoul(Busan).

■ 〈Case〉 귀국 항공편 재확인

Patient: I would like to reconfirm my flight.

MTC(Staff): May I see your air ticket please?

On behalf of you, we will reconfirm your return flight.

Patient: Thank you.

8.2 수하물 정리

Please pack up your luggage and check out the hotel before 12:00 pm.
Please make sure if you leave anything behind before you leave the room.

- ⟨Case⟩

MTC(Staff): Did you pack up your personal belongings?

Patient: Yes, I did.

MTC: Shall we move now?

A mini-bus is waiting outside.

Patient: OK.

How long does it take from here to the airport?

MTC: It will take about one hour.

8.3 호텔 퇴실

Check out시에 주고받을 수 있는 대화는 호텔 서비스에 대한 만족도, Shuttle bus 대기시간 등이다.

The check out time is 12:00 pm.

- ⟨Case⟩ 호텔 퇴실

MTC(Staff): The check out time is noon. 12 o'clock(12 : 00 pm).

Patient: I see.

MTC: Please get ready to leave the room before 12:00 pm.

Patient: OK.

- ⟨Case⟩ 호텔 퇴실

MTC(Staff): Good afternoon?

Are there any inconveniences[1] while you stayed at this hotel?

Participant: No, I am satisfied with the hotel service.

MTC: I am happy to hear that.

Well, the mini-bus is waiting for you in front of the hotel.

8.4 버스 탑승장소 안내

탑승장소는 현관에서 가까운 곳으로 결정한다.

■ 〈Case〉 탑승장소 문의

Patient: Where is the bus stop bound for Gimpo(Incheon, Gimhae) Airport.

MTC(Staff): The bus stop is on the right hand side of the entrance.

The bus departs for Gimpo(Incheon, Gimhae) Airport at 2:30 pm.

It will take about one hour from the hotel to the airport.

■ 〈Case〉 인원 점검

MTC(Staff): Ladies and gentlemen. This mini-bus is bound for Gimpo(Incheon, Gimhae) International Airport. Did you enjoy your stay in Seoul(Busan). How was your stay in Korea?

Patient: I had a great time.

MTC: Before we start, please check if you bring your passport with you and personal belongings.

Patient: How long does it take from here to the airport?

MTC: It will take about one hour and 30 minutes to the airport by bus.

We start toward the airport at least three hours before departure for departure procedures.

When you arrive at the Airport, fill out a departure statement and check in baggage and receive seat assignment on the 2nd floor.

---

1) inconvenience: 불편

8.5 공항으로 출발

■ 〈Case〉 공항으로 출발

MTC(Staff): Are you ready to leave?

Please be sure to double check if you have passports and airline tickets with you.

Patient: OK.

■ 〈Case〉 공항으로 출발

MTC(Staff): Korean Air Line(Asiana Airlines) is scheduled to depart on 3 o'clock.

We have 2 hours and a half before departure.

Patient: Do we have enough time to buy something?

MTC: I think we have enough time to check in and buy some souvenirs for your family members at the airport duty free shop.

■ 〈Case〉 공항으로 출발

MTC(Staff): In front of the hospital there is a blue-colored mini-bus.

Please get on the bus.

Patient: Thank you.

MTC: Please check out the destination on the bus window.

8.6 공항도착

■ 〈Case〉 공항도착

MTC(Staff): Here we are.

Let's get off the bus.

The driver will unload[2] your luggage from the bus and you take your own luggage in front of the bus

---

2) unload: 내리다

unload luggage from conveyor belts

Patient: Thank you.

■ 〈Case〉 공항 수속카운터로 이동

MTC(Staff): Do you have your passport and airline tickets with you?

Patient: Yes, I do.

MTC: Let's stand in a queue to check in.

Patient: I really enjoyed staying in Korea.

MTC: I do hope I will have another chance to serve you.

Please present your passport and airline tickets to the check-in staff.

Please, put your luggage on the weighing machine.

■ 〈Case〉 영송

MTC(Staff): If you find any adverse effect, after your return to America(Canada)[3]

please let us know.

Patient: Thank you for your kindness.

■ 〈Case〉 영송

MTC(Staff): Did you enjoy your staying in Korea?

Patient: Yes, I did.

I would love to visit Korea again.

■ 〈Case〉 영송

MTC(Staff): Once you have finished your medical treatment, you should receive a follow-up care.

I will give you a call to check your condition in a couple of weeks.

Patient: I see.

MTC: When you receive our call, you will be able to get

help with any ongoing or new side effects or symptoms you might be experiencing.

Patient: OK.

---

3) adverse effect: 부작 = adverse reaction, side effects, ill effects

produce an adverse reaction, harmful aftereffects

have no side effects

be free from side effects

Chapter 9

사후관리(Follow UP Call)

Do you have any other symptoms after you return home?
Do you experience any side effects after you start taking
the medicine.
Do you develop any new symptoms after you start taking
the medicine.

Please tell me if you have any other side effects that bother you.
If you notice any other adverse effects, please let me know.

■ 〈Case〉 사후관리

MTC(Nurse): Hello This is the international healthcare center of ABC Hospital.
Is this Mr. Johns?

Patient: Yes, I am.

MTC: I hope this is a good time to call.
If you are contacted at a time that is inconvenient[1] for you, please let
me know.

Patient: It is OK.

MTC: I just want to check up on your health condition, as you have been
receiving medication(Oriental Medicine) for a month until now.

Patient: I think the medication works for me.

---

1) inconvenient: 불편한

I don't have any side effect.

MTC: How are you feeling these days after taking our medication(Oriental Medicine)?

Patient: I feel I am much healthier.

■ 〈Case〉 사후관리

MTC(Nurse): Hello. This is ABC Hospital.

Is this Mr.(Mrs.) Johns?

Patient: Yes, I am.

MTC: I hope this is a good time to call.

I will call you at more convenient time or you can arrange the most convenient time to call you later.

Patient: It is OK.

Thanks for giving me a call.

MTC: How are you finding the medicine?

Is it helping with the pain already?(I wonder if the medicine is helping reduce the pain.)

Patient: I feel much improved, but the herbal medicine[2] tastes bitter.

MTC: We understand the herbal medicine is not very tasty, but if you continue to take the herbal medicine routinely as prescribed by the doctor, it will have great health effects and threat the root causes of your pain, so that it will not reoccur[3] in the future.

Patient: Thanks for your advice.

MTC: If you experience any problem with delivery and receiving medicine on time or any other concerns with the medicine, please don't hesitate to tell us or contact us in the future.

We want to provide the best of the best services to our Patients.

Patient: I see.

MTC: Do you want to continue receiving the herbal medicine?

---

2) herbal medicine: 한약
3) reoccur: 재발하다.

Patient: I want to receive three more packs of herbal medicine.

■ 〈Case〉 사후관리

MTC(Nurse): Hello. This is the international healthcare center of ABC Hospital. Is this Mr.(Mrs.) Johns?

Patient: Yes, I am.

MTC: I hope this is a good time to call.

Patient: It is OK.

MTC: I just want to check up on your health condition as well as the medications. I am going to ask you a few questions.

Patient: OK.

MTC: How are you feeling?

Patient: I am feeling wonderful.

MTC: Did you vomit after taking the dose?

Patient: No.

MTC: Are you having new symptoms since your return to America(Canada)?

Patient: No.

MTC: Are you taking all of your prescribed medications?

Patient: Yes, I am.

MTC: I thank you for your time in answering my questions.

Patient: Thanks for your calling.

본서의 내용에 대해서 궁금한 점이 있거나, 부족한 점이 있거나, 비록 본서에서 다루지 못했지만 다음 번 교정에서 추가·수정했으면 하는 의견이 있으시면 저자에게 fatherofsusie@hanmail.net 으로 직접 문의하시거나 blog.daum.net/fatherofsusie의 방명록에 궁금한 점과 의견을 남겨주시기 바랍니다.

한 광 종 ─────────────────────────────

한국의료관광·컨벤션연구원 원장
Email : fatherofsusie@hanmail.net
blog.daum.net/fatherofsusie
facebook : www.facebook.com/johngwangjong.han

〈강의〉
양산대학교 의료관광과
원광보건대학교 의료관광코디네이션과
인제대학교 국제경상학부 의료관광전공

〈저서〉
국제회의 영어
국제회의 실무영어
국제회의 실무영어회화
의료관광 실무영어
의료관광 실무영어회화
Excel 활용 의료경영 통계분석(의료관광·병원경영)
Excel 활용 마케팅통계조사분석(보건·의료관광·관광경영 사례중심)
SPSS 활용 통계조사분석(관광경영·보건·의료관광 사례중심)
국제의료관광코디네이터 1차 필기시험 예상문제집
컨벤션기획사 1차 필기시험 문제풀이 해설집
컨벤션기획사 2차 실기시험 문제풀이 해설집

English Conversation for Global Healthcare
(의료관광 실무영어회화)

2014년 1월 10일 초판 1쇄 인쇄
2014년 1월 15일 초판 1쇄 발행

저 자 한   광   종
발행인 寅製 진   욱   상

발행처  백산출판사
서울시 성북구 정릉3동 653-40
 등록 : 1974. 1. 9. 제 1-72호
 전화 : 914-1621, 917-6240
 FAX : 912-4438
http://www.ibaeksan.kr
editbsp@naver.com

값 20,000원
ISBN 978-89-6183-822-1